"This book is very timely! After three decades of endless stories about clerical sexual abuse in the Catholic Church, and almost invariably useless gestures to deal with it, the time is now for much more far-reaching structural reforms, including those proposed by this author."

– **A. A. J. DeVille,** *Associate Professor of Psychology, University of Saint Francis, USA*

CELIBACY, SEMINARY FORMATION, AND CATHOLIC CLERICAL SEXUAL ABUSE

Does the current celibate, semi-monastic, and all-male seminary formation contribute to the persistence of clerical sexual abuse in the Roman Catholic Church?

Applying sociological theories on socialization, total institutions, and social resistance as the primary conceptual framework, and drawing on secondary literature, media reports, the author's experience, interviews, and Church documents, this book argues that the Catholic Church's institution of the celibate seminary formation as the only mode of clerical training for Catholic priests has resulted in negative unintended consequences to human formation such as the suspension of normal human socialization in society, psychosexual immaturity, and weak social control against clerical sexual abuse. The author thus contends that celibate training, while suitable for those who do live in religious or monastic communities, is inappropriate for those who are obliged to live alone and work in parishes. As such, an alternative model for diocesan clerical formation is advanced.

A fresh look at the aptness – and effects – of celibate formation for diocesan clergy, this volume is the first to relate the persistence of Catholic clerical sexual abuse to celibate seminary formation, exploring the structural links between the two using sociological arguments and proposing an apprenticeship-based model of formation, which has numerous advantages as a form of clerical training. It will therefore appeal to scholars and students of religion, sociology, and theology, as well as those involved with seminary formation.

Dr. Vivencio O. Ballano is the Chairperson of the Master of Arts in Sociology, Graduate Studies Program, and Associate Professor 5 at the Department of Sociology, Polytechnic University of the Philippines (PUP), Manila. He received his master's (theology) and doctoral (sociology) degrees from the Ateneo de Manila University. He has published four Scopus-indexed books under the imprint Springer Nature. His fifth book entitled *In Defense of Married Priesthood* was published by Routledge in 2023. Dr. Ballano has also published several Scopus-indexed journal articles on the sociology of law, religion, media piracy, postdisaster management, digital education, and Catholic social teaching. He underwent ten years of diocesan and religious seminary training before becoming a sociologist.

Routledge Studies in the Sociology of Religion

A platform for the latest scholarly research in the sociology of religion, this series welcomes both theoretical and empirical studies that pay close attention to religion in social context. It publishes work that explores the ways in which religions adapt or react to social change and how spirituality lends meaning to people's lives and shapes individual, collective and national identities.

Polish Catholicism between Tradition and Migration
Agency, Reflexivity and Transendence
Wojciech Sadlon

Religion, Spirituality and Secularity among Millennials
The Generation Shaping American and Canadian Trends
Sarah Wilkins-Laflamme

Anti-Atheist Nation
Religion and Secularism in the United States
Petra Klug

Celibacy, Seminary Formation, and Catholic Clerical Sexual Abuse
Exploring Sociological Connections and Alternative Clerical Training
Vivencio O. Ballano

For more information about this series, please visit: www.routledge.com/Routledge-Studies-in-the-Sociology-of-Religion/book-series/RRSR

CELIBACY, SEMINARY FORMATION, AND CATHOLIC CLERICAL SEXUAL ABUSE

Exploring Sociological Connections and Alternative Clerical Training

Vivencio O. Ballano

LONDON AND NEW YORK

Designed cover image: © Shutterstock

First published 2024
by Routledge
4 Park Square, Milton Park, Abingdon, Oxon OX14 4RN

and by Routledge
605 Third Avenue, New York, NY 10158

Routledge is an imprint of the Taylor & Francis Group, an informa business

© 2024 Vivencio O. Ballano

The right of Vivencio O. Ballano to be identified as author of this
work has been asserted in accordance with sections 77 and 78 of the
Copyright, Designs and Patents Act 1988.

All rights reserved. No part of this book may be reprinted or
reproduced or utilised in any form or by any electronic, mechanical,
or other means, now known or hereafter invented, including
photocopying and recording, or in any information storage or retrieval
system, without permission in writing from the publishers.

Trademark notice: Product or corporate names may be trademarks
or registered trademarks, and are used only for identification and
explanation without intent to infringe.

British Library Cataloguing-in-Publication Data
A catalogue record for this book is available from the British Library

ISBN: 978-1-032-72249-8 (hbk)
ISBN: 978-1-032-64679-4 (pbk)
ISBN: 978-1-032-72247-4 (ebk)

DOI: 10.4324/9781032722474

Typeset in Sabon
by Apex CoVantage, LLC

Dedicated to His Holiness Pope Francis

and All Seminary Formators

CONTENTS

Acknowledgments   *xiv*

PART I
Introduction   **1**

1   Introduction   3

Book's Overview 3
   Background 3
   The Research Gap 5
   Celibate Seminary Training and CSA 7
Main Objectives and Arguments 10
The Sociological Approach 11
Summary of Parts and Chapters 13
Methodology 14
Theoretical Orientation 15
   Socialization Theory 16
   The Total Institution Theory 16
      The Seminary as a TI Social Structure 17
      The Need for Alternative Clerical Training 18
   Social Resistance Theory 19
Conclusion 21
References 22

x Contents

PART II
**Celibate Clerical Training, Human Formation,
and Clerical Sexual Abuse**   **27**

2   Shifting Method in Catholic Clerical Training
and Human Formation Against Sexual Abuse   29

Introduction 29
Tracing Clerical Formation in the RCC 32
   Apprenticeship 32
   Seminary Clerical Training 35
Socialization and Human Maturity in Clerical
   Training 37
Consequences of Shifting Methods in Clerical
   Training 39
   Covert Clerical Resistance 40
   Psychosexual Immaturity 42
   Lack of Social Control Against CSA 43
Conclusion and Recommendation 45
References 45

3   Celibate Seminary Formation, Total Institution,
and Clerical Sexual Abuse   49

Introduction 49
The Foundation of Celibate Seminary Formation 52
The Characteristics of TI 54
   The Seminary as a TI 56
   Retention of the Seminary Clerical Training 57
Negative Unintended Consequences of Seminary
   Training 59
   Disruption of Normal Human Socialization 59
   Disregarding Married Priesthood 60
   Human Immaturity 61
   Weakening of Social Control Against CSA 62
Alternative Clerical Training for Diocesan Married
   Priesthood 63
Conclusion 64
References 65

4   Gender and Sexuality Formation in the Seminary
and Clerical Sexual Abuse   68

Introduction 68
Clerical Training in the Seminary as a TI 73

Contents **xi**

Sexual Intimacy in Seminary Structure 75
  Scarcity of Professional Counselors 76
  Gender Training in the Seminary 76
  Clerical Celibacy as Sign of Manhood 78
Seminary Curriculum and Sexuality Development 80
  Poor Socialization with Women 81
  Unrealistic Training in Sexuality 82
  Lack of Preparation for Sexuality of Parishioners 84
Seminary Social Structure, the Parish, and CSA 86
Conclusion 88
References 88

5 Celibate Clerical Formation, Social Resistance,
   and Sexual Abuse in the Catholic Church   93

Introduction 93
Theoretical Orientation 99
  Clerical Celibacy and Social Resistance 99
  Passive Resistance and the Backstage 100
Passive Resistance and Seminary Formation 102
  Informal Seminary Socialization 103
  Major Passive Resistant Acts During Formation 105
    Living Double Lives 105
    Pornography 108
    Compulsive Masturbation 109
    Night Life and Secret Romance 110
Summary and Conclusion 113
References 114

PART III
Major Forms of Clerical Sexual Abuse and Seminary
Formation   **119**

6 Heterosexual Clerical Sexual Abuse and Seminary
   Formation   121

Introduction 121
Theoretical Foundation 126
  Socialization, Sex, and Gender in Society 126
  RCC Teaching and Seminary Gender
    Socialization 127
  Third Order Gender for Celibate Priests 129

xii Contents

*Gender Socialization in the Seminary as a Total
Institution (TI) 130*
*Celibate Seminary Training and Psychosexual
Immaturity 132*
CSA by Immature Heterosexual Priests 134
Conclusion 135
References 136

7 Homosexual Clerical Sexual Abuse and Seminary Formation 140

Introduction 140
Misconceptions on Homosexual CSA 143
*Blaming Homosexuals for CSA and the
Priesthood 145*
*Church Stand on Homosexuality and Seminary
Formation 147*
Implications of Blaming Gay Priests for CSA 149
The Need for Specialized Formation for Gays 151
Conclusion 153
References 154

8 Child Clerical Sexual Abuse, Pedophilia, and Seminary
Formation 157

Introduction 157
  Pedophile Clerical Sexual Abuse in the Catholic
    Church 157
  Understanding the Structural Causes of Pedophile
    cCSA 159
  Chapter's Research Objectives and Main
    Arguments 160
Theoretical Foundation 161
  Socialization Theory 161
  The Seminary as a TI 163
  Celibate Seminary Formation and Pedophile
    CSA 164
*The Structural Limitations of the Seminary Against
Pedophilia 165*
  Inadequate Seminary Screening Methods 165
  Lack of Experts and Program for Pedophilia 168
    Regressed and Fixated Pedophiles 169
    Blending Abilities of Pedophiles 170

Implication of Seminary Flaws to Clerical Ministry
   Against cCSA 171
     Occurrence of cCSA Before Discovery and Diocesan
       Response 171
     Weak Detection System for cCSA in the Parish
       and Cover-Ups 173
   Conclusion and Recommendation 174
   References 175

PART IV
Alternative Clerical Training and Apprenticeship   **181**

9   Exploring Alternative Clerical Training and Married
    Priesthood in Current Age   183

   Introduction 183
   Reestablishing Apprenticeship in Contemporary
     Times 187
     Inculturation and Clerical Training in Contemporary
       Age 188
     Married Priesthood 190
     Open Priesthood 192
     Allowing Normal Socialization 194
   Academic Training in Sociology and the Social
     Sciences 195
   Utilization of Telepresence and Digital Networks 197
   Provisions for Clerical Marriage and Confluent
     Relationship 198
   Lay Empowerment in Clerical Formation and
     Behavior 200
   Conclusion 202
   References 203

Index   206

ACKNOWLEDGMENTS

This book on clerical celibacy, seminary formation, and Catholic clerical sexual abuse that applies the sociological-theological approach is a product of painstaking sociological research and writing. This journey would not have been possible without the generous help of the following people who prepared me academically and inspired me for the task:

To all my sociology professors of the Ateneo de Manila University, for providing me a rigorous training in the sociological enterprise. A special thanks to Dr. Ricardo G. Abad, Professor Emeritus of the Sociology-Anthropology Department at the Ateneo de Manila University, my wise advisor, and friend throughout my sociological training, for his continuous support and inspiration.

To all my Jesuit theology professors at the Loyola School of Theology, Ateneo de Manila University, for providing me an in-depth theological formation. A special thanks to the late Fr. John Schumacher, S. J., Fr. Joseph Smith, S. J., Fr. Thomas Green, S. J., and Fr. Romeo Intengan, S. J., for inspiring me to become a scholar and researcher.

To all my colleagues and co-faculty at the CSSD led by Dean Raul Sebastian and Department of Sociology and Anthropology at the PUP led by Prof. John Dalupang, for their encouragement and warm support.

To Mr. Neil Jordan, Senior Editor of Routledge, for his guidance and assistance for the entire publication process. Also, to his assistant, Ms. Gemma Rogers, for helping in the contract process and production.

To the two blind peer reviewers of the book proposal and sample chapters for recommending the publication of this book, as well as to the Routledge Editorial Board for final approval and book contract.

To my wife, Emily, and my children, Joanne Faye, and Johann Karl for their loving support and inspiration.

To our Lord Jesus and Mama Mary for the blessing and guidance in my apostolate of writing – doing research and publishing as my own way of serving the Church and society.

PART I

Introduction

1

INTRODUCTION

Book's Overview

Background

For the Roman Catholic Church (RCC), the seminary is the suitable and ideal place for the formation and preparation of future priests for evangelization. "Formation, as the Church understands it, is not equivalent to a secular sense of schooling or, even less, job training. Formation is first and foremost cooperation with the grace of God" (USCCB 2005, #68). To Pope John Paul II (1992, # 8), "The formation of future priests . . . and lifelong assiduous care for their personal sanctification in the ministry and for the constant updating of their pastoral commitment is considered by the Church one of the most demanding and important tasks for the future of the evangelization of humanity." The RCC as a sacerdotal church cannot accomplish its spiritual mission without priests and clerical formation for future priests.

"The Church continues to place the highest value on the work of priestly formation, because it is linked to the very mission of the Church, especially the evangelization of humanity: 'Go, therefore, and make disciples of all nations'" (Mt 28:19) (USCCB 2005, #9). Forming future priests into another Christ in the current celibate seminary structure as the exclusive institution for clerical training is indeed a noble task in the RCC. "Without priests the Church would not be able to live that fundamental obedience which is at the very heart of her existence and her mission in history" (Pope John Paul II 1992, #1).

This noble task of forming future celibate priests in the seminary, especially diocesan priests, who are considered the frontliners of the Church's

DOI: 10.4324/9781032722474-2

4 Introduction

evangelizing mission is not without a serious challenge in the contemporary world. In recent years, the RCC has been plagued with cases of sexual scandals by priests who are products of the present celibate seminary training. Most research and investigations on clerical sexual abuse (CSA) in the RCC has revealed that the primary cohort of sexually abusive priests consists of immature heterosexual diocesan priests who underwent the exclusive, all-male, and celibate priestly training (Frawley O'Dea 2004; John Jay College Report 2004; De Weger 2022). Thus, one wonders: Does the current celibate seminary formation have something to do with the persistence of CSA in the RCC?

To the priest-therapist and author A. W. Richard Sipe (1990), CSA is the Catholic hierarchy's crisis itself that needs structural reform and investigation into the celibate seminary formation. To Catholic bishops, however, CSA is fundamentally a grave sin that needs repentance and forgiveness. It is only an internal matter for the Church to resolve. To ultimately address and avoid it, Catholic bishops recommended prayer for both abusive priests and their victims. To Pope John Paul II (1993), for instance, whose papacy dealt with most of the sexual abuse scandal in the RCC, prayer should be the preferred response to CSA. In his address to the visiting Irish bishops in Rome, he asked the bishops to pray for the victims as well as for abusive priests who suffered much because of pressure of the surrounding culture.

After decades of revelations on CSA by the media, civil and ecclesial investigations, and scientific research, the RCC has finally improved its response to clergy sexual misconduct but it still retained the basic moral view that CSA is a grave sin rather a crime. Adopting a stricter response against clergy sexual abuses in the RCC, Pope Francis declared a policy of zero tolerance against CSA (Pope Francis 2017). "Since his election in 2013, Francis has taken some steps to root out sexual abuse in the church and to put in place practices to protect children" (Reuters 2017, para. 3). Despite this development, victims' group was unhappy and wished that the Pope could have done more for the victims, especially by holding bishops who tolerated CSA or covered it up to be more accountable (Reuters 2017).

Consistent with the RCC's overall moral view of CSA against children, adolescents, and adults by abusive priests, Pope Francis too sees sexual abuse in the RCC as a horrible sin. In his letter to the RCC adopting a zero tolerance against CSA, he declared: "Allow me to say with all clarity that sexual abuse is a horrible sin, completely opposed to and in contradiction to what Christ and the Church teach us" (Pope Francis 2017, para. 4). Despite Francis's zero tolerance policy against CSA, the Church still underscores the belief that criminal sexual abuse by clergy should be sanctioned by the Church internally – if at all – under canonical commands of contrition and forgiveness, and not by civil authorities (Logan 2003). Thus, after decades of church pronouncements condemning clergy sexual misconduct, victims remain unsatisfied with the church officials' response to CSA and hope that the Catholic hierarchy could have done enough to address its structural roots in the RCC.

The Research Gap

In search of the major structural factors that contribute to the persistence of CSA in the RCC, scholars began employing different research approaches. Some focused on a single-issue cause approach to comprehend the endurance of CSA in the RCC. This includes relating CSA to the mandatory clerical celibacy (e.g., Scheper-Hughes and Devine 2003; Adams 2011; Kasomo 2012), clericalism (e.g., Sipe 1990; Doyle 2006; Benkert and Doyle 2009; Plante 2020), decline of clerical spirituality (e.g., Cross and Thoma 2006; Pargament, Murray-Swank, and Annette 2008), or homosexuality (e.g., Boisvert and Goss 2005; Cozzens 2006; Kraschl 2020). Others employ a more integrated approach that explored a mix of sociocultural factors such as power, sexuality, institutional culture, hierarchicalism, clericalism, patriarchy among others, to understand CSA's major causes (e.g., Doyle 2006; Keenan 2018, 2010; Ballano 2019; Plante 2020; Hadebe 2022).

Catholic theologians too have contributed to this search for the major enablers of CSA in the RCC beyond the moral and spiritual stance of the Catholic hierarchy. Some view Catholic CSA as facilitated by structural factors in the RCC such as hierarchalism and lack of moral leadership as enabling clergy sexual misconduct (Keenan 2018; Hogan 2021; Kwon 2022; Mescher 2023). To them, hierarchicalism or the too much emphasis on the hierarchical ecclesial powers of bishops and clerics in the RCC, which is the promoter of clericalism, that is, the exaggerated cultural belief on the spiritual powers of the clergy in the RCC, is the primary enabler that allows sexually abusive priests to act with impunity in the Church. To the theologian James Keenan (2018), hierarchicalism downplays the moral accountability of priests and bishops in clergy sexual misconduct that results in a culture of cover-up for CSA cases in the RCC.

To the Jesuit Fr. Hans Zollner (2022), a leading member of the Vatican committee against child clerical sexual abuse who recently resigned from his post, the lack of moral responsibility to create a safeguarding culture in the Church is primarily enabling the persistence of CSA in the RCC. Thus, he highlighted the moral responsibility of ecclesiastical authorities to create safe spaces and relationships within the Church, as well as listening to victims and survivors of abuse as the cornerstone of credibility and promoting the Christian faith against CSA. He also recommended that the RCC should also develop a more child-centric theology and church culture to prevent child clerical sexual abuse (Zollner 2019).

Despite this growing scientific and theological research on the nature and causes of CSA, scholars agree that more remains to be known about clergy

6 Introduction

sexual misconduct in the RCC (Calkins, Sque, and Addington-Hall 2015). One limitation of the current approach is that most scientific studies on CSA are done by psychologists, psychiatrists, and psychotherapists who tend to focus on the micro level, lacking in structural perspectives. Furthermore, the present theological research and analysis on CSA, although citing some structural aspects of CSA, fundamentally remain moral and normative in perspective, thus in need of the scientific research and holistic approaches of modern sociology to fully understand the facts and social patterns behind clergy sexual abuse. The structural approaches of sociology that investigate CSA through its distinct mode of holistic analysis of social issues called "sociological imagination" (Mills 2000) is manifestly lacking.

And yet investigators and scholars acknowledged the need of scientific research that seeks to understand CSA's situational and structural contexts (John Jay College Report 2004; Keenan 2018; Ballano 2023). Sociological analysis that relates to the persistence of CSA in the RCC to the current RCC's social structures on mandatory clerical celibacy and exclusive semi-monastic celibate seminary formation is overlooked by scholars and Catholic theologians. But offenders of sexual abuse in the RCC are all celibates and graduates of the current seminary formation and, thus, attracting the attention of sociologists to investigate whether the mandatory clerical celibacy and celibate clerical training are largely contributing to the persistence of clergy sexual scandals in the Church.

The prevailing research on seminary formation and clerical ministry in the RCC tends to focus on the trends of seminary formation as well as historical appraisal of ecclesial policies and their implementation process (e.g., Schuth 1999, 2016), psychological evaluation of seminary candidates (e.g., Isacco et al. 2020; McGlone and Sperry 2020), effectiveness of the psychological tools in screening applicants (e.g., Isacco et al. 2020), suitability of candidates to the priesthood (e.g., Sperry 2003; Isacco et al. 2020; Plante 2020; Isacco, Songy, and Plante 2022), and adequacy of the human formation in seminary training (e.g., Duffy 1992; Meek et al. 2004; Hoesing and Hogan 2021).

There is a paucity of sociological literature that directly explores the structural links between the current celibate seminary priestly training and the continuing CSA in the RCC. Several studies have suggested that the current celibate seminary formation, which produces problematic male heterosexual diocesan priests – the type of priests that is often cited in the present CSA research and investigations as the main group of sexual abusers in the RCC – as a major enabler of clergy sexual misconduct (e.g., Sipe 1990; John Jay College Report 2004; Frawley O'Dea and Goldner 2007; Reisinger 2022). The RCC's Council of Trent in the 16th century and the Second Vatican Council (Vatican II), a universal gathering of all bishops with the Pope in the early 1960s to update church teachings to modern times, acknowledged that celibacy is not an essential requirement for the priesthood and is thus optional for future priests (Vogels 1993).

Celibate Seminary Training and CSA

Conversely, Vatican II declared that the RCC aims to maintain both the current practice of celibate and married priesthood, which are legitimately flourishing in the Eastern Churches – implying that married priesthood is indeed a valid social calling and a holy vocation (*Presbyterorum Ordinis* [Order of Priests] 1965, para. 16). The imposition of clerical celibacy in the 11th and 12th centuries by the Second and Fourth Lateran Councils has resulted in the adoption of a celibate clerical training as the only mode for Catholic priestly formation when the seminary was instituted by the Council of Trent in the 16th century.

With the absence of option to choose married priesthood, which has long been recognized by the RCC as a valid social calling to Catholic priesthood, aspirants are "forced" to join the celibate clerical formation, which was structurally designed for religious and monastic priests who are presumed to possess the rare gift of celibacy. The present closed, exclusive, semi-monastic, and all-male seminary organization, which the sociologist Erving Goffman (1968) calls "total institutions (TI)," is said to produce sexually repressed immature priests (Frawley O'Dea 2004; Madden 2010; *Boisvert* and *Goss* 2021).

Indeed, there is an implicit sociological connection between the celibate seminary training and the endurance of CSA in the Church (Sipe 1990, 2003) that needs structural exploration by sociologists. Although there are cultural variations of seminary formation in the universal RCC, the current pattern of the celibate clerical training that separates seminarians from the real social world has greatly stunted the human and sexual maturity of future priests, which is a major factor in the persistence of CSA in the RCC. As Frawley O'Dea (2004, 129–130) aptly observes:

> Central to this cohort of abusers is their psychosexual immaturity. Many of these priests entered seminaries when they were as young as 14 years old. Throughout their adolescence, sexuality was wholly dissociated from the verbally validated and symbolically processed realm of life. They simply were not to have sex of any kind, talk about sex of any kind, or think about sex about any kind. Celibacy was a rule, but these boys, later men, were given no guidance for growing to mature manhood in which celibacy could become a comprehensible, freely made choice.

Anderson (2016, 846) also highlights the interplay between individual and communal aspects in the persistence of CSA in the RCC:

> Senior clergy in the Roman Catholic Church tend to attribute the harm of child sexual abuse (CSA) solely to individual clergy offenders. The basis

of their assessment is a belief that "sin is a personal act," meaning it is the fault of an individual and not properly of the wider clergy community (Catechism of the Catholic Church, 1994, 457), that the individual cleric may be socialized by numerous and powerful factors that may result in personal tendencies and defects, but their influence does not limit his responsibility for a personal act of sin. . . . They effectively deny there is an interplay between the social dimension of the clergy community and the individuated agency of clergy offenders.

(Anderson 2016, 846)

Thus, the continuing CSA in the RCC is a product not only of personal choice but also of structural and organizational enablers. Priest sexual offenders, for instance, "do not make entirely autonomous choices to abuse children. Rather, their capacity to exercise agency in this matter is substantially influenced by a particular clerical masculinity in a patriarchal order as upheld and demanded by the clergy community" (Anderson 2016, 847). In sociology, one cannot dissociate human action from social structure.

As the criminologist Marie Keenan (2011) contends, the CSA issue is not only personal but also organizational in nature. The blame should be focused not only on personal weaknesses but also on the structural defects of the RCC. To her, the RCC is a closed institution that "encourages practices that actually exacerbate loneliness and emotional immaturity and demands absolute obedience to a centralized leadership without accountability or checks and balances" (Terry 2015, 145).

And one of these practices in the RCC that can exacerbate loneliness and emotional immaturity of Catholic priests is placing young men in their late adolescence or early adulthood in an "abnormal," celibate, semi-monastic, and all-male social environment of the seminary for several years, without sufficient professional guidance on their human and sexual development. The present seminary structure isolates candidates from their usual human and sexual socialization in society as young adults. This type of exclusive clerical formation is also closed to married priesthood in case heterosexual diocesan seminarians opt to join a married presbyterate.[1]

After the highly regulated communal seminary training, newly ordained secular priests are immediately assigned in the semi-autonomous social structure of the parish without safety nets such as a strong social support from the presbyterate or family life in married priesthood to resist CSA. Thus, with the absence of communal life and social bonding, clerical behavior is deprived of regulation that can greatly inhibit sexual deviance or any rule-breaking behavior. Research by Dean Hoge (2002), for instance, revealed that new priests are struggling to cope with loneliness and lack of social support due to celibacy during their first five years in the ministry.

The sociological control theories on crime and deviance assume that rule-breaking or delinquent acts occur because of a weak social bonding in society (Hirschi 1969). Thus, they view social bond and social control of people's behavior as crucial to preventing crime and deviant acts and maintaining social order. "Social control involves mechanisms of integration aimed at securing order and stability at the societal level, despite increasing trends of growing individualism and cultural diversity" (Deflem 2015, 31).

Social control can be internal and external. External control can consist of law enforcement apparatuses to apprehend abusive and undisciplined individuals. But internal social control or self-discipline is socially acquired through proper socialization of the self. Disciplined individuals internalized social norms and developed habits and dispositions or what the Pierre Bourdieu (2020) calls habitus that inhibits them break rules with the absence of guardians or external social control in the environment.

For Catholic priests to develop the habitus of self-discipline, internal social control, and moral leadership (Hogan 2021; Mescher 2023), healthy and realistic training in human development and sexuality should be given to seminarians. Clerical training should then include adequate psychosexual formation, preferably part of the formal seminary curriculum, aside from the spiritual, academic, and pastoral training inside the seminary. If new priests, after long years of seminary training, still do not acquire this habitus of self-discipline and remain sexually immature, then the current celibate seminary formation needs to be sociologically investigated to understand its major structural flaws. Reforms in clerical formation and strengthening of external social control for clerical behavior are necessary to counteract CSA in the RCC.

The quest for structural enablers of CSA should then begin with the present celibate seminary structure, the breeding ground for Catholic priests. One needs to sociologically analyze the appropriateness of the social structure of the celibate seminary formation for future priests, especially for diocesan clerics who are found to be prone to CSA in the parish (John Jay College Report 2004). Unlike religious and monastic priests who are communally supported by their religious orders, diocesan priests face a myriad of clerical problems without a strong social bond, such as loneliness, burn-out, spiritual dryness, and the temptation to commit CSA, which are embedded in the social structure of parish priestly life.

Sociologists believe that human action could not be separated from the social structure that conditions it (Giddens 1984; Hays 1994). Thus, the persistence of CSA in the RCC, which is structurally linked to clerical celibacy and celibate seminary formation, needs sociological investigations. "Social structures are patterns of action and behavior that exist over and beyond activities and purposes of individuals but in turn depend on individual action for their reproduction and continuation" (Sewell Jr. 1992, 3). The sociologist

10 Introduction

George Homans (1975, 53) refers these structures to "those aspects of social behavior that the investigator considers relatively enduring or persistent."

The British sociologist Anthony Giddens (1984) sees human agency (action) in the context of social structure and integrates action and structure. Furthermore, Haslanger (2015, 4) contends that:

> [i]ndividuals exist within social structures; we are part of social structures. We work for organizations. . ... In the case of structured wholes, the behavior of their parts is constrained by their position in the whole, and such constraints are relevant to explaining the behavior of the parts.

The celibate male priesthood model that frames the social structure of the current seminary formation has an impact on the human action of seminarians and priests who, in turn, reinforce the RCC's celibate social structure. Exploring the sociological connections between the celibate seminary formation and the persistence of CSA can be of great help for the RCC to improve clerical training, especially in searching for alternative methods of priestly formation for diocesan priests, who are more prone to commit CSA in the parish. This chapter primarily introduces the book's main objectives and arguments, sociological approach, summary of parts and chapters, methodology, and theoretical orientation.

Main Objectives and Arguments

The main objective of this book is to sociologically explore how the celibate clerical formation in a semi-monastic, all-male, and exclusive environment of the seminary contributes to the persistence of CSA, especially among Catholic priests in the RCC. Specifically, it aims to understand how the celibate seminary structure and socialization have resulted in the unintended consequences of producing psychosexual immature seminary graduates with repressed sexuality who are vulnerable to CSA when ordained and assigned in the parish.

Applying sociological theories on socialization, total institutions, and social resistance as the main conceptual framework and drawing on secondary literature, media reports, the author's experience, interviews, and Church documents, this book argues that the RCC's adoption of celibate seminary training disrupts the normal human socialization of priestly candidates that can lead to poor human formation, psychosexual immaturity, and weak social control against CSA.

It contends that the current celibate seminary formation is structurally contributing to the formation of psychologically immature and sexually repressed diocesan priests – the most common type of sexual abuse offenders in the RCC – who lack social control against CSA in the lonely lifestyle of the parish. Owing to lack of option, heterosexual diocesan seminarians who felt called to married priesthood are constrained to undergo the present celibate seminary training, which can inevitably result in serious psychosexual problems that can significantly obstruct their normal human and sexual development to resist CSA.

It recommends an alternative clerical training based on the historically grounded apprenticeship model that is open to married priesthood. Married priesthood, which provides familial social bonding that inhibits CSA, is more suitable for diocesan priests who normally live a solitary life in the parish. The current seminary formation is only suitable to religious and monastic priests who will continue to join their religious communities after ordination. In fact, the present celibate seminary formation copied most aspects of monastic and religious life. Celibate priesthood can be best lived in a community of fellow celibates in a religious or monastic setting.

The celibate seminary training and celibate priesthood are, however, unsuitable for diocesan clerics who will be obligated to live and work in the lonely life of the parish without direct behavioral supervision and social bonding with their local bishops and presbyterate. Sociological research and literature on crime and deviance generally recommend some sort of social bonding and communal life to minimize rule-breaking behavior such as CSA in the RCC. Thus, this book advocates seminary reforms in the current seminary training and calls for the reestablishment of the apprenticeship clerical training that is open to married for diocesan clergy to generally inhibit CSA in the RCC.

The Sociological Approach

Applying sociological theories on socialization, total institutions, and social resistance, this book attempts to establish the sociological and structural connections between the Catholic celibate seminary formation and the persistence of CSA, especially among male heterosexual diocesan priests. Behavioral issues are beyond the expertise of many clerics, religious, and seminary formators who are primarily educated in the normative disciplines of philosophy and theology, lacking in empirical perspectives and methodologies of sociology and the social sciences. Thus, clerics and seminary formators need the scientific research on seminary formation and CSA as well as the guidance of sociologists and social scientists to improve clerical training of diocesan clergy, given in the growing complexity of the contemporary world.

Although psychological and psychiatric approaches are adequately utilized in CSA research, sociological research perspectives are apparently neglected in CSA investigation literature. The academic dialogue between Catholic theologians, sociologists, and seminary formators is necessary to fully understand how the issues of celibacy and seminary formation are connected to the endurance of CSA in the RCC. Thus, this book attempts to address this need.

Most research and literature on seminary formation applies the philosophical and theological perspectives that tend to focus on the academic and spiritual formation of seminarians, unintendedly neglecting human formation that must be guided by sound scientific research and sociological investigation. As Fr. Eugene Duffy (1992, 5999) argues, "The whole work of priestly formation would be deprived of its necessary foundation if it lacked a suitable human formation." Mature clerical spirituality presupposes mature humanity of priests, which should be adequately developed during clerical formation.

The adoption of seminary clerical training by the Council of Trent in the 16th century and abandonment of the long tradition of apprenticeship for clerical formation since the time of Christ have led to spiritualization of clerical training. It inadvertently suspended the normal adult socialization of seminarians inside the highly supervised seminary training that bans all forms of open discussion on sexuality. The controversial book *From the Depths of Our Hearts* (2020) by Cardinal Robert Sarah – and allegedly coauthored by Pope Benedict XVI – inappropriately assumes that "attacking celibacy" is equated to "attacking the church."

This book argues that the RCC's prescriptions on clerical celibacy and celibate seminary training are not dogmatic in nature. They belong to the realm of church discipline and morality, which have behavioral aspects, thus subject to the scientific research of sociologists and social scientists before their application by seminary rectors and formators. Post-Vatican II documents on clerical formation stress the importance of sociological research as an aid to seminary formation (Pope John Paul II 1992).

Thus, sociological scientific research is necessary to understand how the celibate clerical formation contributes to the persistence CSA in the RCC in contemporary times. An intensive sociological investigation of the human formation in celibate seminary training is vital to comprehend why male diocesan heterosexual priests is the primary cohort of sex offenders in the RCC. No less than Pope John Paul II (1992) has acknowledged that the first area of clerical formation that needs to be seriously attended to in the seminary is the human formation of seminarians and that sociological research is an indispensable aid in this regard (*Presbyterorum Ordinis* 1965).

The current seminary structure as a total institution (TI) (Goffman 1968), however, fundamentally separates the seminarians' normal life from the real world, offering them only limited opportunities for psychosexual growth. Human formation in exclusive clerical training could be abnormal if candidates live outside of normal life situations while participating in academic and spiritual training. Thus, one inquires: How can seminarians receive adequate human formation if they are primarily housed in a TI structure without the necessary agents of socialization such as parents, friends, women, and ordinary people for their human and sexual development?

The seminary cannot sufficiently mimic the real human experience outside the seminary no matter how holistic the seminars and exposures are structured in the seminary program by formators. In a TI social structure, members surrender, "willingly or unwillingly, the loss of their autonomy and a curtailment of their freedom. They faced the possible failure to mature responsibly and developed a tendency to nurture and 'under life,' 'a sub-culture.'" (Madden 2010, 34). "Every seminary has its own human formation program, but this is largely consisting of group seminar work and the opportunity for an individual to meet with a professional counsellor" (Oakley 2017, 231). This is an insufficient substitute for the normal adult socialization process in society for diocesan seminarians who will be exposed to the real secular world in the parish environment after ordination.

The recommendations of *Pastores Dabo Vobis* [I Shall Give you Shepherds] (Pope John Paul II 1992) on priestly formation that prioritizes human development for future priests could not be authentically realized if the seminary social structure remains an exclusive organization that largely distances seminarians from the real world. Future diocesan priests could not develop a strong social control against CSA if they themselves are deprived of the realistic opportunities for human and sexual maturity inside a semi-monastic, all-male, and highly supervised environment of the seminary as a TI.

Summary of Parts and Chapters

This book has four major parts. The first part provides an overview of the book and its sociological approach to understand the structural links between the celibate seminary training in a TI social structure and its negative unintended consequences to the human and sexual development of seminarians and their ability to resist CSA after ordination and assignment in the parish. It argues that the poor human formation and repressed sexuality in the seminary unintendedly produce in immature priests, especially diocesan clerics, who could become humanly weak to resist CSA in the parish.

The second part analyzes the sociological interconnection between the celibate seminary training, human formation, passive social resistance, and CSA. It begins with Chapter 2, which briefly discusses how married priesthood and optional celibacy with roots in apostolic times have been shifted by the RCC to the obligatory celibate priesthood in the 11th and 12th centuries that paved the way for the establishment of celibate seminary formation in the 16th century. Chapter 3 examines the seminary structure as a TI created by the Council of Trent and fundamentally retained by Vatican II and its unintended consequences to the human development and social control of diocesan priests against CSA.

14 Introduction

Chapter 4 focuses on the negative unintended consequences of the adoption of celibate seminary formation as the only mode of clerical training to the human sexuality of seminarians. It argues that the TI social structure of the seminary represses human sexuality, resulting in social resistance and compensatory behaviors that are prone to sexual indiscretion and CSA. Finally, Chapter 5 contends that CSA and other forms of clerical sexual deviance are expressions of passive social resistance by Catholic priests who covertly oppose the mandatory clerical celibacy. It provides some anecdotal qualitative evidence to show how seminarians passively resist and circumvent the seminary celibacy and chastity rule through the informal and hidden sexuality curriculum and socialization such as pornography, masturbation, visiting nightclubs and watching lewd shows, as well as keeping secret romantic relationship during formation.

The third part of this book explores the sociological connections between the celibate seminary clerical formation and the three major types of CSA in the RCC, as well as an alternative diocesan clerical formation based on the historically grounded apprenticeship clerical training. Chapter 6 examines how the current social structure of the celibate seminary formation contributes to the persistence of CSA committed mostly by heterosexual celibate diocesan priests. Chapter 7 investigates homosexual CSA and seminary formation. Chapter 8 assesses how the present seminary structure hinders the identification of seminarians with pedophilic disorder, allowing them to get ordained and engage in child clerical sexual abuse.

The last part consists of Chapter 9, which recommends an alternative clerical training to the current celibate seminary formation for diocesan priests. It explores a new model of clerical training that reestablishes the traditional clerical training of apprenticeship. This training is open to inculturation or adaptation of priestly formation in the contemporary world and to married priesthood, as well as provides greater social control against CSA. It recommends reforms in the current priestly training, such as enhancing the sociological and social science training of seminarians, utilizing telepresence and online networks for priestly formation, introducing canonical provisions that allow married priesthood, involving competent lay leaders in clerical formation, and regulating of clerical behavior by the laity to counteract the temptations of CSA among diocesan Catholic priests.

Methodology

Although it utilizes some sociological insights based on the experience of the author as a former diocesan and religious seminarians for 10 years and personal interviews with some seminarians and priests on passive resistance specifically in Chapter 5, this book largely relies on documentary and archival data from secondary literature and research studies (Long-Sutehall et al.

2011; Largan and Morris 2019). They consist mainly of textual data based on doctrinal and theological documents of the RCC, journal articles, monographs, books, and media reports. These references were organized and synthesized to establish the book's main argument and objective, as well as of those in the chapters.

The secondary data analysis (SDA) of this book reuses the textual data originally intended for other purposes to advance new theoretical and methodological knowledge (Irwin and Winterton 2012). It aims to pursue its research objectives that are different from the original analysis of the secondary sources. In this kind of study, the researcher and author of this book utilized the collected data of other researchers to achieve different research objectives (Wickam 2019).

This research specifically employed the SDA method and systematic literature review to search for the relevant published materials to support the book's objectives and arguments. Under this process, the author first searched for relevant materials online, identifying relevant databases and search terms, and established a search strategy to locate the appropriate online materials for the study (Booth, Papaioannou, and Sutton 2012). The research techniques and search terms were conceived on the basis of the book's research questions. The collected secondary data from the literature that deals with Catholic clerical celibacy, seminary formation, and clerical sexual abuse were organized and interpreted by sociological theories on socialization, total institution, and social resistance to construct the book's main arguments.

Theoretical Orientation

This book applies an eclectic sociological theoretical framework to interpret the secondary textual data but primarily relies on the sociological theories of socialization, total institutions, and social resistance as the main conceptual framework. Aside from the preliminary chapters, it first applies the socialization theory to show how the current celibate seminary structure is problematic for future heterosexual diocesan priests who are constrained to undergo the celibate seminary training in the absence of the option for married priesthood.

Then, it applies Erving Goffman's total institution theory to interpret the negative unintended consequences of celibate seminary training to diocesan priests' resistance against CSA. It also adopts Scott's theory on social resistance to interpret clerical social resistance against the mandatory celibacy that begins during the seminary training and continues in the ministry after ordination. Because of obligatory clerical celibacy, heterosexual diocesan seminarians who may decide to become married priests are forced to undergo the celibate priesthood training that can lead to human and psychosexual underdevelopment and vulnerability to CSA when assigned to the parish.

16 Introduction

Socialization Theory

Socialization refers to "the learning process that deals with the acquisition of the necessary orientations for satisfactory functioning in a role" (Hoy and Woolfolk 1990, 283–284). It is a lifelong process that commences from birth and ends up to death. It has two fundamental stages: primary and secondary. Primary socialization is the basic and initial social training for individuals in society as human beings. It involves "learning the rules of behavior, norms and values that can be treated at early ages and that is informational and emotional baggage of any person" (Crisogen 2015, 331). The "secondary socialization is the process by which an individual learns the basic values, norms, and behaviors that are expected of them outside the main agency of the family" (Nickerson 2023, para. 1).

The "secondary socialization takes place during adolescence and adulthood, and is mainly achieved through peer groups, work colleagues, and clubs or societies" (Nickerson 2023, para. 4). "Socialization and education are the processes directly related to the overall development of an individual. These processes prepare individuals and ensure their inclusion in various social spheres and cultural integration" (Terziev and Vaseliva 2022). In religious organizations such as the Catholic seminary, "socialization is concerned with the learning content and process by which an individual adjusts to a special role in an organization. It is a learning progress through which individuals learn organizational values, norms, informal networks and required skills" (Ge, Su, and Zhou 2010, 167).

Organizational socialization is often understood as the process through which individuals acquire knowledge about and adjust to their work context (Van Maanen and Schein 1979; Fisher 1986). In the RCC, those who want to become priests are required to undergo the usual organizational socialization of the celibate seminary training, where they are formed spiritually and educated in philosophy and theology. Candidates for the priesthood who are normally in their late adolescent and young adult years leave their normal socialization in society to enter the TI structure of the seminary. These young men are still in the secondary socialization stage,[2] which includes dating and entering into romantic relationships with women as part of their growing up as humans and sexual beings. But this stage is shortened by their living in the secluded TI environment of the seminary.

The Total Institution Theory

Future priests who enter Catholic seminaries do not only suspend their secondary socialization but also undergo the process of resocialization, a new social learning wherein individuals enter a distinct exclusive institution and learn a new set of social norms that aims to radically alter their identity. The

Canadian-born sociologist Erving Goffman defines this type of institution for resocialization as TI, that is, "a place of residence . . . where a large number of like-situated individuals cut off from the wider society for an appreciable period of time, together lead an enclosed, formally administered round of life" (Goffman 1968, xiii).

Goffman (1968) contends that in a TI, compliance must appear to be absolute, or punishment may be swift. He identifies characteristics that qualify systems as TI, such as those who enter exclusive institutions both voluntarily and involuntarily, which are established to care for people who are presumed to be both incapable and harmless. In his book, *Assylums*, Goffman considers TI to be those that separate the interaction between members and nonmembers and where members work, play, and sleep in the same place under one set of authorities, following one overall plan. Individuals undergo totalizing practices beyond their control such as mortification of self to serve the needs of the institution (Jenkins, Burton, and Holmes 2022).

People in a TI environment behave differently in face-to-face private interactions compared to public conversations, which are being monitored by authorities, suggesting Michel Foucault's work on panopticism (Manokha 2018). Panoptic surveillance is a means of exertion of power and control and may in fact cause someone to exercise the sovereign's power over themselves without any direct coercion (Foucault 1975). Inside the seminary, panoptic gaze or surveillance by seminary formators on the seminarians' daily activities like eating, sleeping, interacting, studying, and praying is normally done in accordance with the RCC's overall plan to make future priests celibate and Christ-like.

The Seminary as a TI Social Structure

The seminary can be classified as a TI like the military camp, asylum, etc. As a TI, the seminary is an exclusive place for residence, work, study, and training where members live alike, isolated from society, and administered formally by a set of officers (Benelli and Da Costa-Rosa 2002).

> The seminary is purposely structured to train each seminarian to see himself as another Christ, completely surrendered to the will of God as made known to him by his superiors. As a major part of this process, the seminary had a set of operational rules to be strictly obeyed. These were approved by the bishops and administered by a single authority, the rector.
> *(Madden 2010, 34)*

Entering a TI such as the seminary can unintendedly arrest the normal socialization of individuals in society. The semi-monastic, secluded, and all-male organization of the seminary is an abnormal social environment. Whatever social learning a person acquires during secondary socialization in

18 Introduction

society can be shortened once he enters the seminary. It is therefore normal to expect seminarians to experience psychosexual immaturity if long years of their life are spent inside a cloistered environment without adequate socialization with people, especially women.

This book explores how the seminary social structure hinders the seminarians' human and sexual growth, making them weak in social control against CSA once ordained and assigned in the parish. What has been repressed during the TI environment of the seminary will normally surface as compensatory behaviors such as CSA once the new priest is assigned in the autonomous lifestyle of the parish. But unlike ordinary lay people in the Church who undergo the normal socialization process in society, Catholic priests experience bracketing in their psychosexual development, an unintended effect of cloistering seminarians in the seminary as a TI organization with its emphasis on spiritual, academic, and pastoral formation.

Heterosexual seminarians who have inclination to married priesthood are inappropriately socialized in the celibate seminary training resulting in sexual repression, immaturity, and lack of self-control that can lead to weak social resistance against CSA. This book contends that the current seminary structure is suitable only for monastic and religious priests but not for diocesan priests who generally live an independent life in the parish despite their vow of obedience and fraternal communion with their brother priests and bishops (see Tirabassi, Porada, and Fiebig 2015).

The Need for Alternative Clerical Training

In 2001, the Seminary Sexuality Education Survey, conducted by Sally Conklin, revealed that the seminary training for clergy does not address the sexuality-related needs of congregants. It concluded that "those preparing for ministry were not helped to understand their own sexual values or behaviors, and where there were courses in sexuality, they were not required or connected to the core curriculum" (The Role of Sexuality Education Within Seminaries 2002). A 2008 survey of progressive clergy further revealed that two-thirds of the respondents disagreed when asked whether they were adequately prepared by their seminaries concerning sexual orientation, gender identity, and gender expression issues in preparation for their ministry (Haffner and Palmer 2009).

Ott and Winters (2011, 59) specifically argue that an institutional shift is needed to achieve a healthy and responsible seminary:

A sexually healthy and responsible seminary provides training in sexuality issues so that seminary graduates and ordained clergy emerge as trained religious professionals who can deal with the complexity of sexual matters – in a healthy, constructive, and appropriate manner. Formation of religious professionals and clergy requires more than a renewal of the curriculum. It requires an institutional shift toward becoming a sexually healthy and responsible seminary that models respect and dignity for all persons.

The current seminary formation is nonresponsive to the development of sexually healthy and responsible priests who will be assigned in the parish. The TI structure of the seminary is incompatible with the loosely regulated structure of the parish for new priests, which can lead to personal crisis and vulnerability to CSA in the absence of a strong communal support and social bonding. Without the social bonding offered by married priesthood, which provides a strong direct and indirect behavioral social controls against sexual deviance, diocesan clerics can be personally weak against the strong temptations of clergy sexual misconduct and other clerical challenges of contemporary life.

As Stephen Rosetti (2013, para. 4) observes: "The challenges facing priests today are much different than they were only a few decades ago. Formation and support for priests in ministry must focus more intently on these contextual changes and must make significant adjustments." The Medieval world that enacted the mandatory clerical celibacy in the 12th century was different from the modernizing world of Vatican II. But today's contemporary age, which is characterized by globalization, constant evolution in communication and technology, social alienation, and emerging forms of personal and social relationships, is vastly different from the Medieval and Modern world (Pieterse 2019; Ritzer and Dean 2021; Trask 2021).

Vatican II's pronouncements on the priesthood and celibacy were done more than 60 years ago, a period when the process of globalization of the world had not yet incorporated the invention of the Internet, virtual reality, and Information Communications Technologies (ICTs), to name a few, that radically altered people's relationships and intimacy (Giddens 2002). Thus, the RCC needs to adjust its current celibate clerical training to respond to the signs of the times. And one of these important adjustments is to create an alternative clerical training that reestablishes married priesthood and the apprenticeship style of clerical formation, especially for diocesan priests who are most prone to CSA in the lonely life of the parish.

Social Resistance Theory

Aside from the socialization and TI theories, this book also utilizes the theory of James C. Scott on social resistance to argue that CSA is a form of passive social resistance by male heterosexual priests against the current mandatory clerical celibacy that begins in seminary formation. Research and literature on CSA reveal that the most common form of sexual abuse is not committed by gay and pedophile priests but by male heterosexual priests who are mostly

20 Introduction

diocesan clerics (John Jay College 2004). Although child clerical sexual abuse has been highlighted by most media reports and CSA research, the fact remains that most common form of Catholic CSA in the RCC is committed not by gay or pedophile priests but by heterosexual secular priests who resist covertly against the clerical celibacy.

The application of the passive resistance theory of James C. Scott (1989) to interpret the current clerical violations to celibacy has apparently been overlooked in the clerical celibacy and seminary formation research and literature. To Scott (1989), who wrote the popular book *Weapons of the Weak*, social resistance can be active and passive. Active resistance such as mass actions and demonstrations are manifest and observable opposition, while passive is hidden and subtle. In this book, Scott highlights the importance of people's every day or passive resistance rather than the active, open, and confrontational types of political resistance such as revolts, insurrections, and other forms of violent political actions to achieve social change.

Passive resistance refers to everyday forms of resistance that are different from the more typical forms of political resistance dominating the historiography of subordinate groups. In his study of peasant resistance, passive acts of resistance can consist of the small arsenal or acts against the powerful "such acts as foot-dragging, dissimulations, false compliance, feigned ignorance, desertion, pilfering, smuggling, poaching, arson, slander, sabotage, surreptitious assault and murder, anonymous threats, and so on" (Scott 1989, 32–62). Scott (1985, 1990) argues that these small acts of courageous challenge to the microscopic control of behavior can give moments of dignity and self-respect for resisters. They can eventually grow powerful enough to challenge the status quo. Passive resistance can also refer to the practice of using meanings and symbols that contest a dominant power, affirming that power can emanate from below in ways people make sense of their world (Hollander and Einwohner 2004).

Although there is no comprehensive data on the clerical practice of celibacy, some authors suggest that there is widespread opposition and violation of the obligatory celibacy law. Kasomo Daniel (2012, 92), for instance, estimated that

> only ten percent of all priests and bishops successfully abstain from sex during their priesthood. Ninety percent engage in sex, 50 percent continuously and 40 percent periodically. Of those, 30–50 percent are homosexually oriented, and their sexual activity is comparable to heterosexual priests and bishops.

Richard Sipe (1995), a priest psychotherapist and popular author on CSA in the RCC, also estimated that 50% of the Catholic clergy is sexually active and suggested that their sexual gratification is done in opposition to their vows of celibacy. The imposition of mandatory clerical celibacy has generated strong and enduring social resistance from married clerics or priests with illicit marital unions. Those who feel that their vocation is married priesthood but are unable to pursue it because of celibacy law largely express their social resistance covertly or passively.

This book devotes Chapter 5 to examine some of the passive resistant acts of diocesan seminarians in the informal and hidden seminary curriculum that silently opposes celibacy and chastity. Clerical resistance against the obligatory celibacy starts in the seminary and continues in priestly ministry that can lead to CSA without effective guardianship in the parish. Resistant acts against celibacy and continence in seminary formation includes pornography, compulsive masturbation, visiting nightclubs and watching strip shows, and establishing and maintaining illicit romantic relationships with women outside the seminary. In sum, it argues that heterosexual diocesan candidates who have inclination to married priesthood are inappropriately socialized in the celibate seminary training resulting in passive social resistance, psychosexual immaturity, lack of self-control, as well as vulnerability to CSA once ordained and assigned in the solitary life of the parish.

Conclusion

This chapter established the basic orientation of the book in terms of the study's social background, sociological approach, main objectives and arguments, methodology, theoretical framework, and the overview of the major sections and individual chapters. It aimed to address the lack of sociological and structural investigations that connect the current mandatory clerical celibacy and celibate seminary training to the persistence of CSA, especially among diocesan clerics in the RCC. It primarily applied the sociological theories of socialization, total institutions, and social resistance to understand how the shift in clerical training from apprenticeship to seminary formation in a TI structure has resulted in negative unintended consequences such as the suspension of the normal human development of seminarians in society, closure of the option of married priesthood, and passive resistance against celibacy.

It was argued that married priesthood and alternative clerical training that is based on the apprenticeship model that is immersed in the real world are better suited for diocesan priests to avoid poor human formation and sexual repression that can lead to psychosexual immaturity and vulnerability to CSA. It recommended a reestablished apprenticeship priestly training that is open to married priesthood for diocesan clergy to counter the persistence of CSA among diocesan priests who are products of the current celibate seminary formation.

Notes

1 The normal training of Catholic priests in the seminary is about ten years and usually spent for the academic degrees of philosophy and theology and other psycho-spiritual training. There are seminary experiments that allow seminarians to study in universities and live in formation houses in the city or near academic institutions. But this is more of an exception rather than the general rule. Seminarians usually live and study in a remote seminary exclusively for celibate priesthood.
2 The "secondary socialization is the stage immediately following the primary phase the young (and later the adult) acquires a series of statuses and consequently successive roles, with integration into various group structure and wider institutional. This type of socialization takes place within educational institutions and professional or formal structures of various groups" (Crisogen 2016, 4).

References

Adams, Kenneth. 2011. "Clergy Sexual Abuse: A Commentary on Celibacy." *Sexual Addiction & Compulsivity: The Journal of Treatment & Prevention* 10 (2–3): 91–92. https://doi.org/10.1080/10720160390230583.

Anderson, Jane. 2016. "Socialization Processes and Clergy Offenders." *Journal of Child Sexual Abuse* 25 (8): 846–865. https://doi.org/10.1080/10538712.2016.1 241333.

Ballano, Vivencio O. 2019. *Sociological Perspectives on Clerical Sexual Abuse in the Catholic Hierarchy: An Exploratory Structural Analysis of Social Disorganization.* Singapore: Springer Nature.

Ballano, Vivencio O. 2023. *In Defense of Married Priesthood: A Sociotheological Investigation of Catholic Clerical Celibacy.* London: Routledge.

Benedict XVI, and Robert Cardinal Sarah. 2020. *From the Depths of Our Hearts: Priesthood, Celibacy, and the Crisis of the Catholic Church.* San Francisco, CA: Ignatius Press.

Benelli, Sílvio José, and Abílio Da Costa-Rosa. 2002. "The Production of the Subjectivity on the Institutional Context of a Catholic Seminary." *SciELO – Scientific Electronic Library Online.* https://doi.org/10.1590/S0103-166X2002000200003.

Benkert, Marianne, and Thomas P. Doyle. 2009. "Clericalism, Religious Duress, and Its Psychological Impact on Victims of Clergy Sexual Abuse." *Pastoral Psychology* 58: 223–238. https://doi.org/10.1007/s11089-008-0188-0.

Boisvert, Donald, and Robert Goss. 2005. *Gay Catholic Priests and Clerical Sexual Misconduct: Breaking the Silence.* London: Routledge.

Boisvert, Donald, and Robert Goss. 2021. *Gay Catholic Priests and Clerical Sexual Misconduct: Breaking the Silence (Gay and Lesbian Studies).* London: Routledge.

Booth, Andrew, Diana Papaioannou, and Anthea Sutton. 2012. *Systematic Approaches to a Successful Literature Review.* Los Angeles, CA: SAGE.

Bourdieu, Pierre. 2020. *Habitus and Field: General Sociology*, Volume 2 (1982–1983). Trans. By Peter Collier. New York, NY: Wiley.

Calkins, Cynthia, Fargo Jamison, Jeglic Elizabeth, and Karen Terry. 2015. "Blessed Be the Children: A Case-Control Study of Sexual Abusers in the Catholic Church." *Behavioral Science & the Law* 33 (4): 580–594. https://doi.org/10.1002/bsl.2193. PMID: 26294387.

Catechism of the Catholic Church. 1994. *Catechism of the Catholic Church.* Homebush, NSW: St. Pauls.

Crisogen, Disca Tiberiu. 2015. "Types of Socialization and Their Importance in Understanding the Phenomena of Socialization." *European Journal of Social Science Education and Research* 2 (4): 331–336. https://doi.org/10.26417/ejser.v5i1.

Crisogen, Disca Tiberiu. 2016. "Types of Socialization and Their Importance in Understanding the Phenomena of Socialization." *European Journal of Social Science Education and Research* 3 (1): 1–10.

Cozzens, Donald. 2006. *Freeing Celibacy*. Collegeville, MN: Liturgical Press.

Cross, Richard, and Daniel Thoma. 2006. "The Collapse of Ascetical Discipline and Clerical Misconduct: Sex and Prayer." *The Linacre Quarterly* 73 (1): 1–114. https://doi.org/10.1080/20508549.2006.11877771.

De Weger, Stephen Edward. 2022. "Unchaste Celibates: Clergy Sexual Misconduct against Adults—Expressions, Definitions, and Harms." *Religions* 13 (5): 1–27. https://doi.org/10.3390/rel13050393.

Deflem, Mathieu. 2015. "Deviance and Social Control." In *The Handbook of Deviance*, edited by Goode Eric, 30–44. Malden, MA: Wiley-Blackwell.

Doyle, Thomas P. 2006. "Clericalism: Enabler of Clergy Sexual Abuse." *Pastoral Psychology* 54 (3): 189–213. https://doi.org/10.1007/s11089-006-6323-x.

Duffy, Eugene. 1992. "I Will Give You Shepherds: The Formation of Priests." *The Furrow* 43 (11): 597–606.

Fisher, C. D. 1986. "Organizational Socialization: An Integrative View." *Research in Personnel and Human Resources Management* 4: 101–145.

Foucault, Michel. 1975. *Discipline and Punish: The Birth of the Prison*. Translated by Alan Sheridan. New York: Vintage Books.

Frawley O'Dea, Mary Gail. 2004. "Psychosocial Anatomy of the Catholic Sexual Abuse Scandal." *Studies in Gender and Sexuality* 5 (2): 121–137. https://doi.org/10.1080/15240650509349244.

Frawley O'Dea, Mary Gail, and Virginia Goldner, eds. 2007. *Predatory Priests, Silenced Victims: The Sexual Abuse Crisis and the Catholic Church*. London: The Analytic Press/Taylor & Francis Group.

Ge, Jianhua, Xuemei Su, and Yan Zhou. 2010. "Organizational Socialization, Organizational Identification and Organizational Citizenship Behavior." *Nankai Business Review International* 1 (2): 166–179. https://doi.org/10.1108/20408741011052573.

Giddens, Anthony. 1984. *The Constitution of Society: Outline of the Structuration Theory*. Oakland, CA: University of California Press.

Giddens, Anthony. 2002. *Runaway World: How Globalisation Is Reshaping Our Lives*. London: Profile Books.

Goffman, Erving. 1968. *Asylums: Essays on the Social Situation of Mental Patients and Other Inmates*. 1st ed. New York, NY: Anchor Books.

Hadebe, Nontando. 2022. "The Crisis of Sexual Abuse Scandal as Catalyst for Reform in the Catholic Church." In *Sexual Reformation? Theological and Ethical Reflections on Human Sexuality*, edited by Manitza Kotze, Nadia Marais, Ven Velden, and Nina Muller, 45–60. Eugene, OR: Wipf and Stock Publishers.

Haffner, D. W., and T. Palmer. 2009. "Survey of Religious Progressives: A Report on Progressive Clergy Action and Advocacy for Sexual Justice". www.religiousinstitute.org/sites/default/files/research_reports/surveyofreligiousprogressivespublicreportapril2009withcover.pdf.

Hirschi, Travis. 1969. *Causes of Delinquency*. Berkeley, CA: University of California Press.

Hays, S. 1994. "Structure and Agency and the Sticky Problem of Culture." *Sociological Theory* 12 (1): 57–72. https://doi.org/10.2307/202035.

Haslanger, Sally. 2015. "Social Structure, Narrative and Explanation." *Canadian Journal of Philosophy* 45 (1): 1–15.

Hoesing, Paul, and T. Hogan, eds. 2021. "You Can't Measure That . . . Can You? How a Catholic Seminary Approaches the Question of Measuring Growth in Human and Spiritual Formation." *Journal of Spiritual Formation and Soul Care* 14 (2): 254–275. 275. https://doi.org/10.1177/19397909211040518.

Hogan, Linda. 2021. "Moral Leadership: A Challenge and a Celebration." *Theological Studies* 82 (1): 138–155. https://doi.org/10.1177/0040563921993456.

Hoge, Dean R. 2002. *The First Five Years of the Priesthood: A Study of Newly Ordained Catholic Priests*. Collegeville: Liturgical Press.

Hollander, Jocelyn A., and Rachel L. Einwohner. 2004. "Conceptualizing Resistance." *Sociological Forum* 19 (4): 533–554.

Homans, George C. 1975. "What Do We Mean by Social Structure?" In *Approaches to the Study of Social Structure*, edited by Blau Peter. New York: The Free Press.

Hoy, Wayne. K., and Anita E. Woolfolk. 1990. "Socialization of Student Teachers." *American Educational Research Journal* 27 (2): 279–300. https://doi.org/10.3102/00028312027002279.

Irwin, Sarah, and Mandy Winterton. 2012. "Qualitative Secondary Analysis and Social Explanation." *Sociological Research Online* 17 (2): 1–12. https://doi.org/10.5153/sro.2626.

Isacco, A., K. Finn, D. Tirabassi, K. A. Meade, and T. G. Plante. 2020. "An Examination of the Psychological Health of Applicants to the Catholic Priesthood and Diaconate." *Spirituality in Clinical Practice* 7 (4): 230–245. https://doi.org/10.1037/scp0000229.

Isacco, Anthony, David G. Songy, and Thomas G. Plante. 2022. "Psychological Evaluations of Clergy Applicants in the Catholic Church: Answering Frequently Asked Questions." *Spirituality in Clinical Practice* 9 (2): 127–139. https://doi.org/10.1037/scp0000294.

Jenkins, Danisha, Candace Burton, and Dave Holmes. 2021. "Hospitals as Total Institutions." *Nursing Philosophy* 23 (2): 12376–12379. https://doi.org/10.1111/nup.12379.

John Jay College Report. 2004. "The Nature and Scope of Sexual Abuse of Minors by Catholic Priests and Deacons in the United States 1950–2002." *USCCB*. www.bishop-accountability.org/reports/2004_02_27_JohnJay/.

Kasomo, Daniel. 2012. "The Psychology Behind Celibacy." *International Journal of Psychology and Behavioral Sciences* 2 (4): 88–93. https://doi.org/10.5923/j.ijpbs.20120204.03.

Keenan, James F. 2018. "Vulnerability and Hierarchicalism." *Melita Theologica: Journal of the Faculty of Theology, University of Malta* 68 (2): 129–142.

Keenan, Marie. 2010. "Are We Killing Our Priests?" *UCD Research Repository*. http://hdl.handle.net/10197/8605.

Keenan, Marie. 2011. *Child Sexual Abuse and the Catholic Church: Gender, Power, and Organizational Culture*. 1st ed. London and New York: Oxford University Press.

Kraschl, Dominikus. 2020. "Sexual Abuse of Minors and Clerical Homosexuality: Comments on a Puzzling Correlation." In *The Abuse of Minors in the Catholic Church*, edited by Anthony Blasi, and Lluis Oviedo, 262. London: Routledge.

Kwon, David. 2022. "Clergy Sexual Abuse and an Ethics of Recognition: An Example of the # ChurchToo Movement in South Korea." *Journal of the Society of Christian Ethics* 42 (2): 345–362.

Largan, Claire, and Theresa Morris. 2019. *Qualitative Secondary Research: A Step-by-Step Guide*. London: SAGE Publications.

Logan, Wayne A. 2003. "Criminal Sanctuaries." *Harvard Civil Rights-Civil Liberties Law Review* 38 (2): 321–391.

Long-Sutehall, Tracy, Magi Sque, and Julia Addington-Hall. 2011. "Secondary Analysis of Qualitative Data: A Valuable Method for Exploring Sensitive Issues With an Elusive Population? *Journal of Research in Nursing* 16 (4): 335–344. https://doi.org/10.1177/1744987110381553.

Madden, James John. 2010. "Monastic Regime at Banyo Seminary: An Oral and Social History of the Pius XII Seminary, Banyo (1941–2000)." PhD Dissertation submitted to University of Southern Queensland. https://core.ac.uk/download/pdf/11047581.pdf.

Manokha, Ivan. 2018. "Surveillance, Panopticism, and Self-discipline in the Digital Age." *Surveillance and Society* 16 (2): 219–237. https://doi.org/10.24908/ss.v16i2.8346.

McGlone, Gerard, and Len Sperry. 2020. "Psychological Evaluation of Catholic Seminary Candidates: Strengths, Shortcomings, and an Innovative Plan." *Spirituality in Clinical Practice* 7 (4): 262–277. https://doi.org/10.1037/scp0000240.

Meek, Katheryn Rhoads, Mark R. McMinn, Todd Burnett, Chris Mazzarella, and Vitaliy L. Voytenko. 2004. "Sexual Ethics Training in Seminary: Preparing Students to Manage Feelings of Sexual Attraction." *Faculty Publications – Graduate School of Clinical Psychology*. Paper 154. http://digitalcommons.georgefox.edu/gscp_fac/154.

Mescher, Marcus. 2023. "Chapter 8: Clergy Sexual Abuse as Moral Injury: Confronting a Wounded and Wounding Church." *Journal of Moral Theology* 3 (CTEWC Book Series 3): 122–139. https://doi.org/10.55476/001c.72061.

Mills, C. Wright. 2000. *The Sociological Imagination*. New York, NY: Oxford University Press.

Nickerson, Charlotte. 2023. "What Is Secondary Socialization." *Simply Sociology*, March 17, 2023. https://simplysociology.com/secondary-socialisation.html.

Oakley, Fr David. 2017. "Seminary Education and Formation: The Challenges and Some Ideas About Future Developments." *International Studies in Catholic Education* 9 (2): 223–235. https://doi.org/10.1080/19422539.2017.1360613.

Ott, Kate M., and Amanda J. Winters. 2011. "Sex and the Seminary: Preparing Ministers for Sexual Health and Justice." *American Journal of Sexuality Education* 6 (1): 55–74. https://doi.org/10.1080/15546128.2011.547368.

Pargament, Kenneth I., Nichole A. Murray-Swank, and Mahoney Annette. 2008. "Problem and Solution: The Spiritual Dimension of Clergy Sexual Abuse and Its Impact on Survivors." *Journal of Child Sexual Abuse* 17 (3–4): 397–420. https://doi.org/10.1080/10538710802330187.

Pieterse, Jan Nederveen. 2019. *Globalization and Culture: Global Melange*. New York: Rowman & Littlefield.

Plante, Thomas G. 2020. "Clergy Sexual Abuse in the Roman Catholic Church: Dispelling Eleven Myths and Separating Facts from Fiction." *Spirituality in Clinical Practice* 7 (4): 220–229. https://doi.org/10.1037/scp0000209.

Pope John Paul II. 1992. *Pastores Dabo Vobis* [I Shall Give you Shepherds]: *Pope John Paul's Post-Synodal Exhortation on the Formation of Priests in the Circumstances of the Present Day*. Vatican: Libreria Editrice Vaticana. www.vatican.va/content/john-paul-ii/en/apost_exhortations/documents/hf_jp-ii_exh_25031992_pastores-dabo-vobis.html.

Pope John Paul II. 1993. "Letter to the United States Bishops." *Libreria Editrice Vaticana*. www.vatican.va/content/john-paul-ii/en/letters/1993/documents/hf_jp-ii_let_19930611_vescovi-usa.html.

Pope Francis. 2017. "Zero Tolerance Sexual Abuse Policy." L 'Osservtore Romano Weekly Edition in English, October 6, 2017, p. 5. In *ETWN*, "Zero Tolerance Sexual Abuse Policy." www.ewtn.com/catholicism/library/zero-tolerance-sexual-abuse-policy-7696.

Presbyterorum Ordinis [Order of Priests]. 1965. *Decree on the Ministry and Life of Priests, Promulgated by Pope Paul VI*. Vatican: The Vatican Archives. www.vatican.va/archive/hist_councils/ii_vatican_council/documents/vat-ii_decree_19651207_presbyterorum-ordinis_en.html.

Reisinger, Doris. 2022. "Reproductive Abuse in the Context of Clergy Sexual Abuse in the Catholic Church." *Religions* 13 (3): 198. https://doi.org/10.3390/rel13030198.

Ritzer, George, and Paul Dean. 2021. *Globalization: A Basic Text*. 3rd ed. Hoboken, NJ: Wiley-Blackwell.

Rosetti, Stephen J. 2013. "The First Five Years: How the Church Can Support Young Priests in a Secular Age." *America: The Jesuit Magazine*, December 23, 2013. www.americamagazine.org/issue/first-five-years.

Reuters. 2017. "Pope Declares 'Zero Tolerance' for Sexual Abuse in Catholic Church." *The Guardians*, January 3, 2017. www.theguardian.com/world/2017/jan/03/pope-declares-zero-tolerance-for-sexual-abuse-in-catholic-church.

Scheper-Hughes, N., and John Devine. 2003. "Priestly Celibacy and Child Sexual Abuse." *Sexualities* 6 (1): 15–40. https://doi.org/10.1177/1363460703006001003.

Schuth, Katarina, OSF. 1999. *Seminaries, Theologates, and the Future of Church Ministry: An Analysis of Trends and Transitions*. Collegeville, MN: Liturgical Press.

Schuth, Katarina, OSF. 2016. *Seminary Formation Recent History-Current Circumstances-New Directions*. Collegeville, MN: Liturgical Press.

Scott, James C. 1985. *Weapons of the Weak: Everyday Forms of Peasant Resistance*. New Haven, CT: Yale University Press.

Scott, James C. 1989. "Everyday Forms of Resistance." In *Everyday Forms of Peasant Resistance*, edited by Forest D. Colburn, 33–62. New York: Routledge.

Scott, James C. 1990. *Domination and the Arts of Resistance: Hidden Transcripts*. New Haven and London: Yale University Press.

Sewell Jr., William H. 1992. "A Theory of Structure: Duality, Agency, and Transformation." *American Journal of Sociology* 98 (1): 1–29. www.jstor.org/stable/2781 191

Sipe, A. W. Richard. 1990. *A Secret World: Sexuality and the Search for Celibacy*. 1st ed. East Sussex: Brunner-Routledge.

Sipe, A. W. Richard. 1995. *Sex, Priests, and Power: Anatomy of a Crisis*. New York: Brunner/Mazel.

Sipe, A. W. Richard. 2003. *Celibacy in Crisis: A Secret World Revisited*. London: Routledge.

Sperry, Len. 2003. *Sex, Priestly Ministry, and the Church*. London: Liturgical Press.

Terry, Karen. J. 2015. "Child Sexual Abuse Within the Catholic Church: A Review of Global Perspectives." *International Journal of Comparative and Applied Criminal Justice* 39 (2): 139–154. https://doi/org/10.1080/01924036.2015.1012703.

The Role of Sexuality Education Within Seminaries. 2002. *The Case for Comprehensive Sexuality Education Within the Context of Seminary Human and Theological Formation: A Report of the Ford Foundation*. Wayne, PA: The Center for Sexuality and Religion.

Terziev, Venelin, and Silva Vasileva. 2022. "The Role of Education in the Socialization of Individuals." *IJAEDU- International E-Journal of Advances in Education* 8 (22): 70–75.

Tirabassi, Domenick, Kelsey Porada, and Jennifer N. Fiebig. 2015. "Where Two or Three Are Gathered: Catholic Seminarians' Perspectives on Individual Versus Communal Living Arrangements of Diocesan Priests." *Pastoral Psychology* 64: 469–477. https://doi.org/10.1007/s11089-015-0639-3.

Trask, Baahira. 2021. "Love in a Time of Globalization: Intimacy Re-imagined Across Cultural Flows." In *International Handbook of Love*, edited by C. H. Mayer, and E. Vanderheiden. Cham: Springer. https://doi.org/10.1007/978-3-030-45996-3_30.

USCCB (United States Conference of Catholic Bishops). 2005. *Program of Priestly Formation, Fifth Edition*. Washington, DC: USCCB.

Van Maanen, John, and Edgar H. Schein. 1979. "Toward of Theory of Organizational Socialization." *Research in Organizational Behavior* 1: 209–264.

Vogels, Heinz-Jürgen. 1993. *Celibacy: Gift or Law?* Lanham, MD: Rowman & Littlefield.

Wickam, Rita. 2019. "Secondary Analysis Research." *Journal of the Advanced Practitioner in Oncology* 10 (4): 395–400. https://doi.org/10.6004/jadpro.2019.10.4.7.

Zollner, Hans. 2019. "The Child at the Center: What Can Theology Say in the Face of the Scandals of Abuse?" *Theological Studies* 80 (3): 692–710. https://doi.org/10.1177/0040563919856867.

Zollner, Hans. 2022. "The Catholic Church's Responsibility in Creating a Safeguarding Culture." *The Person and the Challenges* 12 (1): 5–21. https://doi.org/10.15633/pch.4233.

PART II

Celibate Clerical Training, Human Formation, and Clerical Sexual Abuse

2

SHIFTING METHOD IN CATHOLIC CLERICAL TRAINING AND HUMAN FORMATION AGAINST SEXUAL ABUSE

Introduction

Clerical sexual abuse (CSA) is probably the greatest scourge that afflicts the Roman Catholic Church (RCC) in contemporary times. To account the roots of CSA in the RCC, research and literature tend to emphasize its psychological, psychiatric, and theological aspects that largely blame clericalism as the main enabler of CSA in the RCC (e.g., Doyle 2003, 2006; Neuhaus 2008; Wilson 2008; Seasoltz 2010; Plante 2020; Ormerod 2022). To the psychologist Thomas G. Plante (2020), clericalism is the main force behind Catholic CSA. To him, clericalism is the misguided perception of the laity that clerics constitute a special spiritual group in the RCC with spiritual powers that enable them to be near to their unsuspecting victims and commit CSA.

Benkert and Doyle (2009) contend that the RCC has taught for centuries that clerics are men set apart from and above others. To them, the difference starts with ordination. By divine action, the priest is special and joined to Christ, making him completely different from the laity. To authors Sipe (1990, 2010), Wills (2000), and Scheper-Hughes and Devine (2003), the main enabler of CSA in the RCC is not clericalism but the mandatory clerical celibacy, which serves as a "halo" that gives abusive priests awesome spiritual powers to access their potential victims.

Sociologically speaking, clericalism as a cultural form is only a manifestation of the RCC's material and social structures that are founded on celibate priesthood that sidelines lay participation in ecclesial governance and the regulation of clerical behavior (Ballano 2023). Thus, Doyle and Rubino (2004, 615) aptly argue that the problem of recurring CSA in the RCC "is not something isolated from the dynamics of the Church's power structures."

DOI: 10.4324/9781032722474-4

Instead of blaming the distorted cultural belief of clericalism, it is necessary to examine how the RCC's social structure, which is founded on clerical celibacy, weakens the institutional system of checks and balances of the Church against CSA.

Clericalism is founded on the high social class and status of celibate clerics such as popes, cardinals, bishops, priests, and deacons in the Church, making them the spiritual and political elite of the RCC as a sacerdotal church (Doyle 2006; Ballano 2023). Under this social structure, the laity becomes subservient to celibate clerics, occupying the lowest social stratum in the RCC's social pyramid. Thus, emerged the culture of clericalism that puts clerics in the pedestal and equates the Church with the Catholic hierarchy.

Despite the growing awareness of the structural roots of CSA in the RCC, the current research and literature tend to disregard the crucial role of the social structure of the exclusive, all-male, semi-monastic, and celibate seminary training that produces immature priests who are vulnerable to CSA. More comprehensive studies on seminary formation have been done by notable authors such as Sr. Katarina Schuth (1999, 2016). However, these studies do not relate to the structural flaws of the seminary clerical training to CSA.

The popular CSA author and priest-therapist, A. W. Richard Sipe, specifically saw the connection between the persistence of CSA in the RCC and celibate seminary training (Sipe 1990, 2003). Unfortunately, sociological analysis that explores the structural connection between CSA and the present structural limitations of celibate clerical training that houses seminarians in a closed institution or what the sociologist Erving Goffman (1961) calls "total institutions" (TI) is apparently absent. Specifically, there is a paucity of an in-depth sociological research on how the shift of clerical formation in the 16th century from apprenticeship to celibate seminary training has resulted in poor human formation and vulnerability of diocesan seminary graduates to CSA once ordained and assigned in the parish.

CSA studies in relation to seminary training tend to focus on micro issues such as poor screening of candidates who have serious psychosexual issues that can lead to CSA, weak evaluation process of psychological fitness of seminary applicants (e.g., Isacco et al. 2020; McGlone and Sperry 2020), ineffectiveness of the psychological instruments (e.g., Isacco et al. 2020), inadequate psychological evaluation (e.g., Sperry 2003; Plante 2020; Isacco, Songy, and Thomaso 2022), poor human formation in the seminary training (e.g., Duffy 1992; Meek et al. 2004; Hoesing and Hogan 2021), as well as the struggles of seminarians against sexual repression and celibate formation (e.g., Frawley O'Dea 2004; Boisvert and Goss 2005; Stanosz 2006).

Yet, Vatican II's *Optatam Totius* [Decree on Priestly Training] (1965) welcomed the opportune aids of modern sociological research in enhancing priestly formation (Pope Paul VI 1965, #2, para. 4). Pope John Paul II's *Pastores Dabo Vobis* [I Shall Give You Shepherds] (1992) specifically recognized sociological research as a tool to improve human formation in clerical training. With no a priori knowledge, modern sociology examines behavioral issues using scientific theories and methodologies to interpret data about people's actions. It offers an empirical foundation for doctrinal or theological interpretation in the RCC. Despite the tremendous potential of sociological research to uncover the negative unintended impact of some ecclesial policies such as mandatory clerical celibacy and the current celibate seminary training, modern sociology, as a social science that can offer scientific and empirical grounding to theological and ecclesial claims, remains underutilized in the RCC (Ballano 2020).

The primary objective of this chapter is to sociologically assess the unintended negative consequences of the shift in the method of clerical training from apprenticeship, which is open to married priesthood, to celibate seminary formation. It also investigate the human maturity of future priests inside the seminary, especially diocesan priests, and their ability to counteract CSA. Celibacy is best achieved in a community of celibates. Structurally, the current celibate seminary is designed for monastic and religious priests who live in religious communities during and after clerical formation. In fact, the Council of Trent, which instituted the seminary in the 16th century, copied much of the social structure of monastic and religious clerical life.

Parish clergy, who serves in dioceses under the leadership of their bishops, does not however live in religious communities after seminary formation. Without social bonding in a religious community or intimate primary group such as the family, which sociologists believe to be crucial in the inhibition of rule-breaking behavior such as sexual abuse, secular priests, who are obligated to live and serve the parish alone most of the time, are unnecessarily exposing themselves to CSA without effective behavioral regulation and guardianship.

This chapter contends that the shift in the general method of clerical training during the 16th century has led to the adoption of a celibate seminary training for diocesan clerics that fundamentally disrupts the normal human development of priestly candidates in society, making heterosexual seminarians humanly immature and weak in their social control against CSA. Research has shown that the sexual orientation of the top group of sexually abusive priests in the RCC is neither pedophile nor homosexual but immature heterosexual who lacked realistic socialization with women. CSA is normally committed by male heterosexual secular priests whose personal maturity and sexuality have been repressed by celibate clerical formation (McDevitt 2012; Armbruster 2022).

To achieve this end, this chapter is structured into three sections. The first section traces briefly the formation of Catholic priests in the RCC, starting with the apprenticeship that started since the time of Christ and the Twelve Apostles up to the time the seminary was institutionalized by the Council of Trent

32 Celibate Clerical Training, Human Formation

as the only organization for priestly training since the 16th century. It explains why the RCC changed the method of priestly formation during this period and its possible consequences to the human maturity of future diocesan priests.

The second section examines and compares the human formation and socialization of future priests in apprenticeship method and the exclusive celibate seminary training. It argues that the apprenticeship system is open to married priesthood and allows priestly candidates to pursue their normal life in society during clerical training and, thus, have greater chances to grow in human maturity. The celibate seminary formation in a TI environment, on the other hand, isolates seminarians from the real world, which can eventually result in human immaturity and vulnerability to CSA in the ministry.

The third section investigates the major negative unforeseen effects of the shift in the method of clerical training to the human development of seminarians that include covert clerical resistance against celibacy that starts in the seminary, psychosexual immaturity, and lack of clerical social control against CSA in the parish and ministry.

Using the sociological theory of socialization and secondary textual data from published journal articles, books, media reports, and church documents, this chapter argues that the apprenticeship style of clerical training that allows candidates to be educated and spiritually formed in the real world can provide more opportunities for diocesan priestly candidates for human and psychosexual growth, as well as stronger personal resistance against CSA, compared to celibate seminary formation, which isolates seminarians from society and thus is ideal for religious and monastic aspirants who are presumed to possess the rare gift of clerical celibacy. The imposition of clerical celibacy played an important role in the shift of clerical formation from apprenticeship to seminary training.

Tracing Clerical Formation in the RCC

Apprenticeship

Since the time of Christ until the creation of the seminary by the Council of Trent in 16th century, clerical training consisted mainly of apprenticeship with priests or bishops and attending secular schools, without being trained in an exclusive formation house away from the world. Clerical training was an open system that allowed candidates with a sacred calling to married priesthood to participate in the formation. Because of clerical immorality and lack of proper education for diocesan clerics during the Medieval period, as well as the threat of Protestant reformation, the RCC established the seminary in the 16th century as an exclusive or total institution for priestly training.

From the time of Christ up to the 16th century or before the Council of Trent that founded the TI of the seminary, priestly training was largely done in apprenticeship within the actual social circumstances of the world. Those who want to become priests or ministers of the RCC with this method were not "separated" from the world but immersed into it with the guidance from a master or veteran cleric. Obinwa (2019, 83) explains the nature of apprenticeship as rooted in the New Testament:

> In the New Testament, priestly formation is also of the model of apprenticeship. Jesus Christ, the eternal High Priest (Heb 5:5–6), had a great multitude as followers or disciples (Mark 3:7–8), who were the nucleus of what we know today as Christians or Christ's faithful (Christi fideles). From among them he chose the twelve apostles "who were to be with him and to be sent out to preach" (Mk 3:14). Being with him (met' autou), is another way of saying that he meant them to learn from him how they would minister as his envoys or apostles and priests among the people of God. So they were with him for three years, understudying him as he took them around while proclaiming the Gospel message (cf. Matt 5–7) and doing his other missionary works.
>
> *(cf. Mark 6:30–44)*

The apprenticeship clerical training was therefore initiated by Jesus, acting as the first formator and the Twelve Apostles as the first clerical candidates (Luke 6:12–16). As narrated by the four Gospels, Christ called his apostles, both married and celibate, to learn his life and ministry. During this apprenticeship period, Christ never required his followers to imitate his celibate life nor instructed them to separate themselves from their wives and families if married while learning from him. In apprenticeship style of clerical training, those aspiring for married priesthood are allowed to join and serve in his ministry.

Thus, Christ's apostles and disciples received their preparation for their ministry by living with him in real-life situations and learning from his teaching and ministry. Jesus acted as the first vocation director for both married men led by St. Peter and celibate disciples such as St. John the Apostle, to join his first clerical training so to speak in the Church. "Jesus did the formation of his disciples according to their context, culture, time and circumstances using that pattern which may be understandable to them, such as using simple parables connecting with their daily lives" (Shazad 2015, 15).

"The style, structure, and method of forming future priests in the early period and throughout the Church history was established under the understanding, need, and circumstance of that time. But as it was passing, it became more formal and official in its approach and criteria" (Shazad 2015, 16). Following Christ's example, the early clerical training before the Council of Trent was informal, with no fixed and official structure prescribed universally by the RCC. Aspirants to the priesthood live their normal lives and return to their homes after their classes of their chosen school or college and spiritual guidance of their assigned formators, such as bishops and/or presbyters. This continued from the first to the fifth centuries.

> Before the Council of Trent (16th century AD), there was no formal seminary for the training of priests; priestly formation was still by apprenticeship as it was in the biblical tradition. In the patristic era. St Eusebius of Vercelli "combined the monastic discipline with a common life for parochial clergy with whom he lived personally." St Augustine of Hippo did the same by converting his Episcopal residence into a cathedral school; a formation centre for both superiors of monastic houses and diocesan bishops, those who would in turn form monks and diocesan priests, thereby making clerical training an affair of both the bishop and the community of Christians within the cathedral parish.
>
> *(Obinwa 2019, 86)*

"From the fourth to fifth centuries, most of the priestly formation was in the form of apprenticeships with local bishops or parish priests, while students stayed in their family homes" (Schuth 2016, 11). Newman (1909), for instance, has suggested that St. John Chrysostom personally instructed some number of students for the priesthood. But this was not widely practiced. Institutions that exclusively trained priests for the RCC still did not exist during this period. There was no historical evidence of a formal program for clerical formation during the first four centuries.

The effort to set up a formal school for clerical training, though not an exclusive organization like a TI, started to emerge in 12th and 13th centuries, the period when Lateral Councils also imposed the mandatory clerical celibacy for all Catholic priests. "At the third Lateran Council in 1179, it was mandated that a priest be appointed to the cathedral and be made responsible and remunerated for the formation of local priests. The Fourth Lateran Council of 1215 further required that this priest should be a theologian who could teach Scriptures and Pastoral theology" (Daboh 2020, 143).

Later, the RCC became dissatisfied with the performance of theologians acting as teachers to clerical candidates. Thus, a separate benefice, which was attached to every cathedral Church in the RCC, was established to hire a headmaster to teach aspirants to the priesthood (Orme 2006). But under this set-up, candidates still resided in their homes. In the 14th–16th centuries before the Council of Trent that created the seminary as a TI, priests were allowed to study in secular universities to improve their knowledge and expose themselves to secular society. This program is open to both religious and diocesan priests. However, few diocesan priests availed of this program as they were normally assigned in the countryside. Only elite clerics from affluent families studied in universities in Parish, Bologna, and Rome during this period (Schuth 2016).

The founders of the Jesuits led by St. Ignatius of Loyola, for instance, attended these universities to enhance their clerical education and preparation. Again, they were not separated from the real world. Clerical candidates who were studying in these universities were allowed to live their own normal lives to interact with other students and ordinary people and not cloistered to an exclusive institution like the seminary.

Seminary Clerical Training

The Council of Trent is "the first council which issues and promulgates decrees with regard to formation, seminary and canonical requirements observed for the priesthood" (Shazad 2015, 18). On July 15, 1563, it legislated clerical formation under its norms on seminaries. It stated that "every cathedral and metropolitan Church was obliged to erect a special institution or seminary for the education of future priests" (Shazad 2015, 18).

> The Council also said that candidates for priestly training must be at least twelve years of age, and must possess the ability of reading and writing, and be of good moral character. The candidates should study letters (literature), humanities, chant or music, ecclesiastical computation, rubrics, Scripture, as well as dogmatic, moral, and pastoral theology.
>
> *(Obinwa 2019, 87)*

> The word "seminary" is from the Latin word *seminarium*, meaning "seed plot," and suggests a place where something is bred, grown, and developed – namely a "hot house" for plants. In the medieval period it was used by the church as the designation for settings where candidates for the priesthood could be nourished and formed in their sacred calling apart from distracting "worldly" influences.
>
> *(Calian 2002, 1)*

The Catholic institution of the seminary as the training ground for priests was largely influenced by the communal life of Western monasticism; thus, its social structure is largely semi-monastic. And after several centuries, the RCC's Second Vatican Council (1962–1965) (Vatican II) retained this semi-monastic and exclusive character of the seminary structure (Oakley 2017), even though diocesan seminarians who would become priests live a solitary life in the parish after ordination.

Although diocesan seminary graduates are exposed to secular society after ordination, Vatican II's document *Optatam Totius* [Decree on Priestly

36 Celibate Clerical Training, Human Formation

Training] still affirmed Trent and retained the exclusive and semi-monastic communal clerical training: The seminary is "a community of young men [which] derives its primary force and fitness to train future priests from its own circumstances and way of life." Specifically, "the seminary college was conceived of as a self-sufficient place where those being prepared for priestly ordination, and those responsible for their education, lived, and worked" (Oakley 2017, 223). And yet the parish where most of the diocesan seminary graduates are assigned has a semi-autonomous social structure that encourages individualism and is vastly different from the highly regulated TI communal life of the seminary.

The early clerical formation before the Council of Trent consisted mainly of the apprenticeship of candidates with local bishops or parish priests. Apprenticeship as a form of clerical formation continued until the 12th and 13th centuries. What triggered to the creation of the seminary as a TI was the dismal state of the moral life and academic preparation of diocesan priests. As Schuth (2016) contends, the rise of the seminary was only a response of the RCC to "the sorry moral condition of the clergy" during this era. During the Middle Ages,

> the ministry of preaching and care for the faithful were neglected. There was also an inadequate academic and spiritual formation of the candidates and as a result, there was an increase in the number of diocesan clerics who were either ignorant or incapable of fulfilling their office. With the need of adequate formation, it is the Council of Trent that realized the birth and realization of the concept of "seminary" as an ecclesiastical institution.
>
> *(Lendakadavil 1989 in Alfonso 2015, 15)*

Trent decreed that every diocese must establish colleges solely for priestly training resulting in the establishment of the seminary. It also emphasized the theological and ascetical training of diocesan priests based on the model of the risen Christ as priest and victim.

The intention of Trent in establishing the seminary was to protect "endangered youth" by removing them from the world and to fortify their priestly vocation (Schuth 2016). Therefore, priestly formation became monastic. Seminaries became isolated from the world, usually located in remote places, away from secular affairs of the city, to shield priestly candidates from worldly temptations. The spiritual training of seminary fundamentally followed the monastic method with strong regimented communal prayer life.

The TI structure of the seminary sought to insulate priestly candidates from the dangers of the world and to form them as celibate priests who would serve the Church. Specifically, Trent institutionalized the seminary precisely to shield seminarians from the temptations of the secular world during clerical formation (Schuth 2016). The seminary was:

> understood to be a coming apart from society, an intensive place of conversion, spiritual growth and the development of a relationship with Christ, the Good Shepherd, as well as the place of academic preparation for priestly ministry. . . . The idea of exclusion from society and the protected growth of a priestly vocation was very much at the heart of life in the post-Tridentine seminary.
>
> *(Oakley 2017, 224)*

Considering the historical and sociological contingencies of the times, it is understandable why the Council of Trent instituted the seminary in the 16th century. Establishing a separate celibate institution for clerical training is part of the RCC's Catholic reform against Protestantism and the desire to improve the quality of the training for Catholic priests. Aside from some religious priests such as the Jesuits, who were educated in top universities of Europe for their philosophical and theological training, many diocesan priests were poorly educated and trained for the priesthood, who were usually assigned in remote rural areas of dioceses. Thus, the Council of Trent mandates Catholic bishops to establish a seminary in their dioceses to improve clerical training. Imposing a celibate type of seminary training was part of the RCC's goal of reforming the clergy and minimizing clerical immoralities largely committed by diocesan priests.

Socialization and Human Maturity in Clerical Training

Peoples' human and sexual maturity depends to a large extent on their exposure to the type of social structure and norms offered to them by institutions of society. Strengthening human resolve against rule-breaking behavior such as CSA would depend on the social upbringing of people or what sociologists call the process of socialization, one important way to explain social reproduction in society (Guhin, Calarco, and Miller-Idriss 2021). The structural functionalist Talcott Parsons (1951, 211) classically views socialization as "a particular part of learning through which actors acquire the requisite orientations for satisfactory function in a role."

Sociologists usually classify socialization into two major stages: the primary and secondary. On the one hand, the primary socialization occurs during the early life of the person, starting from birth up to early adolescence, considered by sociologists as the formative years of the person. Secondary socialization, on the other hand, usually occurs from late adolescence to adulthood. During this stage, the person learns more social norms on how to become human and normally undergoes formal education to further develop his or her human and sexual maturity. When people experience the normal primary and secondary socialization process of becoming human in the real world, they usually interact with agents of socialization such as parents, relatives, friends, as well as the opposite or attractive sex to enable them to become humanly mature and sexually responsible individuals.

However, if people separate themselves from this normal socialization process and undergo what sociologists call resocialization (Goffman 1968) in an exclusive and highly supervised social structure to learn distinct social norms and acquire a new identity, such as in the TI environment of the Catholic seminary, they usually abandon their normalization process and risk their psychosexual development. When the RCC imposed clerical celibacy with finality in the 12th century and institutionalized the seminary in the 16th century, the general clerical training for Catholic priests also shifted from a formation that is open to the normal human socialization in society and married priesthood to a resocialization inside the TI seminary structure that is exclusive and secluded from the real world that only allows celibate priesthood.

The mandatory clerical celibacy and the suspension of the normal socialization of priestly candidates in a TI-style of clerical formation, as well as pressuring all seminarians to undergo the celibate seminary training, can have a tremendous impact on the human and sexual development of future priests. Training people to become future ministers of Christ in the RCC entails not only spiritual and academic formation but also human formation. One can never be spiritually mature unless he or she is humanly mature: Grace builds on nature so to speak.

Human maturity in priestly training could not be achieved by fleeing from the human world but by being immersed into it together with spiritual development. The RCC history has shown that clerical training since the time of Christ until the 16th century consisted mainly of apprenticeship that allowed candidates to live their normal lives during spiritual and academic preparation for the priesthood. Before the Council of Trent, there was no formal seminary training exclusively for those who intend to become celibate priests. Priestly formation was still done by apprenticeship as it was in the biblical tradition (Obinwa 2019).

In apprenticeship clerical training,

> priestly candidates learning from those who already serve as priests is very clearly seen, even in the case of Jesus Christ and his apostles. Through the patristic period to the present day of seminary formation, the same idea still runs, such that seminarians somehow learn not only academic subjects, but also behavioral patterns from their formators/professors.
>
> *(Obinwa 2019, 81)*

In apprenticeship method, clerical training was open to the world and allowed not just celibate presbyterate but also married priesthood.

Compared to seminary training, apprenticeship has greater opportunities for human maturity. It was after the shift of clerical training in the 16th century that changed the clerical formation to a TI structure that resulted in serious negative unintended consequences to the human formation of Catholic priests, especially diocesan priests, that has repercussions up to the present times. The vulnerability of celibate diocesan priests to CSA owing to human immaturity and lack of social safety nets such as married priesthood or intimate diocesan clerical community is one major negative consequence of this TI type of priestly formation. The Council of Trent has made clerical training closed, exclusive, and "other worldly," which forms future priests to be weak in direct social control against CSA.

Consequences of Shifting Methods in Clerical Training

Several sociological and historical contingencies influenced Trent to adopt the exclusive and TI structure of the seminary as the only mode of clerical training. Manicheanism and monasticism that emphasized virginity and celibacy as superior way of following Christ compared to marriage contributed to the legislation of clerical celibacy and copying of some aspects of monastic life in seminary formation (Ballano 2023). The imposition of clerical celibacy, however, which became the basis for a celibate clerical seminary formation, has negative unintended consequences to the life of Catholic priests, especially for secular priests who are usually lonely in the parish.

The intention of the RCC and the Council of Trent to improve the academic and spiritual training of diocesan priests by placing seminarians in exclusive seminary training was indeed noble. But sociologists warn that every policy can have two consequences when implemented in actual social practice: the intended and the unintended. To the American sociologist Robert K. Merton (1936), the unintended consequences can be positive and negative as well as manifest and latent.

Latent negative unintended consequences are the unforeseen negative impact of human action or policy. The creation of the semi-monastic, all-male, and exclusive celibate seminary training has several negative unintended or unforeseen consequences, especially to priestly life in the contemporary times. These consequences were not anticipated by the Pope and bishops during the Council of Trent, who established the seminary institution. Adopting the celibate model of priestly training may be sociologically appropriate during the late Medieval times of the 16th century, but not to growing complexity of the current globalizing era.

Another important negative unintended consequence of the shifting of clerical formation from apprenticeship to exclusive seminary training is the

40 Celibate Clerical Training, Human Formation

social isolation of seminarians from the normal social bonding and inter-action with people in society, which is crucial for psychosexual maturity. Trent established the seminary as what the sociologist Erving Goffman characterizes as a TI like prisons, army barracks, convents, hospitals, boarding schools, or convents. TIs are "total" insofar as they physically confined their members or inmates in an exclusive organization, limiting their access to valued resources: not only material possessions but also time, personal space, and control over one's daily routine.

Goffman (1961) studied in detail the structure, nature, and psychosocial dynamics of "total institutions" while in hospital work in the United States. To him, TI as an exclusive resocialization organization has four key features, namely: "(a) the unfolding of the daily round in the same place and under the same authority; (b) batch living or being treated as part of an anonymous mass; (c) the rigid timetabling and scheduling of activities; and (d) an institutional goal of resocialization" (Scott 2010, 215).

In his book, *Asylums*, Goffman (1961) considers TI as exclusive, generally prohibiting social interaction between insider and outsider and where insiders work, play, and sleep in the same place, with the same coparticipants, under the same authorities and in terms of the same overall plan. "Totalizing practices . . . [can] include 'the mortification of self,' a person within an institution exercises little control, and is essentialized to serve the needs of the institution" (Jenkins, Burton, and Holmes 2022, 1). In a TI environment, members are immersed and enclosed – physically or symbolically – for a long period of time, to the exclusion of other attachments, which fundamentally aim to change their identities. It demands from its members obedience that pervades their entire being and absolute commitment (Scott 2011). Compliance to TI arrangements is absolute and punishment may be swift (Goffman 1961).

Thus, joining a TI would mean that actors are actively and passively controlled by institutional arrangements, making them lacking in autonomy to determine their own fate (Scott 2010). They are pressured to learn and undergo training in a unique way (Wallace 2017). Although this shift from apprenticeship to seminary formation has basically achieved some of the Trent's purpose of improving clerical education and moral life, it has not foreseen the negative unintended effects of detaching seminarians from the real world to their human development and commitment to celibate priesthood.

Covert Clerical Resistance

The British sociologist Anthony Giddens (1984) argues that there is always an interconnection between social structure and human action. The celibate male priesthood model that frames the TI social structure of the seminary formation has an impact on the human agency of formators and future priests

Shifting Method in Catholic Clerical Training **41**

who in turn reinforce the celibate social structure through their actions and compliance. The type of seminary social structure offered by the RCC for the formation of future priests can greatly affect the action and human development of seminarians as well as the type of priesthood available to priestly candidates.

The decision of the RCC to change its policy from optional to obligatory celibacy during the 11th and 12th centuries had serious unintended consequences to the social structure of clerical formation. The change of priestly training from apprenticeship, which is open to married priesthood, to exclusive seminary formation, which is open only to celibate priesthood, has serious consequences. This shift has radically altered the nature of clerical training from one that is open to the secular world to one that is detached from society. This structural change poses a serious challenge to the human and sexual formation of diocesan priestly candidates who are suitable for married priesthood, given the solitary life in the parish, which has no communal support for secular priests.

Although the RCC and the Council of Trent had their own reasons why it dropped apprenticeship and adopted celibate seminary training, the negative unintended consequences to the psychosexual maturity of seminarians are enormous. Clerical candidates who realized that they do not possess the rare gift of celibacy are forced to undergo a repressed psychosexual development of the celibate TI structure of the seminary for lack of options. Taking a lifelong vow of celibacy by those who have no charism into it is silent martyrdom (Cozzens 2006). As Kohanski (2019) argues, clerical celibacy is not a normal condition for human beings. To him, the RCC is attempting to deny reality by suppressing sexuality entirely among its clergy. Christ was clear in the gospels that celibacy is a rare gift (Matthew 19:11f). Thus, he never required his followers to be celibate or to imitate his celibate life and ministry.

Vogels (1993, 8) contends that "the evangelical value of celibacy is charism not a law – indeed the obligation of law actually destroys the effective value of charisms." Married priesthood is a legitimate means of living the vocation of Catholic priesthood; repressing it can lead to various forms of covert resistance to circumvent the mandatory clerical celibacy law (Ballano 2023). Currently, Vatican II recognized the legitimacy of married priesthood and acknowledged the flourishing married clergy in Eastern Catholic churches – implying that married priesthood is indeed a valid social calling and a holy vocation. It also declared that celibacy is not essential to the priesthood (*Presbyterorum Ordinis* [Order of Priests] 1965, para. 16).

Refusing to acknowledge and permit married priesthood for those without the charism of celibacy can lead to what James C. Scott calls passive or everyday resistance. Heterosexual candidates who discerned to enter Catholic priesthood in the married state can passively go through the process of celibate seminary formation and get ordained. However, celibate clerical formation for these candidates can lead to uneasiness and sexual repression, resulting in a life of everyday resistance to celibate life, covertly living double lives and secretly committing sexual abuse in private life to release repressed sexuality when they become priests. Thus, CSA committed by several diocesan priests can be considered a form of ongoing secret opposition by heterosexual clerics the celibacy rule in the RCC, an unforeseen negative effect of celibate seminary formation.

Psychosexual Immaturity

Another negative unintended consequence of adopting the TI seminary clerical formation is the psychosexual immaturity of seminary graduates. The adoption of the one celibate seminary formation for all candidates to the priesthood with its emphasis of transforming seminarians into *Alter Christus* [Other Christ] has inadvertently suppressed human sexuality. Clerical formation usually occurs during late adolescence and young adulthood in the lives of seminarians, crucial years for human and psychosexual maturity.

"Many young men entered the seminary straight after completing their schooling, where their formation contributed to a vulnerability in the clergy community to offend" (Keenan 2012, 146). Their lives are shaped by the controlled environment of the TI communal life of the seminary to develop the spiritualized gender role of the clergy. "Discussion, suggestion, and exploration of sexuality were curtailed, as evidenced in the ban on 'particular friendships' " (Frawley O'Dea 2004, 130). This restriction on any sexual element in friendship serves to form seminarians to the perfect celibate clerical masculinity (Anderson 2016).

In the TI environment of the seminary, seminarians were incorporated into a culture in which open discussion of sexuality is prohibited and where a culture of secrecy is developed (Boisvert and Goss 2005). Socialization processes operate to sustain an established moral code, and, in the case of seminarians who became clergy offenders, their moral education has been identified as a factor in CSA insofar as it prevented human development and the cultivation of healthy relationships (Frawley O'Dea 2004; Keenan 2011). "Seminarians, for example, may well be supported in their practice in a highly regulated environment, where the majority of the teaching faculty are clergy and where laypeople are largely excluded from their classes and seminary living spaces." In the highly regulated environment of the seminary, seminarians have limited interaction with women. The majority of the teachers are priests. Lay people are also excluded in their classes and seminary environment (Plante 2011).

However, once these seminarians are ordained diocesan priests, the communal life of the seminary that regulates their behavior is lost. They usually live alone in the parish and oftentimes find ways to commit sexual deviance and CSA to manage loneliness and other difficulties of celibate life. "Some support may come from confreres and parishioners, but these measures are generally not available in modern society, which they also inhabit." Some priests may receive support from fellow priests and parishioners. But this support may not be easily available for diocesan priests in remote parishes:

> Pope St John Paul II has highlighted the necessity of inculcating in priestly training human formation, spiritual formation, intellectual formation, and pastoral formation. Human formation, for instance, helps priests to become balanced people who are strong and free, capable of bearing the weight of pastoral responsibilities. It helps them to love truth, to be loyal to authorities and respectful to every person, to be able to draw people to Jesus Christ rather than be obstacles to their coming close to him. Indeed, "the priest should be able to know the depths of human heart, to perceive difficulties and problems, to make meeting and dialogue easy, to create trust and cooperation, to express serene and objective judgments."
>
> *(Obinwa 2019, 88)*

But the present semi-monastic seminary formation for human development is inadequate to realistically attain psychosexual maturity since the normal social learning of seminarians in society is disrupted. Experience rather knowledge is the best teacher for human formation. No amount of psychological advice and input on human development and sexuality can replace real interaction with sociocultural agents of society, especially women, for heterosexual diocesan priests to attain authentic human growth. Thus, married priesthood and apprenticeship clerical formation can be the best alternative to the current celibate seminary training for diocesan clergy to address psychosexual immaturity and CSA.

Lack of Social Control Against CSA

The mandatory celibacy was imposed on all Catholic clerics by the Code of Canon Law and Fourth Lateran Council and retained by the Council of Trent and Vatican II. This has become the cornerstone of the current celibate clerical formation that represses the sexuality of seminarians and open discussion on sexuality problems outside spiritual direction. Celibacy is suitable in a religious clerical setting. That is why obligatory celibacy is more appropriate for religious and monastic priests who normally work and live in their religious communities after seminary formation. This is not, however, the case for secular or diocesan celibate priests who usually live a lonely life in the parish after seminary training (O' Doherty 2017).

Married priesthood, if not suppressed in the 11th and 12th centuries by the Second and Fourth Lateran Councils, would have been the most common social calling for Catholic priests, following Christ's counsel that celibacy is a rare gift. The RCC could have avoided the two serious problems of CSA and priest shortage if apprenticeship clerical training and married priesthood are allowed universally. Research studies in psychiatric, psychological, sociological, and other social science disciplines view celibacy as a serious obstacle for clerics to live a happy and healthy psycho-spiritual life, free from CSA (Sipe 1990; Scheper-Hughes and Devine 2003).

Clerical celibacy and ordination do not make Catholic priests superhuman, providing them with religious immunity from CSA and loneliness in the parish. To Canon lawyer and CSA expert Fr. Thomas P. Doyle (2006), celibacy is only a form of clerical garb that heightens people's perception that clerics are special people in the RCC and distinct from the laity. It also strengthens clerical secrecy in sexual life, which hides CSA. It magnifies the glitter of the priesthood as a "better" vocation to marriage, resulting in clericalism. But both celibacy and ordination do not make priests extraordinary people in the RCC. Doyle (2006) contends that priests and bishops remain mortal beings and vulnerable to CSA despite ordination and consecration in the Church.

Clerical celibacy appears to be a better option for religious and monastic priests who live with social bonding, mutual support, and guardianship against CSA in their religious communities – although cover-ups of CSA cases can also happen. This is not, however, the case for solitary diocesan priests who are more suitable for married presbyterate that offers intimacy, mutual support, and behavioral monitoring by their spouses and children. Married priesthood offers a strong social control against CSA for the parish clergy.

Social control refers to the system of "measures, suggestion, persuasion, restraint, and coercion," which coerces individuals to conform to conventional behavior (Sharma 2007). It can be direct and indirect. Direct social control is exerted on a person by members of a primary or intimate group, such as immediate family members (Umberson 1987), while indirect social control is experienced through informal pressures to conform to conventional norms in the local community through the family (Umberson 1987; Sydlitz 1993). Spouses and children of married diocesan clergy can extend the necessary direct social control, while the network of married priests and their families in the diocese can offer indirect social control.

Research has shown that intimate and support groups are important for diocesan priests to overcome loneliness and spiritual dryness (Schnabel and Koval 1979; Büssing et al. 2017), as well as the temptation of CSA in the parish (Ballano 2019). Marriage and family life in diocesan priesthood can indeed provide direct social control and monitoring of the daily activities of priests in the parish, greatly minimizing the deviant opportunities for sexual indiscretion and sexual abuse against parishioners. Specifically, spouses and children of married priests can serve as regulators of clerical behavior who can strongly prevent CSA in the diocesan ministry. Although married priesthood is not a complete guarantee against CSA, it is nevertheless a better alternative and social calling for diocesan clergy compared to celibate priesthood.

Conclusion and Recommendation

This chapter has sociologically explored the structural connection between the persistence of CSA in the RCC and the poor human formation of the current exclusive, all-male, and celibate seminary clerical formation in a TI social structure, which suspends the normal human development of priestly candidates, especially diocesan seminarians. The celibate seminary training also deprives candidates of the option to married priesthood and making them vulnerable to CSA once ordained and assigned in the parish without intimate social bonding offered by a religious community or family life in married priesthood.

The major shift of clerical training from the historically grounded apprenticeship since the time of Christ that is rooted in the real world to an exclusive seminary clerical formation in an isolated social environment by the Council of Trent in the 16th century has resulted in negative unintended consequences that included covert passive resistance against celibacy, psychological immaturity, and a lack of social control by diocesan priests against CSA.

Since the present seminary clerical training is more suitable for religious and monastic priests who continue to live in their religious communities after seminary formation, this chapter recommends the alternative clerical training of apprenticeship and married priesthood for diocesan clergy to best equip secular priests with the necessary direct and indirect social controls against CSA in the lonely life of the parish.

References

Alfonso, Ashley. 2015. "The Role of Accompaniment in Seminary Formation." *Janana-Sanjeevani* 1 (3): 13–23.

Anderson, Jane. 2016. "Socialization Processes and Clergy Offenders." *Journal of Child Sexual Abuse* 25 (8): 846–865. https://doi.org/10.1080/10538712.2016.1241333.

Armbruster, Andre. 2022. "On the Undisclosed Transfer of Abusive Catholic Priests: A Field Theoretical Analysis of the Sexual Repression Within the Catholic Church and the Use of Legitimate Language." *Critical Research on Religion* 10 (1): 61–67. https://doi.org/10.1177/20503032211015282.

Ballano, Vivencio O. 2019. *Sociological Perspectives on Clerical Sexual Abuse in the Catholic Hierarchy: An Exploratory Structural Analysis of Social Disorganization.* Berlin: Springer Nature.

Ballano, Vivencio O. 2020. "The Social Sciences, Pastoral Theology, and Pastoral Work: Understanding the Underutilization of Sociology in Catholic Pastoral Ministry." *Open Theology* 6: 531–546. https://doi.org/10.1515/opth-2020-0132.

Ballano, Vivencio O. 2023. *In Defense of Married Priesthood: A Sociotheological Investigation of Catholic Clerical Celibacy.* London: Routledge.

Benkert, Marianne, and Thomas P. Doyle. 2009. "Clericalism, Religious Duress and Its Psychological Impact on Victims of Clergy Sexual Abuse." *Pastoral Psychology* 58 (3): 223–238. https://doi.org/10.1007/s11089-008-0188-0.

Boisvert, Donald, and Robert Goss. 2005. *Gay Catholic Priests and Clerical Sexual Misconduct: Breaking the Silence.* London: Routledge.

Büssing, Arndt, Baumann, Klaus, Jacobs, Christoph, and Frick, Echard. 2017. "Spiritual Dryness in Catholic Priests: Internal Resources as Possible Buffers." *Psychology of Religion and Spirituality* 9 (1): 46–55. https://doi.org/10.1037/rel0000063.

Calian, Carnegie Samuel. 2002. *The Ideal Seminary: Pursuing Excellence in Theological Education*. Louisville and London: Westminster John Knox Press.

Cozzens, Donald. 2006. *Freeing Celibacy*. Collegeville, MN: Liturgical Press.

Daboh, Habila. 2020. "The Evolution of Seminary Formation from the Apostolic Era to the Council of Trent: A Critical Appraisal." *JORAS* 10: 137–156.

Doyle, Thomas P. 2003. "Roman Catholic Clericalism, Religious Duress, and Clergy Sexual Abuse." *Pastoral Psychology* 51: 189–231. https://doi.org/10.1023/A:1021301407104.

Doyle, Thomas P. 2006. "Clericalism: Enabler of Clergy Sexual Abuse." *Pastoral Psychology* 54 (3): 189–213. https://doi.org/10.1007/s11089-006-6323-x.

Doyle, Thomas P., and Stephen C. Rubino. 2004. "Catholic Clergy Sexual Abuse Meets the Civil Law." *Fordham Urban Law Journal* 31: 549–615. https://ir.lawnet.fordham.edu/ulj/vol31/iss2/6.

Duffy, Eugene. 1992. "I Will Give You Shepherds: The Formation of Priests." *The Furrow* 43 (11): 597–606. http://www.jstor.org/stable/27662296.

Frawley O'Dea, Mary Gail 2004. "Psychological Anatomy of the Catholic Sexual Abuse Scandal." *Studies in Gender and Sexuality* 5 (2): 121–137. https://doi.org/10.1080/15240650509349244.

Giddens, Anthony. 1984. *The Constitution of Society: Outline of the Structuration Theory*. Oakland, CA: University of California Press.

Goffman, Erving. 1961. *Asylums: Essays on the Social Situation of Mental Patients and Other Inmates*. New York: Anchor Books.

Goffman, Erving. 1968. *Asylums: Essays on the Social Situation of Mental Patients and Other Inmates*. 1st ed. New York, NY: Anchor Books.

Guhin, Jeffrey, Jessica McCrory Calarco, and Cynthia Miller-Idriss. 2021. "Whatever Happened to Socialization?" *Annual Review of Sociology* 47 (1): 109–129. https://doi.org/10.1146/annurev-soc-090320103012.

Hoesing, Paul, and T. Hogan, eds. 2021. "You Can't Measure That . . . Can You? How a Catholic Seminary Approaches the Question of Measuring Growth in Human and Spiritual Formation." *Journal of Spiritual Formation and Soul Care* 14 (2): 254–275. https://doi.org/10.1177/19397909211040518.

Isacco, Anthony, Katie Finn, Domenick Tirbassi, and Thomas G. Plante. 2020. "An Examination of the Psychological Health of Applicants to the Catholic Priesthood and Diaconate." *Spirituality in Clinical Practice* 7 (4): 230–245. https://doi.org/10.1037/scp0000229.

Isacco, Anthony, David G. Songy, and Thomas G. Plante. 2022. "Psychological Evaluations of Clergy Applicants in the Catholic Church: Answering Frequently Asked Questions." *Spirituality in Clinical Practice* 9 (2): 127–139. https://doi.org/10.1037/scp0000294.

Jenkins, Danisha, Candace Burton, and Dave Holmes. 2022. "Hospitals as Total Institutions." *Nursing Philosophy* 23 (2): 12376–12379. https://doi.org/10.1111/nup.12379.

Keenan, Marie. 2011. *Child Sexual Abuse and the Catholic Church: Gender, Power, and Organizational Culture*. 1st ed. London and New York: Oxford University Press.

Keenan, Marie. 2012. *Child Sexual Abuse and the Catholic Church: Gender, Power, and Organizational Culture*. New York, NY: Oxford University Press.

Kohanski, Dan. 2019. "Why the Catholic Church Is So Conflicted About Sex." *The Humanist*, January/February. www.academia.edu/38058857/Why_the_Catholic_Church_Is_So_Conflicted_about_Sex?email_work_card=view-paper.

Lendakadavil, Anthony. 1989. *Candidates for the Priesthood*. Shillong: Vendrame Institute Publications.

McDevitt, Patrick J. 2012. "Sexual and Intimacy Health of Roman Catholic Priests." *Journal of Prevention & Intervention in the Community* 40 (3): 208–218. https://doi.org/10.1080/10852352.2012.680413.

McGlone, Gerard, and Sperry, Len. 2020. "Psychological Evaluation of Catholic Seminary Candidates: Strengths, Shortcomings, and an Innovative Plan." *Spirituality in Clinical Practice* 7 (4): 262–277. https://doi.org/10.1037/scp0000240.

Meek, Katheryn Rhoads, Mark R. McMinn, Todd Burnett, Chris Mazzarella, and Vitaliy Voytenko. 2004. "Sexual Ethics Training in Seminary: Preparing Students to Manage Feelings of Sexual Attraction." *Pastoral Psychology* 53 (1): 63–79.

Merton, Robert K. 1936. "The Unanticipated Consequences of Purposive Social Action." *American Sociological Review* 1 (6): 894–904. https://doi.org/10.2307/2084615.

Neuhaus, Ricard John. 2008. "Clerical Scandal and the Scandal of Clericalism." *First Things*, March 2008. www.firstthings.com/article/2008/03/clerical-scandal-and-the-scandal-of-clericalism.

Newman, John H. 1909. *Universities and Seminaries. L École des Hautes Etudes, Historical Sketches*. Vol. Ill. London: Longmans, Green.

Oakley, Fr David. 2017. "Seminary Education and Formation: The Challenges and Some Ideas about Future Developments." *International Studies in Catholic Education* 9 (2): 223–235. https://doi.org/10.1080/19422539.2017.1360613.

Obinwa, Ignatius M. C. 2019. "Revisiting the Formation of Catholic Priests in Nigerian Context: A Perspective of the Biblical Notion of Priesthood." *Ministerium: A Journal of Contextual Theology* 5: 81–95.

O' Doherty, Malachi. 2017. "Former Catholic Priest on the Sad, Lonely Lives of Retired Clergy." *Belfast Telegraph*, January 19, 2017. www.belfasttelegraph.co.uk/news/northern-ireland/former-catholic-priest-on-the-sad-lonely-lives-of-retired-clergy-35378704.html.

Optatam Totius [Decree on Priestly Training]. 1965. *Decree on Priestly Training by Pope Paul VI on October 28, 1965*. Vatican: Vatican Archives. https://www.vatican.va/archive/hist_councils/ii_vatican_council/documents/vat-ii_decree_19651028_optatam-totius_en.html.

Orme, Nicholas. 2006. *Medieval Schools*. New Haven and London: Yale University Press.

Ormerod, Neil. 2022. "The Parable of the Good Samaritan, Clericalism, and the Sexual Abuse Crisis in the Australian Context." *Revista Iberoamericana de Teología*, XVIII (34): 35–56.

Parsons, Talcott. 1951. *The Social System*. New York: Free Press.

Pastores Dabo Vobis [I Shall Give you Shepherds]. 1992. *Pope John Paul's Post-Synodal Exhortation on the Formation of Priests in the Circumstances of the Present Day*. Vatican: Libreria Editrice Vaticana. www.vatican.va/content/john-paul-ii/en/apost_exhortations/documents/hf_jp-ii_exh_25031992_pastores-dabo-vobis.html.

Plante, Thomas G. 2011. "Psychological Screening of Clergy Applicants: Keeping Those Who Might Harm Children and Others Out of Ministry". In *Sexual Abuse in the Catholic Church: A Decade of Crisis, 2002–2012*, edited by Thomas G. Plante, and Kathleen McChesney, 195–203. Santa Barbara, CA: Praeger.

Plante, Thomas G. 2020. "Clergy Sexual Abuse in the Roman Catholic Church: Dispelling Eleven Myths and Separating Facts from Fiction." *Spirituality in Clinical Practice* 7 (4): 220–229. https://doi.org/10.1037/scp0000209.

Presbyterorum Ordinis [Order of Priests]. 1965. *Decree on the Ministry and Life of Priests, Promulgated by Pope Paul VI*. Vatican: The Vatican Archives. www.vatican.va/archive/hist_councils/ii_vatican_council/documents/vat-ii_decree_19651207_presbyterorum-ordinis_en.html.

Schnabel, John F., and Koval, John P. 1979. "Loneliness and Deprivation: The Case of Roman Catholic Priests." *Journal of Sociology & Social Welfare* 6 (3): 410–434. https://scholarworks.wmich.edu/jssw/vol6/iss3/11.

Scheper-Hughes, Nancy, and Devine, John. 2003. "Priestly Celibacy and Child Sexual Abuse." *Sexualities* 6 (1): 15–40. https://doi.org/10.1177/1363460703006001003.

Schuth, Katarina, OSF. 1999. *Seminaries, Theologates, and the Future of Church Ministry: An Analysis of Trends and Transitions.* Collegeville, MN: Liturgical Press.

Schuth, Katarina. 2016. *Seminary Formation: Recent History-Current Circumstances-New Directions.* Collegeville, MN: Liturgical Press.

Scott, Susie. 2010. "Revisiting the Total Institution: Performative Regulation in the Reinventive Institution." *Sociology* 44 (2): 213–231. https://doi.org/10.1177/00380 38509357198.

Scott, Susie. 2011. *Total Institutions and Reinvented Identities.* London: Palgrave McMillan.

Seasoltz, Kevin. 2010. "Clericalism: A Sickness in the Church." *The Furrow* 61 (3): 135–142. www.jstor.org/stable/27809007.

Sharma, Rajendra Kumar. 2007. *Social Change and Social Control.* Chennai: Atlantic Publishers and Distributors.

Shazad, Waqas. 2015. "Formation for Priesthood and Challenges for the Church in Pakistan." *National Institute of Theology.* www.academia.edu/19331009/Formation_for_Priesthood_Challenges_for_the_Church_in_Pakistan.

Sipe, A. W. Richard. 1990. *A Secret World: Celibacy and the Search for Celibacy.* London: Brunner/Mazel.

Sipe, A. W. Richard. 2003. *Celibacy in Crises.* New York and Hove: Brunner-Routledge.

Sipe, A. M. Richard. 2010. "Beneath the Child Abuse Scandal." *National Catholic Reporter,* July 22, 2010. https://www.bishop-accountability.org/news2010/07_08/2010_07_22_Richard_BeneathThe.htm.

Sperry, Len. 2003. *Sex, Priestly Ministry, and the Church.* London: Liturgical Press.

Stanosz, Paul. 2006. *The Struggle for Celibacy: The Culture of Catholic Seminary Life.* New York: Herder & Herder.

Sydlitz, Ruth. 1993. "Complexity in the Relationships Among Direct and Indirect Parental Controls and Delinquency." *Youth & Society* 24 (3): 243–275. https://doi.org/10.1177/0044118X93024003001.

Umberson, Debra. 1987. "Family Status and Health Behaviors: Social Control as a Dimension of Social Integration." *Journal of Health and Social Behavior* 28 (3): 306–319. https://doi.org/10.2307/2136848.

Vogels, Heinz-Jürgen. 1993. *Celibacy: Gift or Law?* Lanham, MD: Rowman & Littlefield.

Wallace, Samuel E, ed. 2017. *Total Institutions.* 1st ed., Kindle ed. London: Routledge.

Wills, Gary. 2000. *Papal Sin: Structures of Deceit.* New York: Doubleday.

Wilson, George. 2008. *Clericalism: The Death of Priesthood.* Collegeville, MN: Liturgical Press.

3

CELIBATE SEMINARY FORMATION, TOTAL INSTITUTION, AND CLERICAL SEXUAL ABUSE

Introduction

The clerical sexual abuse (CSA) scandal in the Roman Catholic Church (RCC) is not a recent phenomenon that started only in the United States with the Boston Globe reports on clerical sexual misconduct in 2002. The Canon lawyer Fr. Thomas P. Doyle (2003) argued that CSA is embedded in the Church's more than 2,000 years of history, citing a steady stream of Church's legal documentation that revealed disciplinary pronouncements from popes and the bishops against CSA from the fourth century up to the present day. Public inquiries and commissions that investigated CSA in other Western and English-speaking countries also indicated that CSA is not only an American phenomenon but a worldwide problem for the RCC (Terry 2015).

One of the commissions investigating CSA in the RCC is the Royal Commission into Institutional Responses that Child Sexual Abuse (2017) of Australia. Its final report claims that a combination of individual and systemic factors enabled CSA, especially child sexual abuse, in the RCC. It particularly highlighted the inadequate human and sexual formation of priests in the seminary as contributing to CSA. Cozzens et al. (2004) have provided in their research a profile of Catholic clergy abusing children and adolescents, especially boys, as psychosexually immature, with their emotional life stuck at an adolescent level of development. They claimed that the requirements of mandatory clerical celibacy have attracted certain types of men to ordained Catholic ministry who are prone to commit sexual abuse against minors. Grattagliano et al. (2018, 812) also contend that:

[s]ome priests conceive of celibacy as the abstention from sexual relations with women. Therefore, they convince themselves that sexual relations

DOI: 10.4324/9781032722474-5

with boys do not contravene their vow of celibacy. The boy is seen simply as a means for obtaining pleasure in all safety. Those most likely to suffer abuse by ministers, the victims, are generally young people with some social or physical lack, who are therefore vulnerable.

The choice of a minor is also preferred because satisfaction is sought outside the commitment of a relationship. The John Jay College Report (2004) revealed that 64% of the accused priests had abused males only, 22.4% females only, and 3.6% had abused both sexes.

Sexual abuse by priests seems to be a reactive behavior . . . [and] a compensation mechanism that attempts to fill a void of affection, erotism, and sexuality. The abuse is seen and rationalized as similar to masturbation or pornography so that it does not tarnish the public function of a church minister.

(Grattagliano et al. 2018, 812)

Priest offenders who are products of seminary formation usually have

few real friends of their own age cohort with whom they can be themselves, with whom they enjoy friendships that are appropriately intimate. . . . [T]hey relate as Catholic clergyman – not as a man who happens to be an ordained priest.

(Cozzens et al. 2004, 6–7)

This loneliness is part and parcel of mandated celibacy that can result in compensatory behaviors such as CSA by a number of priests (Cozzens et al. 2004).

The Royal Commission into Institutional Responses that Child Sexual Abuse of Australia (2017) faulted the ineffective process of selecting, screening, and initial forming of clerical candidates as contributing to the increased risk of CSA. It blamed "the role of human formation and formation to live a celibate life; the challenges of sexuality and sexual orientation; the relationship between formation and clericalism" (Royal Commission into Institutional Responses that Child Sexual Abuse 2017, 588, 569).

Clerical celibacy and celibate seminary training also emerged as a significant enabler of CSA in another commission sponsored by German Bishops' Conference that aimed to identify the major structures that facilitate CSA in the RCC. It revealed several structures and dynamics within the RCC that supported CSA, including the obligatory clerical celibacy (Wamsley 2018). Other research studies also supported this finding of the German bishops, connecting CSA to the mandatory clerical celibacy (Sipe 1990, 2010; Wills 2000; Scheper-Hughes and Devine 2003; Yocum 2013; Li, Liu, and Wan 2022).

Sandra Yocum (2013) specifically views clerical celibacy as enabling CSA. To her, compulsory celibacy is only a "symbolic system of purity" that provides clerics with awesome spiritual powers and divine authority to lead the flock. With this great power, clerics can then easily commit CSA since it is so difficult for the faithful "to accept that 'holy' men could perpetrate sexual abuse" (Yocum 2013). Li, Liu, and Wan (2022) also view clerical celibacy as related to CSA since the former is repressing clerics' inherent sexual drive resulting in a covert resistance to express it in invisible but convenient means. They attributed the persistence of CSA to the suppression of sexual needs of priests by mandatory clerical celibacy in the RCC.

The veteran priest-therapist and author A. W. Richard Sipe, however, specifically relates the persistence of CSA in the RCC to the celibate seminary training of priests (Sipe 1990, 2003). Linking celibacy to CSA necessitates inquiring how the exclusive celibate seminary training built in a closed social structure of what the sociologist Erving Goffman (1961) calls total institutions (TI) and how this set-up structurally contributing to the psychosexual immaturity of diocesan priests and their vulnerability to CSA. It is thus important to investigate the ill effects of isolating diocesan seminarians in TI structure of the seminary to their normal human growth in society and personal capacity to resist CSA. Some organizations have started to relate the current celibate seminary training to CSA.

The National Review for the Protection of Children and Young People (NRPCYP) (2004), for instance, was calling for seminaries to review and improve their screening and formation of seminarians. The NRPCYP affirmed Vatican's 2002 decision to investigate the selection and training of seminarians of all US seminaries and theologates (Stanosz 2004). Screening and training candidates for the priesthood has long been a method in the RCC to test their aptness to Catholic priestly life. And apprenticeship to a senior priest or bishop for clerical formation is a centuries-old tradition in the RCC. But this style of clerical training was changed with the institution of the seminary in the 16th century.

After the Council of Trent (1545–63), the seminary was established to train and educate secular priests in a TI or exclusive institution: "The seminary horarium copied a monastic structure of designated times for communal prayers, meals, study, recreation, silence, and sleep" (Sipe 2003, 241). The council fathers and bishops of the Council of Trent who created the Catholic institution of the seminary in the 16th century had all the good intentions to improve the training of diocesan priests for the good of the Church. But this structural change in clerical training has negative unintended effects to the human growth and personal social control of Catholic clerics against CSA.

The primary aim of this chapter is to investigate the significant negative unintended impacts of the RCC's decision to adopt the celibate seminary formation as the only method of clerical training to the human development

52 Celibate Clerical Training, Human Formation

of priests, especially diocesan clerics. It argues that the adoption of celibate seminary training is inappropriate and has structural flaws in the psychosexual formation of priests who are usually assigned to the autonomous social structure of the parish without the safety net of an intimate group or community that protects them from the temptations of CSA. It recommends the adoption of an alternative clerical formation that is immersed in the world and open to married priesthood for parish clergy.

To achieve this end, this chapter is structured into four major parts. The first part discusses the social background and ecclesial foundation of the current celibate seminary formation for Catholic priests. The second part provides a theoretical framework to analyze the present celibate seminary training using Erving Goffman's theory (1968) on total institutions (TI). The third part examines the unintended ill effects of adopting a celibate seminary training under a TI structure to the psychosexual formation of priests and their capacity to resist CSA in the ministry. The last part suggests some reforms for the clerical formation of diocesan priests to address and minimize CSA in the RCC.

Overall, this chapter contends that the total institution (TI) structure of the seminary instituted by Trent has inherent structural flaws that inadvertently stunt the human growth of diocesan seminarians during the seminary training before they reach psychosexual maturity. It also views the RCC's adoption of the mandatory clerical celibacy as strongly weakening the social control of secular priests against CSA. Diocesan or secular clergy is obligated to work and live alone most of the time in the parish.

The Foundation of Celibate Seminary Formation

The celibate seminary formation is founded on the obligatory clerical celibacy imposed by the RCC in the Second and Fourth Lateran Councils. With this imposition, the Council of Trent later adopted the all-male and celibate seminary training in every diocese or group of dioceses for the training of secular priests since the 16th century. To justify the obligatory celibate priesthood that sidelined the long custom of married priesthood in the RCC, a new gender construction was conceived that saw celibate priests as belonging to a "third" gender. This new gender construction, which had roots in the Gregorian reform movement for celibate priesthood during the Medieval period, is still largely pursued in the current clerical training to justify the obligatory celibate seminary training.

R. N. Swanson (1999), in his essay "Angels Incarnate: Clergy and Masculinity from Gregorian Reform to Reformation," calls this "third order" gender construction as "emasculinity." Under this construction,

the priest is seen as a male whose role was to give orientation and spiritual guidance to other men and women, and whose influence depended, beyond the obvious powers conferred upon him by the church, on his personal authority, based on his own ability to relate to the social circumstances around him, which did not exclude considerations of his gender.

(Romeo Mateo 2021, 542)

This "third order" gender construction of the Gregorian reform movement that idealized celibate masculinity did not suit well with empirical reality as not all priests did possess the charism of celibacy but the gift of married priesthood. Seeing celibate priests as ontologically different from ordinary males had idealized celibate priesthood that makes it humanly impossible without the divine charism or grace of celibacy. Witte Jr. clarifies this humanly impossible ontological status of the celibate clergy:

The clergy were called to higher spiritual activities in the realm of grace, the laity to lower temporal activities in the realm of nature. The clergy were thus distinct from the laity in their dress, in their language and in their livings . . . And they were foreclosed from the natural activities of the laity, such as those of sex, marriage, and family life. These natural, corporal activities were literally beneath the clergy in ontological status and thus formally foreclosed. For a cleric or monastic to marry or to have sex was thus in a real sense to act against nature (*contra naturam*).

(Witte Jr. 2006, 4–5)

The social construction of the new gender of male celibate priests as perpetually permanent, which the current seminary formation tries to socialize to seminarians, is not based on human experience but on some lofty philosophical and theological ideals that are humanly difficult to live by diocesan priests. This construction of a "third order" gender according to the RCC's ideal for celibate clergy disregards the nature of masculinity as a historical and contingent social construct. Masculinity as a category is sociologically contingent in society and not immutable.

"As has been highlighted in a range of academic disciplines, masculinity is a sequence of changing meanings and practices, a fact that demolishes any pre-tensions of immutability" (Romeo Mateo 2021, 542).

Masculinity has been defined as a constructed identity that often fits into a certain way of looking at what it means to be a man. Masculinity is shaped by historical, cultural, and socioeconomic factors. The predominant masculinity by which all other masculinities are gauged within a given society is sometimes referred to as hegemonic masculinity.

(Cozzens et al. 2004, 9)

The ideal priest as projected by this third gender as spiritually strong, sexually pure, and celibate like Christ does not sit well with human experience, which can result in serious difficulties for diocesan priests. Without some sort of safety nets such as marriage and family or an intimate communal life of a religious presbyterate, these priests would be vulnerable when challenged by serious problems of the contemporary parish life such as loneliness and CSA. "As a group . . . priests are overworked, overburdened, lonely, isolated, and socially stigmatized, factors that may lead to sexually inappropriate behaviors" (Lothstein 2004, 169).

Diocesan priests are usually exposed to the sociological contingencies of secular society in the parish. This ideal of the "third gender" and its ontological status of celibate priesthood are pursued by seminary training and are humanly tested after ordination. And research has revealed the weakness of diocesan priests against CSA. It also showed that these priests constitute the largest group of sexual offenders in the RCC (John Jay College 2004). Clerical concubinage and other sexually inappropriate behaviors committed by secular clerics have always been perennial problems in the RCC. Thus, the concept of a third gender for celibate priests does not protect diocesan priests against the challenges of CSA and other priestly problems after ordination.

The third gender construction assumes that clerical celibacy is ontologically connected to Catholic priesthood, making new priests new Christ. Thomas P. Doyle (2006), however, argues that priests despite the spiritual clerical training remain human after ordination. The sacrament of holy orders and the perfect celibate masculinity do not make priests superhuman and sexless (Doyle 2006; Keenan 2015). They remain ordinary mortals, vulnerable to CSA after ordination. The celibate seminary formation that is built on the exclusive and semi-monastic organization or what the sociologist Erving Goffman calls total institution (TI) has unintendedly produced psychologically immature graduates who will be vulnerable to CSA when assigned in the parish.

The Characteristics of TI

Contrary to the primary theological perception of the RCC of the human nature as something fixed, immutable, and determined by natural law, sociology and the social sciences generally believe that people are open systems who constitute their self and human nature through experience in society. Sociologists believe that "people are not born with an intrinsic knowledge of themselves or others. Rather they develop reasoning skills, morality, personality, and a sense of self through social observation, contact, and interaction" (Henslin 2014, 2).

"Individuals learn how to think, behave, and act through contacts and interaction with agents of socialization – those people or groups that influence our self-concept, attitudes, behaviors, or other orientations toward life" (Henslin 2014, 3). And sociologists call this process of learning on how to become human as socialization. Socialization refers to "the learning process that deals with the acquisition of the necessary orientations for satisfactory functioning in a role" (Hoy and Woolfolk 1990, 283).

"Socialization and education are the processes directly related to the overall development of an individual. These processes prepare individuals and ensure their inclusion in various social spheres and cultural integration" (Terziev and Vaseliva 2022). Socialization is a lifelong process that commences from birth and ends up to death. It has two fundamental stages: primary and secondary. In some cases, however, individuals choose or are forced to undergo a special form of socialization that is totally different from the normal experiences of people in society.

This type of socialization is dubbed by sociologists as resocialization, that is, "the process of learning a different set of norms, values, attitudes, and behaviors in a separate or exclusive institution to assume a new identity. This implies entering a new and exclusive organization that provides a distinct socialization and imposes a new identity" (Jenness and Gerlinger 2020). The process of resocialization is closely associated with what the Canadian-born sociologist Erving Goffman calls TI, a unique and exclusive organization that offers a distinct form of social learning and identity.

Goffman coined the term TI as "a place of residence and work where a large number of situated individuals, cut off from the wider society for an appreciable length of time, together lead an enclosed, formally administered round of life" (Goffman 1961, xiii). People who enter this type of organization are generally "cut off from the rest of society and are under almost total control of agents of the institution" (Henslin 2013, 3). Thus, institutionalized practices of TI are constructed to strip members not only of their former identity but also of their humanity.

Dehumanization is often associated with TI as members undergo a constant surveillance of their behavior by authorities and forced to perform practices to achieve the institutional goals regardless of their negative consequences (Malacrida 2005). It causes significant problems for those who undergo this process. Dehumanization in TI promotes anxiety or depression and reduces the need for competition and interaction, damaging their well-being (Ariño-Mateo et al. 2022).

A TI environment that is isolated from the real world does not offer a natural environment for authentic human growth. With the strong behavioral control of TI's authorities, members are being forced to undergo human resocialization process that is often contrary to their personal and gender preferences (Scott 2011). A TI is characterized by a bureaucratic control of the human needs of its members, functioning through a mortification of the self (Goodman 2013). A study by Valeries Jenness and Julie Gerlinger (2020) among transgender women in an American prison, for instance, revealed TI's dehumanizing environment and human suffering, where transgender prisoners were forced to undergo resocialization to become male prisoners instead of allowing their transgender identity and personality to flourish.

In Goffman's description, TI has always functioned in accordance with its established internal rules that organize directly or indirectly the sex life of its members in which sexual relations are often limited, banned, and even sanctioned (Giami 2020). In this case, members have no way to freely actualize their own human and sexual development in normal and real-life circumstances. The TI's set of rules determine what members ought to be as human beings.

The Seminary as a TI

Although not all aspects of Goffman's TI are applicable to the spiritual and academic goals of a Catholic seminary, its four elements such as "members living in the same place and under the same authority, batch living, rigid timetabling and scheduling of activities and an institutional goal of resocialization" (Scott 2010, 215) are evident in this type of organization. As a TI, the seminary is "a place comprising residence, work, study, background, sociability and entertainment, where lots of people living alike but apart from the well-off society lead a reclusive life and formally administrated" (Benelli and Da Costa-Rosa 2003). Its members are governed by a set of ecclesial rules on clerical formation, which is implemented by seminary formators led by the rector.

Despite the experiments of making seminary formation adapted to the current world by the Second Vatican Council (Vatican II), Catholic seminaries are generally TI in structure institutionalized in the 16th century that replaced apprenticeship as the primary method of clerical training since the time of Christ. Vatican II and postconciliar documents on seminary formation still insisted on the communal character of clerical formation, resembling Goffman's specific description of TI. The seminary college, for instance, was conceived of as "a self-sufficient place where those being prepared for priestly ordination, and those responsible for their education, lived and worked" (Oakley 2017, 223).

Like Goffman's TI, Catholic seminaries for priestly formation are generally done in the same place under the authority of the rector and seminary formators appointed by the bishop. All seminarians are treated alike and are required to follow the daily routine of praying, working, and studying. Despite slight cultural variations, all seminaries follow a regimented way of life determined and imposed by seminary formators. Lastly, the enforced activities are based on a rational plan of the RCC documents on seminary formation (e.g., *Optatam Totius* [Decree on Priestly Training] 1965; *Pastores Dabo Vobis* [On Formation of Priests in the Circumstances of the Present Day] 1992; *Ratio Fundamentalis Institutiones Sacerdotalis* [The Gift of the

Priestly Vocation] 2016) to attain the official purpose of forming celibate priests as another Christ (*Alter Christus*), ready to administer the sacraments and manage the parishes for the faithful.

The RCC teaches that "the heart of the spiritual formation in the seminary is rooted in the discipleship of Jesus experienced in the life of the one who offers himself for ordination as a priest. This is central to the future priest's identity and mission" (Oakley 2017, 230). Obedience to the will of God as expressed by ecclesiastical superiors, in the manner of Christ's obedience to God, as the way of becoming another Christ is expressed in the rational plan of the Catholic seminary formation. This plan attempts to create a new self-understanding and identity among seminarians as future celibate priests. The seminary had a set of operational rules, approved by the bishops and administered by seminary rector, to be strictly obeyed by seminarians (Madden 2010).

The seminary also uses the confinement and a totalitarian and "panoptic logic" of a TI to form seminarians to celibate priesthood (Benelli and Da Costa-Rosa 2003). Panoptic surveillance is a means of exerting power and control by seminary formators to exercise sovereign power over seminarians without any direct coercion (Foucault 1975). Thus, there is a kind of superficiality in the social interaction between formators and seminarians inside the tightly controlled social environment of the seminary. But seminarians tend to behave differently during face-to-face and private interactions when away from the gaze of their formators (Manokha 2018). Any human concerns such as sexuality problems are suppressed and addressed only during spiritual direction.

Retention of the Seminary Clerical Training

> From the Tridentine beginnings, the seminary was understood to be a coming apart from society, an intensive place of conversion, spiritual growth, and the development of a relationship with Christ, the Good Shepherd, as well as the place of academic preparation for priestly ministry.
>
> (Oakley 2017, 224)

With the makeover of the seminary by the RCC in order to make it fit for the modern age, the seminary program became informed by sound psychology and pedagogy. However, the Second Vatican Council (Vatican II) and its major document on clerical training *Optatam Totius* [Decree on the Training of Priests] (1965) still retained the seminary formation under a TI social structure for priestly formation (Oakley 2017).

In 1990, the Synod returned to the topic of priestly formation in the modern world. *Pastores Dabo Vobis* [I Shall Give You Shepherds] is the resultant post-synodal apostolic exhortation and the most important document about human formation of clerical training. This was later followed by significant documents on seminary formation such as the publication of a new *Ratio Fundamentalis* (2016), which is clearly founded upon what is described as the "groundbreaking" reflection of *Pastores Dabo Vobis* that emphasized human development of clerical training.

(Oakley 2017)

The RCC has the best intentions to continue the TI structure of seminary formation in contemporary times. However, sociologists recognize the unintended consequences of TI to human action and policy. The German sociologist Max Weber warns people of the iron cage of the unintended consequences of human action. What is intended by people may turn out to be the opposite of what they plan, owing to their inability to anticipate unforeseen events. Thus, the shift of clerical training from apprenticeship, which started since the time of Christ, to a secluded and exclusive institution after the Council of Trent instituted the seminary, has serious unintended negative consequences to the human and sexual maturity of priests.

Council of Trent's manifest intended effect of improving the academic, spiritual, and human development of future diocesan priests away from the temptations of the city may turn out opposite of what is originally planned by the council fathers. Training priests apart from society in a semi-monastic, all-male, exclusive, and celibate seminary or TI can result in psychosexual immaturity and social isolation of seminarians from the real world, cutting them off from the normal socialization with people, especially women. A TI environment can make them weak and vulnerable to sexual abuse and other forms of immoral acts once assigned in the semi-autonomous social structure of the parish.

Undoubtedly, the intention of the RCC to set up the seminary is to produce celibate and highly spiritual priests patterned after the celibate life and ministry of Christ. The decision to set up a diocesan seminary as the only institution for clerical training to improve clerical education and address immorality and abuses of clerics in the late Medieval period was the RCC's way of responding to the signs of the times. But the Council of Trent's celibate seminary training that houses diocesan seminarians in an exclusive, semi-monastic, and highly controlled egalitarian life of the seminary has serious unintended impact on the human growth of seminarians and their capacity to deal with CSA once assigned in the parish.

Sociologists always see two consequences of human action and decision: the intended and the unintended. The intended consequences of the Council of Trent to establish the celibate seminary training for young seminarians in the 16th century might have been good and appropriate from the hierarchy's point of view, but it has serious unintended limitations to the human and sexuality formation of future diocesan priests in dealing with CSA especially in the parish. As Cravatts (2007, para. 3) argues, "the very process of accepting celibacy and entering the priesthood at an emotionally immature age level predispose priests to conflicting notions about human sexuality."

Negative Unintended Consequences of Seminary Training

Disruption of Normal Human Socialization

Entering the seminary as a TI with its rational plan of making seminarians celibate and Christ-like can unintendedly undermine the seminarians' normal secondary socialization in society. With the constant supervision of seminary fathers against any infraction of celibacy and chastity, seminarians tend to develop a culture of secrecy on sexual matters which can extend up to their entire priestly life (Sipe 1990). Indeed, the semi-monastic, secluded, and all-male environment of the seminary is an "abnormal" social environment for the human and sexual development of seminarians.

As Armbruster (2021, 68) argues, "seminary education and socialization must be understood as a transformation of the habitus [personal disposition], as an incorporation of structures of the Catholic Church in the bodies and minds of the future priests." But McGlone and Sperry (2020) noted the major shortcoming in the screening and socialization of seminary candidates is "the lack of communication between the major stakeholders: vocation, formational personnel, and psychologists and a uniformly applied, standardized battery that emphasizes 'suitability' with little or no focus on the 'fit' of candidates for a particular diocese or religious order."

Under the mandatory celibacy set-up that ignores married priesthood as a legitimate priestly vocation, those who left during and after the seminary formation were then deemed unsuitable to Catholic priesthood, instead of being recognized that they may have been called to married priesthood. The TI structure and panoptic surveillance of the seminary can unintendedly encourage external compliance rather than developing personal responsibility and maturity. Candidates can sometimes pass all the seminary requirements without being noticed by formators that it is primarily the will of the parents, specifically mothers, that there should be a priest in the family as a form of social prestige.

This is an unintended consequence of the panoptic structure of the seminary that encourages compliance and secrecy, resulting in the neglect of understanding the inner processes of the seminarian's life. This type of priests with no real priestly vocation usually does not endure in the ministry once parental wishes are fulfilled. The seminary as a TI organization is often seen by church authorities as a doable "human factory" for priests, where candidates can receive the gift of clerical celibacy if they generously respond to the promptings of Holy Spirit. However, this assumption is often unrealistic. Several departures during seminary formation and after the first five years in the priestly ministry (Hoge 2002) suggested that seminarians can submissively undergo the rigid structural requirements of seminary formation and yet leave the ministry after ordination owing to sexual repression and lack of commitment to celibate priesthood.

Disregarding Married Priesthood

Before the Council of Trent established the seminary as the only institution for clerical training, candidates were given the flexibility of choosing the celibate or married priesthood in an apprenticeship style of clerical training. But with the seminary clerical training becomes obligatory, priests and seminarians are forced to disregard any possibility of pursuing married priesthood. Under the current seminary formation, it is assumed that seminarians can receive the gift of celibacy if they are open to the Holy Spirit and subservient to the seminary rules and practices.

This assumption is, however, contrary of Christ's teaching that celibacy is a charism and a personal choice that cannot be imposed on the individual by an institution through a sort of TI clerical training. Sociologically speaking, charism is based on personal traits. In Max Weber's theory on authority, charism is always personal that connects the charismatic leader to his or her followers. Charism is based on a social relationship between the charisma holder and the charisma believer (Lepsius 2017).

Charism is not something based on law or what Weber's calls rational-legal authority, nor based on tradition. Celibacy as a rare charism is personal and only determined by the person as manifested in his or her personal traits and lifestyle and appreciated by believers. Celibate seminary training is not based on rational-legal rules of seminary formation formulated by the RCC. Compliance with seminary rules cannot result in acquiring the personal charism of celibacy.

"If celibacy becomes obligatory, then priests who have no gift to celibacy would obviously suffer the consequences of living a lonely celibate and asexual life in which they are not called for" (Ballano 2023, 2). It is silent martyrdom for candidates with vocation to married priesthood but must undergo a celibate seminary formation and live a lifelong celibate lifestyle contrary to their social calling. Thus, Donald Cozzens (2006) rightly views obligatory clerical celibacy as

> a contradiction in terms, because celibacy is a charism, a gift, a grace that resides in the individual often before the person knows it in his heart. . . . If charismatic celibacy is indeed a jewel in the crown of the priesthood, mandated, obligatory celibacy for individuals not blessed with the charism is a silent martyrdom.

If married priesthood is reinstated in the RCC and an alternative clerical training is available to those who felt called into it, seminarians and priests would not have abandoned their priestly calling altogether, thus preventing the current acute priest shortage experienced by the RCC in contemporary times (Schoenherr 2002). Celibacy is God's gift in which only the person can ascertain it through personal discernment. As Witte Jr. (2006, 5) aptly argues:

> Celibacy was a gift for God to give, not a duty for the church to impose. It was for each individual, not for the church, to decide whether he or she had received this gift. By demanding monastic vows of chastity and clerical vows of celibacy, the church was seen to be intruding on Christian freedom and contradicting Scripture, nature, and common sense.

With the TI structure of the current celibate seminary that emphasizes external compliance to seminary rules, clerical celibacy becomes a law rather than a rare gift that can inadvertently result in psychosexual immaturity of seminary graduates, which can be carried over to clerical life after ordination.

Human Immaturity

The RCC generally blames homosexual priests as largely causing CSA in the RCC, instead of looking up closely on the negative unintended consequences of allowing young teens and adults undergoing formative years to enter the exclusive, semi-monastic, and highly regulated environment of celibate seminary training. In autumn 2005, for instance, it was reported that the Vatican would issue a ban on gays in the priesthood, declaring that celibate homosexual men are inherently unfit for priesthood.

But this decision is contrary to the scientific research findings on CSA. Homosexuality is not directly related to persistence of CSA in the RCC. The priest-therapist, Dr. Leslie Lothstein, for instance, insisted that the sexually active gay priests he treated had sex with age-appropriate men and that even priests who abused minor males were, in fact, mostly heterosexual priests (Frawley O'Dea and Goldner 2007). Grattagliano et al. (2018, 812) contend,

> In fact, it is sexual immaturity, due to entering a seminary at an early age, and the lack of any sexual education, together with a strong vulnerability to narcissism (in relational terms), that leads the subject to turn his attentions to young people of both sexes. The youths are perceived as psychosexual peers.

If majority of Catholic priests who commit CSA in the RCC are not gay priests but immature heterosexual priests, one needs to investigate the socialization of priestly candidates before and during their seminary training. Do all seminary applicants psychosexually mature before they enter seminary

62 Celibate Clerical Training, Human Formation

training? If not, does the current celibate seminary formation under a TI structure develop the psychosexual maturity and socialization heterosexual diocesan seminarians with women in preparation for their diocesan ministry?

Weakening of Social Control Against CSA

One last serious unintended consequence of imposing clerical celibacy and celibate seminary formation in a TI environment is the lack of social control of seminary graduates or new celibate priests against CSA. Social control refers to the system of "measures, suggestion, persuasion, restraint, and coercion," which coerces individuals to conform to conventional behavior (Sharma 2007). It can be direct and indirect. Direct social control is exerted on a person by members of a primary or intimate group, such as immediate family members (Umberson 1987), while indirect social control is experienced through informal pressures to conform to conventional norms in the local community through the family (Umberson 1987; Sydlitz 1993).

Sociological literature on crime and rule-breaking behavior emphasizes the importance of intimate social groups and communities to inhibit deviant behavior. Individuals who exercise absolute privacy owing to the absence and lack of behavioral regulation by an intimate group or community are prone to commit rule-breaking behavior. Sociological theories on deviance often identify social bonding and communal support as crucial in the inhibition of deviance and criminality. One such theory is the social bonding theory (SBT). SBT is a theory that attempts to explain why individuals choose to conform to conventional norms. Its main proponent Travis Hirschi (2002) identified attachment as one of the four bonds that can discourage rule-breaking behavior.

"Attachment" refers to close affectional relationships with others and the extent to which an individual cares about others' expectations (Akers and Sellers 2004). Individuals who are insensitive to society's opinions or judgments have weakened bonds with society. The celibate seminary training and vow of celibacy prepares diocesan priests to a solitary life and absolute privacy in the parish. With the absence of an intimate group such as the family or clerical community, parish clerics normally live and work alone in the parish and expose themselves without some safety nets against CSA.

Empirical evidence shows that priests remain human and do not possess superior spirituality over the laity after celibate training and taking the vow of celibacy. To Thomas Doyle (2006), celibacy is only a sort of clerical garb that strengthens the fantasy that priests are special beings in the Church, making them different from lay people, fortifying clerical secrecy, and increasing the glamour of priestly life. Ordination does not transform clerics into a superhuman group in the RCC who can totally resist CSA. After receiving sacred orders, they remain mortal beings who vulnerable to sin and CSA (Doyle 2006).

The John Jay College of Criminal Justice (2004), which was commissioned by American bishops to study the CSA in the United States, insinuated that CSA could have been minimized if celibacy is optional in the RCC. Most CSA is done by unsupervised celibate clerics, alone with their victims in private places. Thus, Scheper-Hughes and Devine (2003, 20) aptly argue that CSA has everything to do with mandatory clerical celibacy.

[T]he mantle and aura of prestige that has been accorded to Catholic priests allowed them to be treated for generations as special agents of God, as mediators between ordinary humans and the divine. Celibacy endowed Catholic priests with awesome, almost magical, power and authority. Celibate priests were not "ordinary men." It is this aura, this "mystical halo," that the pedophile priests have taken advantage of to gain easy access to naive religious families and their vulnerable children.

(Scheper-Hughes and Devine 2003, 29)

Alternative Clerical Training for Diocesan Married Priesthood

Despite the sincere efforts of the Council of Trent to improve the clerical training of diocesan priests, the institution of the seminary has serious unintended consequences to the human formation of priests. By instituting the celibate seminary formation as the only method of priestly training, one cannot deny the negative unintended effects of forming young mean in their formative years in an abnormal, exclusive, semi-monastic, and highly regulated TI of the seminary. With the shift of the method of clerical training from apprenticeship to seminary formation, the normal socialization and psychosexual development of seminarians are arrested, resulting in human immaturity and vulnerability to CSA once ordained and assigned to the autonomous social structure of the parish.

The imposition of mandatory celibacy, which had become the foundation of the celibate seminary training instituted by Trent, has also led to the suppression of married priesthood and forcing diocesan seminarians to undergo the celibate training, which is basically suitable for religious and monastic priests. This implies hindering the psychosexual development of these seminarians in the highly regulated sexuality environment of the seminary. The primary negative unintended effect of celibate seminary training, which is isolated from the real secular world, is the repression of the normal socialization process and sexuality of many diocesan seminarians whose vocation might have been married priesthood. As Christ said, celibacy is a rare gift and should not be imposed on all who wants to follow him.

If research shows that majority of clerics who commit CSA were not gays but immature heterosexual diocesan priests whose personal and sexual issues were not resolved during seminary training, then the TI formation of the seminary has a lot to do with clerical immaturity and the persistence of this type of CSA in the RCC. These priests were mostly probably called to the priesthood but did not possess the rare gift of celibacy. But owing to lack of alternative clerical training, they were forced to undergo the celibate seminary formation meant only for celibate priesthood and remained in the diocesan ministry with serious sexuality problems and high vulnerability for CSA with their repressed sexuality.

To address the persistence of CSA by diocesan priests, who constitute the main cohort of sexual offenders, the RCC should rethink its current clerical training that is founded on a celibate seminary training and TI social structure. This necessitates reforms in clerical formation for diocesan priests. It involves reestablishing the universal married priesthood as a valid social calling of Catholic priesthood, a custom and tradition in the RCC that is based on Christ's teaching on optional celibacy.

If married priesthood is reestablished, then the RCC can start restructuring the current clerical training that is appropriate for both celibate and married priesthood. The current celibate seminary training maybe retained for religious and monastic priests. But an alternative clerical training that is grounded in human experience in the secular world needs to be established for diocesan seminarians who will opt for married presbyterate. Since married priesthood is like the vocation of marriage for the laity that is immersed in the secular matters, clerical training should not be in a TI structure but one that allows the normal social interaction with women in society. In this case, returning of the historically grounded apprenticeship clerical training – this time adapted to contemporary life – that has long been practiced in the RCC since the time of Christ can be a viable alternative for diocesan priests with a vocation to married priesthood.

Conclusion

This chapter has shown that the persistence of CSA in the RCC is greatly associated with the celibate seminary formation in a TI social structure and the vow of clerical celibacy. It argued that the shift of priestly formation from apprenticeship to an exclusive, semi-monastic, and highly supervised celibate seminary formation not only removes the option of married priesthood but also allows sexual repression, psychosexual immaturity, and a lack of preparation in dealing with the priest's sexuality and his parishioners. Clerical celibacy is a charism that can only be discovered through individual discernment and cannot be imposed by law in TI seminary training. Celibate seminary training and the vow of celibacy have deprived future diocesan priests of the choice to pursue married priesthood and safety nets against CSA in the absence of an intimate social group or religious community in the parish. To address this problem, the RCC should consider reestablishing the universal married priesthood and explore alternative clerical training that is immersed in the world for parish clergy.

References

Akers, Ronald L., and Christine S. Sellers. 2004. *Criminological Theories: Introduction, Evaluation, and Application.* 4th ed. Los Angeles, CA: Roxbury Publishing.

Armbruster, Andre. 2021. "On the Undisclosed Transfer of Abusive Catholic Priests: A Field Theoretical Analysis of the Sexual Repression Within the Catholic Church and the Use of Legitimate Language." *Critical Research on Religion* 10 (1): 61–77.

Ariño-Mateo, Eva, Raúl Ramírez-Vielma, Matías Arriagada-Venegas, Gabriela Nazar-Carter, and David Pérez-Jorge. 2022. "Validation of the Organizational Dehumanization Scale in Spanish-Speaking Contexts." *International Journal of Environment Research and Public Health* 19 (8): 4805. https://doi.org/10.3390/ijerph19084805.

Ballano, Vivencio O. 2023. *In Defense of Married Priesthood: A Sociotheological Investigation of Catholic Clerical Celibacy.* London: Routledge.

Benelli, Silvio José, and Abilio Da Costa-Rosa. 2003. "Study About the Presbyterate Formation in a Catholic Seminary." *Psychology Studies (Campinas)* 20 (3): https://doi.org/10.1590/S0103-166X2003000300008.

Cozzens, Donald. 2006. *Freeing Celibacy.* Collegeville, MN: Liturgical Press.

Cozzens, Donald, William Schipper, Merle Longwood, Marie M. Fortune, and Elaine Graham. 2004. "Clergy Sexual Abuse: Theological and Gender Perspectives." *Journal of Religion & Abuse* 6 (2): 3–29. https://doi.org/10.1300/j154v06n02_02.

Cravatts, Richard. 2007. "L.A. Sex Abuse Settlement Leaves Troubling Questions Unanswered." *The State Journal-Register*, July 25, 2007. www.sj-r.com/story/news/2007/07/25/l-sex-abuse-settlement-leaves/47782055007/.

Doyle, Thomas P. 2003. "Roman Catholic Clericalism, Religious Duress, and Clergy Sexual Abuse." *Pastoral Psychology* 51: 189–231. https://doi.org/10.1023/A:1021301407104.

Doyle, Thomas P. 2006. "Clericalism: Enabler of Clergy Sexual Abuse". *Pastoral Psychology* 54 (3): 189–213. https://doi.org/10.1007/s11089-006-6323-x.

FIgnazio Grattagliano, Rosa Scardigno, Rosalinda Cassibba, and Giuseppe Mininni. 2018. "Holy Crime: Sexual Abuse of Minors by Priests." *Proceedings of the American Academy of Forensic Sciences, 70th Annual Scientific Meeting*, February 19–24, 2018. https://iris.unito.it/handle/2318/1733594#.

Foucault, Michelle. 1975. *Discipline and Punish.* New York: Vintage Books.

Frawley O'Dea, Mary Gail, and Virginia Goldner. 2007. "Abusive Priests: Who They Were and Were Not*." In *Predatory Priests, Silenced Victims*, edited by Frawley O'Dea Mary Gail, and Goldner Virginia. New York: Routledge.

Giami, Alain. 2020. "Institutions' Approach to Sexuality, A Necessity Between Care and Sexual Rights." *Soins. Psychiatrie* 41 (330): 12–16. https://doi.org/10.1016/s0241-6972(20)30100-6. PMID: 33353601.

Goodman, Benny. 2013. "Erving Goffman and the Total Institution." *Nurse Education Today* 33 (2): 81.

Goffman, Erving. 1961. *Asylums: Essays on the Social Situation of Mental Patients and Other Inmates.* New York: Anchor Books.

Henslin, James. 2013. "Chapter 3: Socialization." In *Instructor's Manual, Essentials of Sociology.* London: Pearson.

Hirschi, Travis. 2002. *Causes of Delinquency.* Piscataway, NJ: Transaction Publishers.

Hoge, Dean R. 2002. *The First Five Years of Priesthood: A Study of Newly Ordained Catholic Priests.* Collegeville, MN: Liturgical Press.

Hoy, Wayne K., and Anita E. Woolfolk. 1990. "Socialization of Student Teachers." *American Educational Research Journal* 27 (2): 279–300. https://doi.org/10.3102/00028312027002279.

Jenness, Valerie, and Julie Gerlinger. 2020. "The Feminization of Transgender Women in Prisons for Men: How Prison as a Total Institution Shapes Gender." *Journal of Contemporary Criminal Justice* 36 (2): 1–24. https://doi.org/10.1177/1043986219894422.

John Jay College. 2004. *The Nature and Scope of Sexual Abuse of Minors by Catholic Priests and Deacons in the United States 1950–2002.* Washington, DC: USCCB. www.bishop-accountability.org/reports/2004_02_27_JohnJay/.

Keenan, Marie. 2015. "Masculinity, Relationships and Context: Child Sexual Abuse and the Catholic Church Catholic Church." *Irish Journal of Applied Social Studies* 15 (2): 64–77.

Lepsius, Rainer M. 2017. "Max Weber's Concept of Charismatic Authority and Its Applicability to Adolf Hitler's "Führerstaat."" In *Max Weber and Institutional Theory*, edited by C. Wendt. Cham: Springer. https://doi.org/10.1007/978-3-319-44708-7_8.

Li, Hankun, Lejing Liu, and Wei Wan Wan. 2022. "Understanding and Deconstruct Systematic Catholic Church Sexual Abuse and Trauma." *Advances in Social Science, Education and Humanities Research* 670 (Proceedings of the 2022 3rd International Conference on Mental Health, Education and Human Development (MHEHD 2022)).

Lothstein, Leslie M. 2004. "Men of the Flesh: The Evaluation and Treatment of Sexually Abusing Priests." *Studies in Gender and Sexuality* 5 (2): 167–195. https://doi.org/10.1080/15240650509349246.

Madden, James John. 2010. "Monastic Regime at Banyo Seminary: An Oral and Social History of the Pius XII Seminary, Banyo (1941–2000)." PhD Thesis Doctor of Philosophy, University of Southern Queensland.

Manokha, Ivan. 2018. "Surveillance, Panopticism, and Self-discipline in Digital Age." *Surveillance & Society* 16 (2): 219–237. https://ojs.library.queensu.ca/index.php/surveillance-and-society/index.

Malacrida, Claudia. 2005. "Discipline and Dehumanization in a Total Institution: Institutional Survivors' Descriptions of Time-Out Rooms." *Disability & Society* 20 (5): 523–537. https://doi.org/10.1080/09687590500156238.

McGlone, G., and L. Sperry. 2020. "Psychological Evaluation of Catholic Seminary Candidates: Strengths, Shortcomings, and an Innovative Plan." *Spirituality in Clinical Practice* 7 (4): 262–277. https://doi.org/10.1037/scp0000240.

Oakley, Fr David. 2017. "Seminary Education and Formation: The Challenges and Some Ideas about Future Developments." *International Studies in Catholic Education* 9 (2): 223–235. https://doi.org/10.1080/19422539.2017.1360613.

Optatam Totius [Decree on Priestly Training]. 1965. *Decree on Priestly Training by Pope Paul VI on October 28, 1965.* Vatican: Vatican Archives. www.vatican.va/archive/hist_councils/ii_vatican_council/documents/vat-ii_decree_19651028_optatam-totius_en.html.

Roman Curia, *Ratio Fundamentalis Institutiones Sacerdotalis* [The Gift of the Priestly Vocation]. 2016. Vatican: The Sacred Congregation for the Clergy. www.vatican.va/roman_curia/congregations/cclergy/documents/rc_con_cclergy_doc_20161208_ratio-fundamentalis-institutionis-sacerdotalis_sp.html.

Romeo Mateo, María Cruz. 2021. "A New Priest for a New Society? The Masculinity of the Priesthood in Liberal Spain." *Journal of Religious History* 45 (4): 540–558. https://doi.org/10.1111/1467-9809.12799.

Royal Commission into Institutional Responses That Child Sexual Abuse, Final Report, vol. 16: Religious Institutions Book 2 (Australia: Commonwealth of Australia, 2017), 595. www.childabuseroyalcommission.gov.au/sites/default/files/final_report_-_volume_16_religious_institutions_book_2.pdf.

Scheper-Hughes, Nancy, and John Devine. 2003. "Priestly Celibacy and Child Sexual Abuse." *Sexualities* 6 (1): 15–40. https://doi.org/10.1177/1363460703006001003.

Schoenherr, Richard. 2002. *Goodbye Father: The Celibate Male Priesthood and the Future of the Catholic Church*. Oxford: Oxford University Press.

Scott, Susie. 2010. "Revisiting the Total Institution: Performative Regulation in the Reinventive Institution." *Sociology* 44 (2): 213–231. https://doi.org/10.1177/0038038509357198.

Scott, Susie. 2011. "Introduction." In *Total Institutions and Reinvented Identities. Identity Studies in the Social Sciences*. London: Palgrave Macmillan. https://doi.org/10.1057/9780230348608_1.

Sharma, Rajendra K. 2007. *Social Change and Social Control*. New Delhi: Atlantic Publishers & Distributors Ltd.

Sipe, A. W. Richard. 1990. *A Secret World: Celibacy and the Search for Celibacy*. New York: Brunner/Mazel.

Sipe, A. M. Richard. 2010. "Beneath the Child Abuse Scandal." National Catholic Reporter, July 22, 2010. https://www.bishop-accountability.org/news2010/07_08/2010_07_22_Richard_BeneathThe.htm.

Sipe, Richard. 2003. *Celibacy in Crisis: A Secret World Revisited*. London: Brunner-Routledge.

Stanosz, Paul. 2004. *Reproducing Celibacy: A Case Study in Diocesan Seminary Formation*. Fordham University ProQuest Dissertations Publishing, 2004. 3140903. www.proquest.com/openview/837656b34c4ffa9e63ac6145263e1fa7/1?pq-origsite=gscholar&cbl=18750&diss=y.

Swanson, Robert N. 1999. "Angels Incarnate: Clergy and Masculinity from Gregorian Reform to Reformation 1." In *Masculinity in Medieval Europe First Edition* edited by Dawn Hadley. London: Routledge.

Sydlitz, Ruth. 1993. "Complexity in the Relationships Among Direct and Indirect Parental Controls and Delinquency." *Youth & Society* 24 (3): 243–275. https://doi.org/10.1177/0044118X93024003001.

Terry, Karen J. 2015. "Child Sexual Abuse Within the Catholic Church: A Review of Global Perspectives." *International Journal of Comparative and Applied Criminal Justice* 39 (2): 139–154. https://doi/org/10.1080/01924036.2015.1012703.

Terziev, Venelin, and Silva Vasileva. 2022. "The Role of Education in Socialization of an Individual." SSRN: https://ssrn.com/abstract=4101387; http://dx.doi.org/10.2139/ssrn.4101387.

The National Review Board for the Protection of Children and Young People. 2004. *A Report on the Crisis of the Catholic Church in the United States*. Washington, DC: United States Conference of Catholic Bishops.

Umberson, Debra. 1987. "Family Status and Health Behaviors: Social Control as a Dimension of Social Integration." *Journal of Health and Social Behavior* 28 (3): 306–319. https://doi.org/10.2307/2136848.

Wamsley, Laurel. 2018. "German Bishops' Report: At Least 3,677 Minors Were Abused By Clerics." *NPR Website*, September 25, 2018. https://www.npr.org/2018/09/25/651528211/german-bishops-report-at-least-3-677-minors-were-abused-by-clerics.

Wills, Gary. 2000. *Papal Sin: Structures of Deceit*. New York: Doubleday.

Witte Jr., John. 2006. "The Perils of Celibacy: Clerical Celibacy and Marriage in Early Protestant Perspective." In *Sexuality in the Catholic Tradition*, edited by Cahill Lisa, and Garvey John, 107–119. Lexington, KY: Crossroad Publishers. www.researchgate.net/publication/228137465_The_Perils_of_Celibacy_Clerical_Celibacy_and_Marriage_in_Early_Protestant_Perspective [Accessed November 01, 2022].

Yocum, Sandra. 2013. "The Priest and Catholic Culture as Symbolic System of Purity." In *Clergy Sexual Abuse: Social Science Perspectives*, edited by Claire M. Renzetti and Yocum Sandra, 90–117. Boston: Northeastern University Press.

4

GENDER AND SEXUALITY FORMATION IN THE SEMINARY AND CLERICAL SEXUAL ABUSE

Introduction

The clerical sexual abuse (CSA) crisis that currently besets the Roman Catholic Church (RCC) is happening not just in the United States but also all over the world. It reminds one of the ineptitude of the Church as an institution in dealing with gender and sexuality issues. The persistence of CSA only reflects the culture of repression and secrecy within the RCC (Yip 2003). And the Catholic seminary, which is the primary institution for the formation of celibate priests in the RCC, shares this ineptitude and culture of repression in addressing gender and human sexuality issues. Sexual abuse committed by Catholic clergy reflects the problematic sexuality development of future priests inside the exclusive, all-male, semi-monastic, and highly regulated social and spiritual environment of the Catholic seminary or what the sociologist Erving Goffman (1961) characterized as total institutions (TI).

In seminary clerical formation, which was introduced by the Council of Trent in the 16th century (Alphonso 2015), seminarians are removed from their normal gender socialization and sexuality development in society and housed in an abnormal and highly spiritualized community where sexuality is banned and repressed. Sex is biological in nature and is determined by the person's genitalia, while gender is social and cultural orientation on how people express their masculinity and femininity. Gender refers to all manifestations of masculinity or femininity, which is determined by social learning and culture (Blank 2012). Gender socialization is "the process through which boys and girls learn sex appropriate behavior, dress, personality characteristics, and demeanor" (Rohlinger 2007, 590). Suppressing the normal gender socialization and sexual development of individuals can have serious unintended consequences to their psychosexual maturity.

DOI: 10.4324/9781032722474-6

The seminary as a Catholic institution implements the mandatory clerical celibacy, denying a normal gender and sexuality experience to Catholic priests. As the criminologist Marie Keenan (2015) contends, the RCC's perfect celibate clerical masculinity has effectively deprived Catholic priests of their sexuality and sexual desire. They are expected to be "holy and detached" and "sexless." This type of gender socialization is pursued in the present celibate seminary formation. Thus, with the disruption of the normal gender and sexual socialization inside the "artificial" and exclusive social environment of the seminary, it is inevitable that several diocesan seminarians with no gift to celibacy would become psychosexually immature and personally weak to fight CSA when assigned in the secular world of the parish. To develop self-control in sexual life requires a realistic, adequate, and healthy sexual socialization in society that cannot be realized in the current closed system of the seminary.

A healthy human and sexuality formation in seminary training is crucial in the prevention of CSA in the RCC. Although not without problems because of the situational factors of CSA, self-discipline or interior social control acquired by individuals in an adequate human formation in clerical training is an effective proactive measure to prevent sexual scandals in the RCC. Priests who participated in adequate human formation have more resistance against CSA. As the John Jay College Report (2004, 3) suggested:

> The development of a curriculum of "human formation" as part of seminary education follows the recognition of the problem of sexual abuse by priests. Participation in human formation during seminary distinguishes priests with later abusive behavior from those who did not abuse. The priests with abusive behavior were statistically less likely to have participated in human formation training than those who did not have allegations of abuse.

"From the church's perspective, seminary training should mold the seminarians' views to approximate church teachings in order to assure continuance of church doctrine and to avoid future conflicts between the seminarians and their church" (Hayduk, Strattkotter, and Rovers 1997, 455). An earlier data collected by Martin Rovers (1996) indicated seminarians are willing to adjust their personal views to the Church's teaching, which is included in clerical formation. However, the type of priestly training mandated by the Council of Trent in the 16th century and largely continued by the Second Vatican Council (Vatican II) up to the present may contradict their views, especially by those who feel that married priesthood, not celibate priesthood as officially taught by the RCC, is their vocation.

Owing to a lack of options, they join the exclusive celibate seminary training to become priests. Trent's introduction of the celibate seminary training was a major break from the long tradition of apprenticeship style of priestly training in the RCC that originated since the time of Christ, which is open to married priesthood. Under the old apprenticeship clerical training, candidates did not generally abandon their ordinary human life and gender training as normal adolescents and adults in society. They did not disrupt their usual sexual development while undergoing spiritual and academic training with a veteran priest or bishop. They were not required to stay in an exclusive institution during their priestly formation. They were allowed to live a normal life and stayed in their homes (Schuth 2016; Obinwa 2019).

The apprenticeship system, however, was greatly changed with Trent's institutionalization of the seminary as the only mode of clerical training in the RCC, aiming to protect "endangered youth" or young seminarians from the temptations of the city and to separate them from the world to fortify their priestly vocation (Schuth 2016). The TI clerical training of the seminary has removed seminarians from their normal sexuality development in society and banned informal learning through open discussions on sexuality. Sexuality seminars offered in the seminary formation became substitutes for healthy human experience and social interaction with sociocultural agents in society, specifically women, to develop human and gender maturity.

With the strong seminary regulation that censors sexual matters, seminarians are informally initiated into a culture of secrecy and repression concerning gender and sexuality inside the seminary (Boisvert and Goss 2021), a culture described by the priest psychotherapist Richard Sipe (1990) as the secret world of clerical sexuality – a world of passive resistance (Scott 1989, 1992) against clerical celibacy that seminarians tend to continue after ordination. Further, the present psychological process of screening seminary applicants is inadequate to identify unfit candidates and high-risk individuals to CSA if they become priests (Lassi et al. 2022).

Men who are sexually attracted to peri-pubescent boys (pederasts), for instance, are generally undetectable with the present screening methods for priestly aspirants. Also, gay candidates, who are generally banned by the RCC to join the priesthood because of their being the main cause of sexual scandals in the Church, are also indistinguishable from heterosexual men who join the seminary. Almost all applicants in psychological examinations and interviews say that they are normal and healthy heterosexual men. Despite the new measures introduced by ecclesial authorities to improve seminary training since Vatican II, psychological screening of candidates remains ineffective to prevent and weed out sexually problematic candidates from celibate seminary training.

If celibacy is a rare gift as taught by Christ himself in the gospels (Matthew 19:11f) and married priesthood is recognized by Vatican II as a valid social calling as practiced in Eastern Catholic churches (*Presbyterorum Ordinis* [Order of Priests] 1965, para. 16), then those who join the seminary training to become ministers of Christ were not all called to celibate priesthood. Many diocesan seminarians are probably called to married priesthood but are constrained to join the celibate seminary training, instead of the apprenticeship training that is more suited for married diocesan presbyterate with its normal sexuality socialization. Candidates of this kind would be susceptible to CSA because of their inadequate sexuality training, sexual repression, and psychosexual immaturity as negative unintended consequences of the celibate seminary training if they get ordained and decide to stay in the priesthood.

Thus, to Jay Feierman (2020), a long-term solution to effectively address CSA should include (1) allowing diocesan priests to marry, (2) allowing married persons to become priests, and (3) allowing married persons and women into the Church hierarchy. The current problem of sexual scandals by diocesan priests in the RCC, which is founded on mandatory clerical celibacy and nurtured by a TI social structure, has sociological connections to celibate seminary formation that inadvertently produces psychologically and sexually immature priests who are prone to CSA.

An early study with a random sample of 271 priests who were graduates of celibate seminary training, commissioned by American bishops in 1971, a few years after Vatican II, for instance, revealed that only 6% of priests were maturely developed by seminary training, 29% were developing, while another 57% were underdeveloped and 8% maldeveloped (Kennedy and Heckler 1972). More contemporary research also blames the ongoing psychosexual problems and immaturity of priests as one of the two obstacles that hinder priests to live a spiritually healthy celibate priesthood (Bauman et al. 2019).

The primary objective of this chapter is to sociologically investigate the sexuality and gender development of seminarians under the current TI social structure of seminary formation, which produces psychosexually immature priests who are vulnerable to CSA. Because young diocesan seminarians are cut off from the normal socialization in society when they enter the seminary, the normal process of sexual development is suspended, resulting in psychosexual immaturity. A sociological study by Paul Stanosz (2006) on Catholic seminaries in the United States, for instance, described the struggles of seminarians against celibate seminary formation and discovered that seminaries did not have a forum in which future priests can freely discuss their sexual feelings and appropriate to themselves the academic learning from the celibacy curriculum (Stanosz 2006).

Stanosz (2006) also explored in his study how the suspension of the normal sexuality development of seminarians and absence of open discussion about sexuality in the seminary could result in difficulty for formators in uncovering problematic sexual behaviors during seminary formation, which can lead to psychosexual immaturity and lack of social control against CSA (Stanosz 2006). As Frawley O'Dea aptly observed (2004, 129–130):

Central to this cohort of abusers is their psychosexual immaturity. Many of these priests entered seminaries when they were as young as 14 years old. Throughout their adolescence, sexuality was wholly dissociated from the verbally validated and symbolically processed realm of life. They simply were not to have sex of any kind, talk about sex of any kind, or think about sex about any kind. Celibacy was a rule, but these boys, later men, were given no guidance for growing to mature manhood in which celibacy could become a comprehensible, freely made choice.

To sociologically explore how the inadequate sexuality and gender formation of the current celibate seminary training can unintendedly result in the formation of psychosexual immature diocesan priests, this chapter is divided into four major parts. The first part examines the clerical celibate training in the Catholic seminary as a TI. Although the seminary does not totally resemble the TI that Erving Goffman (1961) described in his work, it nevertheless bears its basic structure. This section specifically investigates the sexuality training and gender socialization of seminarians inside the TI-structure of Catholic seminaries.

The second part closely examines the sexuality training of seminarians inside the TI structure of celibate seminary formation. Specifically, it investigates their sexuality and gender socialization inside the exclusive and highly supervised social environment of the seminary and attempts to illustrate how this kind of training contributes to the psychosexual immaturity and vulnerability of future priests against CSA in the parish.

The third part examines inquires into the socialization of seminarians with women under a celibate seminary formation and how its limitations stunt the sexual maturity of seminarians in dealing with their own sexuality and parishioners' sexuality problems. The last part analyzes the incompatibility between the communal social structure of the celibate seminary formation and autonomous social life of the parish that can lead to the weakening of new priests' social control against CSA in the absence of direct social control offered by marriage and family life in married priesthood.

Catholic seminaries that developed through the years kept their basic TI structure and emphasized spiritual training. "Even when more attention was gradually paid to instruction, the spiritual aspect was still stressed, and the professors were all spiritual directors" (Fagan 1965, 269). "The seminary was meant to train people to the life of prayer and to help them acquire virtues like regularity, dignity, and a sense of obedience" (Fagan 1965, 270). This focus, however, leads to the unintended neglect of the human and sexual development of seminarians. David Melliot, a seminary professor and Catholic priest, confirmed in an interview that seminary administrators were told that under no circumstances were seminary students be allowed to raise or explore issues concerning sexual orientation during the clerical formation. Such issues should only be discussed only in spiritual direction or confidence (Melliot in Boisvert and Goss 2021).

Gender and Sexuality Formation   **73**

This prohibition raises the question whether the seminary as a TI can provide a healthy sexuality and masculinity training to seminarians. Richard Sipe, a veteran psychotherapist of priests, has already warned the RCC of the unintended negative consequences of repressing sexuality of priests in his book *The Secret World* (1990). Current studies on seminary formation and CSA have overlooked the implication of forming seminarians under a tightly controlled environment with no open talk on sexuality for their psychosexual maturity. Applying sociological theories on TI and gender socialization to interpret textual data from published materials, this chapter aims to provide a modest contribution to the lack of sociological literature that relates the psychosexual immaturity of diocesan priests and their vulnerability to sexual abuse to the poor human formation in the seminary. Owing to social isolation and a lack of healthy socialization with women inside the TI structure of the current celibate seminary formation, future priests usually experience psychosexual underdevelopment.

Clerical Training in the Seminary as a TI

The Catholic seminary described by Erving Goffman as a TI (1961) always functions in accordance with its internal rules to direct the sex life of seminarians. And since sexual matters are often ignored, banned, and even sanctioned inside the TI structure of the seminary, psychosexual immaturity is a strong possibility for future priests (Giami 2020). The seminary specifically aims to train seminarians to become celibate and spiritual priests. But this has the negative result of failing to look after the human and sexual development of priestly candidates, which can have disastrous effects on their future diocesan clerical lives, given the various sexuality challenges in the parish.

The overall objective of the current seminary training is to form seminarians into "Alter Christus" (Another Christ):

> Special attention is given to the spiritual, moral, pastoral, and academic training of the seminarians (students). Hence, provision is made for spiritual directors on the staff list for the spiritual life of the seminarians and qualified teachers (lecturers) in Theology and Philosophy for the seminarians' moral, pastoral and academic training to make future priest Christ-like.
>
> *(Adubale and Aluede 2017, 31)*

With the focus on spiritual, academic, and pastoral training, seminary formation results in a lack of attention and seminary personnel who can attend to the seminarians' psychosexual development. As Adubale and Aluede (2017, 31) argue:

> [T]here is no provision made to attend to the seminarians' emotional disposition in relation to their personal, social, academics, and other related

issues. In order words, there are no trained personnel on the staff list to attend to the seminarians' counselling needs, which could be social, emotional, and personal in nature. Any person who assumes such duty of providing counselling services to seminarians, such person may not have the required skills to provide such service for the seminarians.

Assigning full-time professional psychologists or psychotherapists to deal with the unresolved personal and sexual issues of seminarians during seminary formation can be considered a luxury to several Catholic seminaries. Most seminaries do not have permanent and full-time professional counselors or experts who can handle psychosexual problems of seminarians. Oftentimes, it is the spiritual directors, who are not usually trained in the social sciences, who assume this role in spiritual direction. Despite this apparent lack of professional psychologists and psychiatrists, seminary formators provide seminarians with human and sexual formation through sexuality seminars, trainings, and spiritual directions on human growth inside the seminary. However, they tend to ignore sexual issues of seminarians and remain critical of any open discussion on sexual problems and secret romantic or gay relationships inside the seminary that can lead to vocational crises and departures.

"Priests do not and cannot talk about sex, sexual fantasies, or desires. Sexuality is censored and tabooed" (Armbruster 2022, 67) during and after the highly supervised celibate seminary training. A study by Meek et al. (2004) further revealed that conversations about sex and attraction to women in the seminary are regarded as unethical, thus to be repressed and discussed only with spiritual directors. Results of this survey involving seminary graduates indicated that minimal attention is given to sexual issues during seminary formation. Respondents reported that they coped with feelings of sexual attraction only in a private and internal manner.

The TI celibate seminary training is thus leading seminarians to what Richard Sipe (1990) calls the secret world of repressed and covert clerical sexuality. Anything that is openly connected to sex is simply prohibited inside the seminary. And because of this repression, seminarians often experience sexual temptations and engage in various forms of coping mechanism to overcome them such as pornography, having sexual partners, or masturbation (Alphonso 2015; Oldenkamp 2018; Rockenbach 2020).

"In recent years, the growing free exposure to pornography, especially through the internet, is a special problem in the life of the seminarians. Masturbation is another unhealthy condition which seminarians get caught up with" (Alphonso 2015, 1), given the repressed environment of the seminary. The priest psychotherapist Richard Sipe (2003) confirmed that masturbation is quite common among seminarians. In one Philippine college seminary, for instance, an express lane confessional box is improvised to accommodate several seminarians with the sin of masturbations.[1] Compulsive masturbation, which can be a serious sign that seminarians do not probably possess the rare gift of celibacy, is sometimes interpreted by formators as mere sin and human weakness.

Sexual Intimacy in Seminary Structure

A healthy sexual intimacy for priests needs relational closeness with other persons. This closeness can be emotional, sexual, social, intellectual, and recreational. It can be attained through friendship, kinship, and belonging to an institution (Popovic 2005). A healthy sex life also implies satisfying intimate relationships, which have been associated with lower levels of risky sexual behaviors (Lam, Morrison, and Simeesters 2009). But an unhealthy sexual life with various "unmet sexual needs, the lack of closeness, or unwanted sexual experiences are detrimental to psychological and sexual functioning and can lead to sexual disorders" (McDevitt 2012, 209).

Although the ecclesial document *Pastores Dabo Vobis* [I Shall Give Shepherds] emphasized human formation of seminarians, much is still to be done to form the healthy sexual life of seminarians in preparation for the priesthood. Under the present TI structure of the seminary, the normal sexual maturity of seminarians is arrested. They are largely isolated from the real world and normal interaction with agents of human maturity such as parents, peers, relatives, friends, women, and other social networks in society, which are necessary for authentic psychosexual development.

In the TI environment of the seminary, real human experiences are denied and normal conversations about sex and sexuality are sanctioned by seminary fathers who expect seminarians to become celibate ministers. Any romantic correspondence between seminarians and women is censored by seminary formators for the obvious reason that the seminary prepares aspirants to celibate priesthood and not to marriage. The Prefect of Discipline of the seminary or the seminary formator in-charge of discipline normally monitors suspicious letters or communications that suggest romantic relationship. In one seminary, the Prefect called some seminarians to read their love letters themselves in order that they could not deny their secret romantic relationship with women outside the seminary.[2] Seminarians who violate the seminary celibacy rule normally face expulsion in a regular semestral or year-end evaluation by formators for being unfit to a celibate priestly life.

"Prior to the exposure of sexual misconduct by clergy, a man's emotional and psychological health was not normally investigated when he entered the seminary. Indeed, for years, sex and sexuality were topics not openly discussed with future priests" (Investigative Staff of Globe 2002). While seminarians were taught that celibacy is a charism and a requirement for the priesthood, they were often left alone to figure out how to humanly live the lifetime commitment to celibacy. Seminary formation encourages seminarians to avoid sexual temptations but are not professionally guided inside the seminary owing to lack of in-house experts on gender and sexuality issues who can supplement the spiritual and academic clerical formation.

Scarcity of Professional Counselors

With the lack of professional experts in the seminary who can teach academic courses on human sexuality and personally guide seminarians in their sexual problems, some priests may never have had the opportunity to explore their own sexuality and may not have learned during seminary formation on how to accept themselves as sexual beings and deal with their sexual urges openly and appropriately (Gregoire and Jungers 2010). Sexual matters during seminary formation are always hidden in a secret world where only the seminarians or priests and their spiritual directors know the problem. And spiritual directors are usually trained in philosophy and theology but not in human psychology and sexuality. Thus, sexuality problems are kept hidden in the secret world of clerical sexuality when they become priests.

In one study among Nigerian theologate seminarians, Adubale and Aluede (2017) disclosed that there is a scarcity of competent counselors in Catholic seminaries to handle human and sexuality problems. It also revealed that most of the seminarians (59.9%) seek the assistance of their spiritual directors and other priests in the seminaries in place of counselor(s) because of the apparent lack of professional psychologists. Having experts in the seminary for gender and sexual problems of seminarians as well as effective screening applicants to the seminary are important to ensure that future priests are in sound mental and sexual health.

The common sexual problem of masturbation, for instance, is normally resolved in the confession box, rather than recognizing that this problem may be an indication that the seminarian may have a serious difficulty in coping with celibate seminary formation and may be more suitable to married priesthood if allowed in the RCC. Furthermore, seminarians still hold on to the traditional gender view and sexuality that complicate their understanding of a healthy sexual life. An empirical study by Medora Barnes (2022) that examined the sex and gender views of Roman Catholic undergraduate seminarians in the United States, for instance, has revealed that many still held traditional views on gender, sexuality, and masculinity despite seminary formation.

Gender Training in the Seminary

The gender training in the seminary only reflects the institutional understanding of the RCC on gender and sexuality. In recent years, the Church has been opposing the emergence of the so-called gender theory or gender ideology (Bracke and Paternotte 2016; Case 2016). It rejects perspectives that view gender differences as the result of historical and cultural forces (Congregation for Catholic Education 2019). The RCC fundamentally sees men and women as different and yet complementary and equal in both nature and social roles (Congregation for Catholic Education 2019). It contends that denying the distinction and complementarity between a man and a woman can weaken the family as a vital institution in society (Congregation for Catholic Education 2019).

The newer teachings of the RCC on gender and sexuality, as well as Pope John Paul II's doctrine on the "theology of the body," have greatly shaped the conservative and rigid understanding of gender that permeates the entire universal church. They also influenced Catholic institutions such as the seminary. In recent years, the RCC is espousing an "anti-gender" position in response to feminism, contraception, sexual liberation, and changes in gender beliefs in the Western world (Bracke and Paternotte 2016). Although some Catholic theologians attempted to assume a more positive view of sex, they remain within the parameters of the present doctrine and theology of the body of the RCC (Capecchi 2020).

The traditional perspective of the RCC, which sees gender as ahistorical and immutable, has influenced Catholic institutions such as the seminary. Despite long years of seminary training on human development through training and seminars, seminarians still view gender in the traditional sense. In a qualitative study by Medora Barnes (2022) that involved in-depth interviews with seminarians in the United States, it revealed that future priests largely followed the RCC's traditional and ahistorical view of gender. In this research, seminarians rejected the interactionist and social constructionist models of gender and relied strictly on biological theory where sex and gender are seen as a unified and fixed concept. It also showed that they believed in "essential male inclusivity," arguing that all people who are assigned as male at birth have equal claim to manhood.

The traditional gender view of manhood in the RCC contrasts with the contemporary inclusive masculinity view, which is based on increasingly liberal perception and a rapid decline in homophobia, where men are no longer required to behave according to traditionally masculine behaviors to be accepted as men (Anderson 2009; McCormack 2011; Anderson and McCormack 2018). "Inclusive masculinity theory" argues that a rapid decline in homophobia and homohysteria – the cultural fear of being homosexualized – has led contemporary men who no longer feel they need to perform hypermasculine or traditionally masculine behaviors to be accepted as men (Anderson 2009; McCormack 2011; Anderson and McCormack 2018).

A study by Nontsokile Maria Emmanuela Khwepe (2016) on seminarians' view of gender in a Catholic seminary in South Africa also revealed adherence to traditional gender and cultural practices. It also showed their view of priesthood masculinity

> as patient, strong, serving, and enduring and sacrificing, which are also regarded as the characteristics of a "real man." In this regard . . . to be a man and to be a priest cannot be different from one another since masculinity is seen as a prerequisite for priesthood masculinity and vice versa.
>
> *(Khwepe 2016, vi)*

To be a celibate priest who gives up marriage is seen as a sign of true masculinity.

To justify the social construction of a new gender created by mandatory clerical celibacy, the RCC had conceived of a "third gender" for male celibate priests whose primary role is to celebrate the Eucharist, pure and clean from sexual and marital impurities. Celibate priests are described unambiguously as men and the expanding range of clerical actions should be done in "a manly fashion" (Miller 2003). Under this gender construction, which has a philosophical and theological foundation,

> the priest is seen as a male whose role was to give orientation and spiritual guidance to other men and women, and whose influence depended, beyond the obvious powers conferred upon him by the church, on his personal authority, based on his own ability to relate to the social circumstances around him, which did not exclude considerations of his gender.
>
> *(Romeo Mateo 2021, 542)*

This "godly" concept of "third gender" is obviously spiritualized and ahistorical, which overlooks the humanity of celibate priests and historicity of gender as a social construct. After all, ordination does not alter the gender, humanity, and sexuality of seminarians, making them superhumans. Clerics remain mortals and vulnerable to the temptation of sexual abuse after receiving ordination or the sacrament of Holy Orders (Doyle 2006).

Clerical Celibacy as Sign of Manhood

The giving up of marriage and adoption of clerical celibacy is a sign of true manhood under the RCC's "third gender" construction of celibate priesthood. Thus, for the Catholic hierarchy, gays becoming celibate priests is not a sign of true manhood. They are not sacrificing marriage since their attraction is on the same sex. Thus, bishops are hesitant to accept homosexual seminarians to the priesthood who are seen to be lacking in manhood: Homosexuals are not sacrificing their own marriage by becoming priests.

Gender and Sexuality Formation   **79**

An older statement from Rome, for example, revealed the RCC's reluctance to accept homosexuals to the priesthood. As early as 1961, the RCC, through its Sacred Congregation for the Religious, had warned that the people afflicted with the evil tendencies to homosexuality or pederasty should be prohibited to enter the priesthood. In more recent times, Pope Benedict XVI opposes the entry of gays to the seminary and the priesthood. To him, gays only make the Catholic priesthood a refuge for their lack of desire for heterosexual marriage:

> [h]omosexuality is incompatible with the priestly vocation. Otherwise, celibacy itself would lose its meaning as a renunciation. It would be extremely dangerous if celibacy became a sort of pretext for bringing people into the priesthood who don't want to get married anyway. For in the end, their attitude toward man or woman is somehow distorted, off-center, and, in any case, is not within the direction of creation of which we have spoken.
>
> *(Benedict XVI and Seewald 2010, 151–152)*

Commenting on seminary training in the United States, Donald Cozzens and others (2004) also contend that

> the seminary environment is not conducive to the free exploration of what it means to be a male in today's American culture. Unlike the encouraging freedom and growth for ordinary college students, seminarians undergo some stifling elements in the Catholic seminary system. The increased homophobia that has resulted from Vatican statements about homosexuals in the seminary and priesthood creates an environment in which young men may find it difficult to explore their sexuality in a chaste celibate way.
>
> *(Cozzens et al. 2004, 11)*

Homophobia and the fear of allowing gays to enter the priesthood are, however, rejected by some research studies that showed that the primary group who are committing CSA in the RCC are not gays but immature heterosexuals who have unresolved personal issues and lacking in self-control (John Jay College Report 2004; Frawley O'Dea and Goldner 2007; Keenan 2011; Terry et al. 2011; De Weger 2022). They revealed that gays are not the main offenders of CSA in the RCC. The Catholic hierarchy's blaming of gays for sexual scandals is only scapegoating for its failure to effectively address CSA and cover-ups of abuse cases in the Church (Boisvert and Goss 2021). Thus, it is important to investigate the socialization of male heterosexual seminarians with women during the seminary training to understand why they also became attracted to young children and minors when ordained and assigned in the ministry.

80 Celibate Clerical Training, Human Formation

Most sexually abusive heterosexual priests have deep psychological problem with the opposite sex, which were not properly addressed during seminary formation. The seminarians' lack of intimacy with women can sometimes transform into attraction with young people under their pastoral care. As Frawley O'Dea (2004, 130) contends:

> Some priests who became predators developed the heretofore prohibited "particular friendships" with teenage boys they were charged with supervising. At some point, the sexual urges and the relational yearnings for intimacy, including touch, contained within the adolescently organized priest, took hold and a line was crossed. Once the dam of pent-up longings and sexual strivings burst, too many priests continued to seek sexual satisfaction and relational adulation with adolescent boys who were entrusted to their care.

Seminary Curriculum and Sexuality Development

Despite the stress on human formation in Pope John Paul II's post-apostolic exhortation *Pastores Dabo Vobis* [I Shall Give you Shepherds], which is incorporated in the *Program for Priestly Formation* (PPF #50), the focus of seminary formation is still on the spiritual and academic training of the seminarians. No psychological, sociological, and social science courses that directly deal with human sexuality and maturity and their relevance to celibate priesthood are formally offered in the curriculum. Frawley O'Dea (2004) argues that seminarians are taught in the seminary not to engage in sex and talk about sex of any kind but were not guided on how to appreciate celibacy as freely given choice.

The formal curriculum of college seminaries in the United States, for instance, includes several courses in philosophy and undergraduate theology but none on human development and sexuality that use sociological and the social science research and perspectives. Before college seminaries are admitted to theological seminaries before ordination, they should acquire:

> a bachelor's degree or its equivalent from an accredited institution. Sufficient education in philosophy, which the Code of Canon Law states as a biennium, is understood in the United States to be at least 30 semester credit hours, plus the out-of-classroom work associated with each credit hour traditionally expected in American higher education. A minimum of 12 semester credit hours is required in appropriate courses of undergraduate theology.
> *(The content of such courses is outlined in norms 178 and 179 under*
> *"Intellectual Formation – College Seminaries: Norms")*

Formal courses on the sociology, anthropology, and psychology of human sexuality are apparently missing in the formal curriculum despite the RCC's emphasis on human formation. As understood by the PPF, formation for Catholic priests remains largely spiritual and thus underappreciating the importance of human maturity as the foundation of a mature priestly spirituality. The RCC states that "[f]ormation, as the Church understands it, is not equivalent to a secular sense of schooling or, even less, job training. Formation is first and foremost cooperation with the grace of God" (USCCB 2005, #68). Spiritualizing clerical formation and neglecting psychosexual formation pose serious problem to the social control of priests against CSA in the parish and ministry.

Poor Socialization with Women

Although the primary stage of socialization is crucial for the formation of the person's personality and gender identity, secondary socialization during adolescence and adulthood is also significant to the person's life. The socialization of early adulthood, for instance, which coincides with the age bracket of most candidates who enter the seminary, is crucial in determining the person's human and sexual maturity. "Many diocesan seminarians are in the stage of emerging adulthood. This developmental level is characterized by five features: age of identity exploration, possibilities, self-focus, instability, and a feeling of being in-between" (Abano and Bedoria 2023, 315).

The disposition of priestly aspirants who entered the seminary is normally transformed by the highly exclusive and spiritual clerical training, living in a semi-monastic environment with fellow male candidates to the priesthood. Thus, candidates develop a religious or Catholic habitus – to borrow Pierre Bourdieu's concept (1977) – but not the sexuality habitus of a normal adult. Understanding how the seminary formation contributes to CSA in the RCC also requires investigating the secondary socialization of seminarians inside the seminary. Most candidates to the priesthood who enter the all-male seminary are in their late adolescence or young adulthood, a crucial phase when they should have been experiencing normal interaction, friendship, dating, and intimate relationship with women.

The imposition of an all-male and exclusive seminary training to pursue the celibate clerical identity inadvertently deprives seminarians of the opportunities to mature in relationships with women. Most seminary instructors are priests and men. It is rare to see attractive female teachers. Seminarians only see young women during exposures, weekly day offs, or semestral breaks. The academic and spiritual focus of seminary training to establish the new identity for seminarians as another Christ has unintendedly resulted in psychosexual immaturity and greater vulnerability to CSA after ordination. Frawley O'Dea (2004) observes that most abusers in the

RCC are sexually immature priests who entered seminaries at younger age and taught not to talk about sex and women and without guidance on how to deal with celibacy as a free choice.

One study showed that seminaries failed to prepare seminarians to understand their own sexual values and behaviors. Seminary courses on sexuality were often optional and unrelated to the core curriculum (The Role of Sexuality Education Within Seminaries 2002). Donald Cozzens et al. (2004, 12) argue that sexual issues such as

> masturbation cannot be discussed as a natural part of healthy psychosexual development since it is always considered a grave matter and most likely a mortal sin. Rather than reaching some level of integration, the young seminarian may see any sexual desire as an evil that must be avoided lest he fails in his spiritual commitment. Sexuality may become something that is seen as evil and in need of suppression rather than as something integrated into a healthy male image and masculinity.

According to Dr. Leslie Lothstein, Director of Psychology at the Institute of Living, "the social ecology of seminary training for Catholic priests isolates them from women, so you have an all-male society in which a hierarchical structure is very profound, in which the people at the top share traits of invincibility, invulnerability, omnipotence, omniscience."

Given the strict panoptic surveillance of seminary fathers, any attempt to establish or maintain romantic relationship with women, which is usually interpreted by seminary formators as a sign of vocation to marriage, is greatly hindered by the celibate seminary environment. Thus, it is difficult for seminarians to mature in intimate relationships and meaningful relationships with women in actual human circumstances if they have not done so before seminary training because of the strict supervision of seminary formators and social isolation of the seminary.

Unrealistic Training in Sexuality

Although seminaries offer some alternative programs to develop human maturity, requiring students to take courses and attend workshops on sexuality, the seminarians' gender and sexual formation remains inadequate (Gregoire and Jungers 2004). These programs, courses, or workshops on sexuality could not substitute the normal socialization and sexual development of individuals in society, unless clerical training reestablishes the apprenticeship style of clerical training that immerses candidates in the real world. It is, therefore, normal to expect seminarians to experience sexual immaturity in dealing with women if long years of their adolescent life and young adulthood are spent inside a cloistered environment of the seminary without sufficient

Gender and Sexuality Formation **83**

contacts with the outside world and meaningful interactions with sociocultural agents of human growth, specifically women, for celibate priests.

Aside from regular interaction with women and other sociocultural agents for sexual maturity, sexual concerns are generally suppressed during formation. Sexual matters are treated with secrecy, which could only be spoken with spiritual directors who are not normally professional psychologists or behavioral scientists (Stanosz 2004). Sexuality in the seminary is therefore largely repressed and discussed only with spiritual directors who might also have their own unresolved sexuality issues.

Thus, a case of a blind leading another blind.

For some men, the institutional life in the same-sex environment may have served to further postpone social and sexual development. For these men, at the age of their ordination in their mid- to late twenties, they were intellectually and physically adults, but emotionally they remained far younger.

(Cravatts 2007, para. 5)

This is one reason why heterosexual priests are attracted to children and young adolescents who mistook them as part of their cohort because of psychosexual immaturity (Frawley O'Dea 2004).

Seminarians' temptations about sexuality will lead to sexual violations if not managed carefully (Meek et al. 2004). These sexual temptations usually pertain to the challenges in human form involving pornography and masturbation (Alphonso 2015). Therefore, there is a need to maintain a balance to build healthy relationships with the opposite sex, the community, and the formators to achieve a healthy sexuality (Naparan et al. 2022).

But this task seems insurmountable for heterosexual seminarians, especially those who felt being called to married priesthood given the social isolation of the seminary. "As human as they are, seminarians also experienced the attraction to the opposite sex. Many of them struggled in the seminary formation because of the temptation to engage in an intimate relationship with ladies and abandon the priestly vocation" as some seminarians testified (Naparan et al. 2022, 621–622):

The temptation in relation to sexuality is really affecting my life in the seminary. This temptation really allowed me to decide what it is that I want to be whether I want to be a priest or a married man.

– P8

When I was in the seminary, there was a time that I had a girlfriend. I came to a point that I want to quit the seminary formation and marry her. I wanted to meet her parents and tell them of our situation.

– P9

When I had my studies later in my priestly formation in another country, I met a lady who tried to convince me to be with her and quit my priestly vocation. She said that together, we can earn a living in that country.

– P10

The problem with the current celibate and TI seminary structure is that it does not distinguish between those seminarians who might have a potential vocation to married priesthood or marriage. Falling in love with women does not necessarily mean that the seminarian has no priestly vocation but may be called to married priesthood. Owing to mandatory celibacy and the lack of alternative clerical training for a married clergy, falling in love and difficulties in dealing with sexuality inside the seminary are usually interpreted as a calling to marriage and not to married priesthood.

Lack of Preparation for Sexuality of Parishioners

One serious unintended consequence of the seminary type of clerical training that can lead to CSA is the lack of preparation of seminarians in dealing with their parishioners' sexuality problems. The "spiritualization" of seminary formation can have an unintended negative impact on the ability of diocesan priests to deal with sexuality problems of their flock. Seminary training ought to prepare priests to interact with women and attractive people in the parish. But this seems not to be the case.

In her book, *Sex, Priestly Ministry, and the Church*, Len Sperry (2003), for instance, argues that the current clerical formation has resulted in unhealthy repression and stunted the psychological development of priests. Once a young priest leaves the structured culture of the seminary, emotionally immature, unsure of his true sexual state and impulses, it is likely that he acts in defiance of the Church's stringent requirement of celibacy and would encounter temporal temptations (Cravatts 2007). Thus, Ott and Winters (2011, 59) suggest an institutional shift toward a sexually healthy and responsible seminary formation that trains sexually healthy and religious professionals:

> A sexually healthy and responsible seminary provides training in sexuality issues so that seminary graduates and ordained clergy emerge as trained religious professionals who can deal with the complexity of sexual matters – in a healthy, constructive, and appropriate manner. Formation of religious professionals and clergy requires more than a renewal of the curriculum. It requires an institutional shift toward becoming a sexually healthy and responsible seminary that models respect and dignity for all persons.

"Being a priest has a religious as well as a sexual dimension – and thus the Catholic Church also has a sexual dimension, because it must deal with the sexuality of these newly minted priests who are still, after all, socialized men"

(Armbruster 2022, 66). Making sexual matters taboo and unethical inside seminary formation can be considered an initiation process to Catholic clergy's secret world of sexuality (Sipe 1990). "The Catholic Priest Habitus does not allow priests to express sexual feelings, let alone sexuality" (Armbruster 2022, 69). Thus, the seminary formation has taught seminarians to keep secrets about sex and sexuality, gradually initiating them to the resistant clerical world against celibacy (Sipe 1990).

Seminarians who enter the seminary give up their normal socialization in society and suppress anything that has to do with dating, romance, and intimacy with the opposite sex. This situation does not properly prepare them to deal with their parishioners' sexuality problems after ordination. An early seminary sexuality education survey conducted Sally Conklin in 2001, for example, showed that the seminary training for clergy did not address the sexuality-related needs of their parishioners. A study by Ott and Winters (2011) also indicated that only a handful of seminaries, specifically in the United States, were actively preparing their seminarians to address their own sexual needs as well as of those they intend to administer in the parish. It further revealed the overwhelming need for improvement in sexuality education for seminarians and overall program for sexual health in seminaries.

The current TI celibate seminary training generally not only encourages seminarians to repress their own sexuality but also deprives them of an adequate preparation to deal with their parishioners' sexuality problems in the ministry. Clergy and other religious professionals have a unique opportunity and responsibility to guide congregations and communities on a number of sexuality-related concerns. Many perceive religious professionals and the clergy, regardless of training, to be capable of dealing with marital counseling and sexual dysfunction (Conklin 2000), teen sexual development and relationships (Clapp, Helbert, and Zizak 2003), and family planning decisions (Ellison and Goodson 1997).

Sexual issues of Catholic priests are not usually addressed and even understood within the Church because of the emphasis on clerical role as spiritual mentor and advisor. Thus, people tend to think of priests as normal human beings with similar temptations and lusts (Francis and Turner 1995). Furthermore, "beliefs about clerical superiority and separateness prevented them from socializing positively with other gendered subjects, including children, resulting in developmental conflict and suppressed emotions" (D'Alton, Guilfoyle, and Randall 2013, 698).

When parishioners seek out clergymen for help during periods of suffering, they often assume that their priests are immune from ordinary suffering and that the priests' special relationship with God insulates them from doubt, imperfection, melancholia, and all forms of mental illness.

(Lothstein 2004, 168)

As spiritual leaders in the parish, "priests are likely to have more extensive contact with women than with men in their ministerial work and, given the intimate nature of ministry, they are likely to be challenged more frequently than other men to enter into close relationships" (Nestor 1993, 134–135). Research has shown that some priests who counsel parishioners developed sexual relationships with them as well as commit sexual abuse. A 2008 survey among progressive clerics confirmed this lack of preparation in the seminary on how to deal with sexuality in the parish. It revealed that two-thirds of the respondents disagreed that they were adequately prepared by their seminaries concerning sexual orientation, gender identity, and gender expression issues before their priestly ministry (Haffner and Palmer 2009): "The Catholic priesthood is electively mute about the sexuality in its midst. . . . [P]riests soothing their loneliness in the arms of beloved women or men. Further, the act of finding words, of developing a vocabulary, is prohibited" (Frawley O'Dea 2004, 133–134).

Seminary Social Structure, the Parish, and CSA

The sexual orientation in the seminary is totally different from secular society that surrounds the parish where diocesan seminarians are obligated to work after ordination. In the parish, newly ordained priests are normally exposed to women with no censorship on sexual matters like seminary training. Once seminary graduates became secular priests, the secluded and monitored seminary environment is replaced by an autonomous social structure of the parish with parish clergy generally enjoying absolute privacy. One study suggests that a communal life after seminary training is preferred by several diocesan seminarians (Tirabassi, Porada, and Fiebig 2015).

This ideal cannot happen in abnormal, secluded, and all-male celibate seminary formation where sexuality is repressed and normal interaction with women is lacking. The goal of the current seminary training of making seminarians celibate priests without distinguishing vocations to celibacy, marriage, or married priesthood for its seminarians is the major obstacle of forming sexually mature priests. The seminary formation should not only be focused on the spiritual, academic, and pastoral training of seminarians but also on how to diversify clerical training in accordance to their vocation in life. Since the primary goal of seminary formation is training celibate clerics, anything that is connected to sexuality and marriage is effectively suppressed by seminary formators; thus, one cannot expect seminarians to grow and mature in sexual life under this highly regulated social environment.

The TI seminary training is incompatible with the semi-autonomous lifestyle of diocesan priesthood. The incompatibility between the communal and highly controlled environment of the seminary and the semi-autonomous social structure of the parish implies evaluating the adequacy and appropriateness of the human and sexual development of seminarians in the seminary. The current seminary in a TI structure was originally conceived to train celibate religious and monastic priests after the imposition of mandatory clerical celibacy in the 11th and 12th centuries. This type of priests usually continues to live in their religious communities after ordination. This is not, however, the case for secular or diocesan priests who are usually obligated to live alone in the parish after seminary training.

The regulated freedom in the seminary is then suddenly replaced by absolute privacy in the parish after ordination for diocesan priests, away from the gaze of seminary formators, testing their social control and sexual maturity when faced with the temptations of CSA. As Frawley O'Dea (2004, 130) aptly observes:

> the protected collegial environments of seminaries shielded their residents from many worldly phenomena and temptations while providing camaraderie something akin to sleep-away camp lasting more than a decade. After ordination, however, these young men arrived in parishes often staffed by older priests, parishes, and ostensible mentors shortly to be convulsed by the liberalization of the Church ushered in by Vatican II. Frequently assigned to handle youth activities, the priest, juggling his adolescent psychosexual development and his sense of priestly power, was suddenly surrounded by idealizing young people living their teenage years very differently than he had.
>
> Catholic priests are particularly stressed in their work, a situation correlated with a variety of psychological and somatic disorders (Kilburg, Nathan, and Thoreson 1986; Labier 1986). Moreover, with an aging priesthood (the average age of priests is 57) and fewer men entering the priesthood, there are enormous demands on priests to cover more than one parish and to be always available to everyone. As a group, therefore, priests are overworked, overburdened, lonely, isolated, and socially stigmatized, factors that may lead to sexually inappropriate behaviors.
>
> *(Lothstein 2004, 168)*

In 20 years after the Second Vatican Council, it is estimated that between 70,000 to 100,000 priests worldwide left the priesthood to marry (Sweeney 1992). Priestly departures continued in recent years. In the 1990s, it was found in a research by Hoge (2002) that 15% of those ordained left the ministry within their first five years in the priesthood because of celibacy. It was also revealed that a high dissatisfaction among active and resigned priests with celibate formation, owing to its lack of depth and openness concerning celibacy and sexuality inside the seminary (Hoge 2002). Thus, it is high time for the RCC to reconsider reforming clerical training and reestablish the traditional apprenticeship style that does not disrupt the normal human and sexual development of candidates to the priesthood during clerical training. This type of priestly formation is also open married priesthood and, thus, provides alternative clerical formation for those with genuine calling to the married presbyterate.

Conclusion

This chapter has shown that the adoption of the celibate seminary training that suspended the normal socialization and sexual development of seminarians has serious unintended negative impact on the sexual maturity of diocesan priests and their capacity to resist the temptation to commit CSA once ordained and assigned in the parish. Despite seminary formation, seminarians still held traditional and conservative views on gender that reflect the RCC's ahistorical and anti-gender stance. The shift of clerical training from apprenticeship to a seminary clerical training that is built on a TI social structure has serious negative impact on the gender and sexuality development of diocesan seminarians who will be assigned in the semi-autonomous social structure of the parish and obligated to live and work alone with no social and spiritual support from a religious community.

Sexuality seminars and training are mere palliatives as healthy sexuality is acquired through real experience and socialization in society. To address clerical sexual immaturity and vulnerability of secular priests to CSA requires an alternative diocesan clerical training such as an apprenticeship style of clerical formation that is open to married priesthood and grounded on the real world rather than on a secluded and exclusive TI structure of the seminary.

Notes

1 Shared to the author in an informal conversation by seminarian informants.
2 Based on the personal knowledge of the author as a college diocesan seminarian who witnessed this type of problems with his coseminarians.

References

Abano, John Dave A., and Chris John C. Bedoria. 2023. "Assessing Grit of Emerging Adult Diocesan Seminarians in Negros Island, Philippines." *Technium Social Science Journal* 43: 314–326.
Adubale, Andrew A., and Oyaziwo Aluede. 2017. "A Survey of Counselling Needs of Seminarians in Catholic Major Seminaries in Nigeria." *Asia Pacific Journal of Counselling and Psychotherapy* 8 (1): 29–40. https://doi.org/10.1080/21507686.2016.1260610.
Alphonso, Ashley. 2015. "The Role of Accompaniment in Seminary Formation." *Janana-Sanjeevani* 1 (3): 13–23. https://web.archive.org/web/20180410060658id_/http://jdv.edu.in/wp-content/uploads/2017/07/8.pdf.
Anderson, Eric. 2009. *Inclusive Masculinity: The Changing Nature of Masculinities.* London: Routledge.

Anderson, Eric, and McCormack Mark. 2018. "Inclusive Masculinity Theory: Overview, Reflection and Refinement." *Journal of Gender Studies* 27: 547–561.

Armbruster, Andre. 2022. "On the Undisclosed Transfer of Abusive Catholic Priests: A Field Theoretical Analysis of the Sexual Repression Within the Catholic Church and the Use of Legitimate Language." *Critical Research on Religion* 10 (1): 61–77.

Barnes, Medora W. 2022. "Catholic Seminarians on 'Real Men', Sexuality, and Essential Male Inclusivity." *Religions* 13 (352): 1–14. https://doi.org/10.3390/rel13040352.

Bauman, Klaus, Eckhard Fricj, Chrsitoph Jacobs, and Arndt Bussing. 2019. "Spiritual Dryness and Celibacy of Priests – Discernment of Ongoing Spiritual Journeys from Relational and Psychosocial Immaturities." *Pastoral Psychology* 68: 605–617. https://doi.org/10.1007/s11089-019-00886-1.

Benedict XVI, and Seewald Peter. 2010. *Light of the World: The Pope, the Church and the Signs of the Times.* San Francisco: Ignatius Press.

Blank, Hanne. 2012. *Straight: The Surprisingly Short History of Heterosexuality.* Boston: Beacon Press.

Boisvert, Donald, and Robert Goss. 2021. *Gay Catholic Priests and Clerical Sexual Misconduct.* New York: Routledge.

Bourdieu, Pierre. 1977. *Outline of a Theory of Practice.* Vol. 16. Cambridge: Cambridge University Press.

Bracke, Sarah, and Paternotte David. 2016. "Unpacking the Sin of Gender." *Religion & Gender* 6: 143–154.

Capecchi, Christina. 2020. "Christopher West Rolls Out His 2020 'Made for More' Tour. The Catholic Spirit." https://thecatholicspirit.com/news/local-news/christopher-west-rolls-out-his-2020-made-for-more-tour/ [Accessed June 25, 2023].

Case, Mary Anne. 2016. "The Role of the Popes in the Invention of Complementarity and the Vatican's Anathematization of Gender." *Religion & Gender* 6: 155–172.

Clapp, Steve, Kristen Leverton Helbert, and Angela Zizak. 2003. *Faith Matters: Teenagers, Religion and Sexuality.* Fort Wayne: Life Quest.

Congregation for Catholic Education. 2019. "Male and Female, He Created Them." In *Towards a Path of Dialogue on the Question of Gender Theory in Education.* Vatican City: Congregation for Catholic Education.

Conklin, Sarah C. 2000. "Six Billion and Counting Compel Sexuality Study in Churches." *The Clergy Journal* 76 (6): 3–5.

Cozzens, Donald, William Schipper, Merle Longwood, Marie M. Fortune, and Elaine Graham. 2004. "Clergy Sexual Abuse: Theological and Gender Perspectives." *Journal of Religion & Abuse* 6 (2): 3–29. https://doi.org/10.1300/j154v06n02_02.

Cravatts, Richard. 2007. "L.A. Sex Abuse Settlement Leaves Troubling Questions Unanswered." *Delaware Online*, July 25, 2007. www.delawareonline.com/story/news/2007/07/25/l-sex-abuse-settlement-leaves/47783198007/.

D'Alton, Paul, Michael Guilfoyle, and Patrick Randall. 2013. "Roman Catholic Clergy Who Have Sexually Abused Children: Their Perceptions of Their Developmental Experience." *Child Abuse & Neglect* 37 (9): 698–702. https://doi.org/10.1016/j.chiabu.2012.12.001.

De Weger, Stephen Edward. 2022. "Unchaste Celibates: Clergy Sexual Misconduct Against Adults—Expressions, Definitions, and Harms." *Religions* 13 (5): 1–27. https://doi.org/10.3390/rel13050393.

Doyle, Thomas P. 2006. "Clericalism: Enabler of Clergy Sexual Abuse." *Pastoral Psychology* 54 (3): 189–213. https://doi.org/10.1007/s11089-006-6323-x.

Ellison, Christopher G., and Patricia Goodson. 1997. "Conservative Protestantism and Attitudes Toward Family Planning in a Sample of Seminarians." *Journal for the Scientific Study of Religion* 36: 512–529.

Fagan, Seán. 1965. "The New Approach to Seminary Training." *The Furrow* 16 (5): 267–276.

Feierman, Jay R. 2020. "Sexual Abuse of Young Boys in the Roman Catholic Church an Insider Clinician's Academic Perspective." In *The Abuse of Minors in the Catholic Church: Dismantling the Culture of Cover-ups*, edited by A. Blasi, and L. Oviedo. London: Routledge.

Francis, P. C., and N. R. Turner. 1995. "Sexual Misconduct Within the Christian Church: Who Are the Perpetrators and Those They Victimize?" *Counseling and Values* 39: 219–227.

Frawley O'Dea, M. G. 2004. "Psychological Anatomy of the Catholic Sexual Abuse Scandal." *Studies in Gender and Sexuality* 5 (2): 121–137. https://doi.org/10.1080/15240650509349244.

Frawley-O'Dea, Mary Gail, and Virginia Goldner, eds. 2007. *Predatory Priests, Silenced Victims*. 1st ed. London: Routledge.

Giami, Alain. 2020, "Institutions' Approach to Sexuality, A Necessity Between Care and Sexual Rights." *Soins. Psychiatrie* 41 (330): 12–16. https://doi.org/10.1016/s0241-6972(20)30100-6. PMID: 33353601.

Goffman, Erving. 1961. *Asylums: Essays on the Social Situation of Mental Patients and Other Inmates*. New York: Anchor Books.

Gregoire, Jocelyn, and Chrissy Jungers. 2004. "Sexual Addiction and Compulsivity Among Clergy: How Spiritual Directors Can Help in the Context of Seminary Formation." *Sexual Addiction and Compulsivity* 11 (1): 71–81. https://doi.org/10.1080/10720160490458256.

Gregoire, Jocelyn, and Crissy Jungers. 2010. "Sexual Addiction and Compulsivity Among Clergy: How Spiritual Directors Can Help in the Context of Seminary Formation." *Sexual Addiction & Compulsivity* 11 (1–2): 71–81. https://doi.org/10.1080/10720160490458256.

Hayduk, Leslie A., Rainer F. Stratkotter, and Martin W. Rovers. 1997. "Sexual Orientation and the Willingness of Catholic Seminary Students to Conform to Church Teachings." *Journal for the Scientific Study of Religion* 36 (3): 455–467.

Haffner, Debra W., and Palmer, Timothy. 2009. "Survey of Religious Progressives: A Report on Progressive Clergy Action and Advocacy for Sexual Justice." www.religiousinstitute.org/sites/default/files/research_reports/surveyofreligiousprogressivespublicreportapril2009withcover.pdf.

Hoge, Dean R. 2002. *The First Five Years of Priesthood: A Study of Newly Ordained Catholic Priests*. Collegeville, Minnesota, MN: Liturgical Press.

Investigative Staff of Globe. 2002. "Church Allowed Abuse by Priest for Years: Aware of Geoghan Record, Archdiocese Still Shuttled Him From Parish to Parish." *Boston Globe*, January 6, 2002. www.bostonglobe.com/news/special-reports/2002/01/06/church-allowed-abuse-priest-for-years/cSHfGkTIrAT25qKGvBuDNM/story.html.

John Jay College Report. 2004. "The Nature and Scope of Sexual Abuse of Minors by Catholic Priests and Deacons in the United States 1950–2002." *USCCB*. www.bishop-accountability.org/reports/2004_02_27_JohnJay/.

Keenan, Marie. 2011. *Child Sexual Abuse and the Catholic Church: Gender, Power, and Organizational Culture*. 1st ed. London and New York: Oxford University Press.

Keenan, Marie. 2015. "Masculinity, Relationships and Context: Child Sexual Abuse and the Catholic Church Catholic Church." *Irish Journal of Applied Social Studies* 15 (2): 64–77.

Kennedy, Eugene C., and Victor J. Heckler. 1972. *The Catholic Priest in the United States: Psychological Investigations*. Washington, DC: U.S. Catholic Conference.

Khwepe, Nontsokile Maria Emmanuela. 2016. "The Construction of Masculinity by the Seminarians of the Roman Catholic Church: "A South African Study." Master's thesis in Clinical Psychology submitted to the School of Psychology, University of KwaZulu-Natal, Pietermaritzburg. http://hdl.handle.net/10413/15208.

Kilburg, R., P. Nathan, and R. Thoreson, eds. 1986. *Professionals in Distress: Issues, Syndromes and Solutions in Psychology*. Washington, DC: American Psychological Association.

Labier, D. 1986. *Modern Madness: The Hidden Link Between Work and Emotional Conflict*. New York: Touchstone.

Lam, Stephanie R., Kimberly R. Morrison, and Dirk Smeesters. 2009. "Gender, Intimacy, and Risky Sex: A Terror Management Account." *Personality and Social Psychology Bulletin* 35 (8): 1046–1056. https://doi.org/10.1177/01461 67209336 607.

Lassi, Steffano, Lisa Asta, Amedeo Cencini, Ernesto Caffo, and Hans Zollner. 2022. "Reviewing the Use of Psychological Assessment Tools in the Screening and Admission Process of Candidates to the Catholic Priesthood or Religious Life." *Spirituality in Clinical Practice* (Advance online publication). https://doi.org/10.1037/scp0000305.

Lothstein, Leslie M. 2004. "Men of the Flesh: The Evaluation and Treatment of Sexually Abusing Priests." *Studies in Gender and Sexuality* 5 (2): 167–195. https://doi.org/10.1080/15240650509349246.

McDevitt, Patrick J. 2012. "Sexual and Intimacy Health of Roman Catholic Priests." *Journal of Prevention & Intervention in the Community* 40: 208–218. https://doi.org/10.1080/10852 352.2012.680 413.

McCormack, Mark. 2011. "Hierarchy Without Hegemony: Locating Boys in an Inclusive School Setting." *Sociological Perspectives* 54: 83–101.

Meek, Katheryn Rhoads, Mark R. McMinn, Todd Burnett, Chris Mazzarella, and Vitaliy Voytenko. 2004. "Sexual Ethics Training in Seminary: Preparing Students to Manage Feelings of Sexual Attraction." *Pastoral Psychology* 53 (1): 63–79.

Miller, Maureen C. 2003. "Masculinity, Reform, and Clerical Culture: Narratives of Episcopal Holiness in the Gregorian Era." *Church History* 72 (1): 25–35.

Naparan, G., M. Canoy, F. D. Mahinay, and J. E. Villaflor. 2022. "Walking on Hot Coals: A Phenomenological Study on Dealing With Temptations in the Seminary." *Millah: Jurnal Studi Agama*. https://doi.org/10.20885/millah.vol21.iss3.art1.

Nestor, Thomas F. 1993. "Intimacy and Adjustment Among Catholic Priests." Dissertations. 3320. https://ecommons.luc.edu/luc_diss/3320.

Obinwa, Ignatius M. C. 2019. "Revisiting the Formation of Catholic Priests in Nigerian Context: A Perspective of the Biblical Notion of Priesthood." *Ministerium: A Journal of Contextual Theology* 5: 81–95.

Oldenkamp, Nathan G. 2018. "Addressing the Need for Greater Social Competence of Lutheran Brethren Seminary Students Entering Pastoral Ministry." Doctoral Thesis, Bethel University, Spark Repository. https://spark.bethel.edu/etd/480.

Ott, Kate M., and Amanda J. Winters. 2011. "Sex and the Seminary: Preparing Ministers for Sexual Health and Justice." *American Journal of Sexuality Education* 6 (1): 55–74. https://doi.org/10.1080/15546128.2011.547368.

Pope John Paul II. 1992. *Pastores Dabo Vobis [I Shall Give you Shepherds]: Pope John Paul's Post-Synodal Exhortation on the Formation of Priests in the Circumstances of the Present Day*. Vatican: Libreria Editrice Vaticana. www.vatican.va/content/john-paul-ii/en/apost_exhortations/documents/hf_jp-ii_exh_25031992_pastores-dabo-vobis.html.

Popovic, Miodrag. 2005. "Intimacy and Its Relevance in Human Functioning." *Sexual and Relationship Therapy* 20: 31–49. https://doi.org/10.1080/14681 99041233 1323 992.

Presbyterorum Ordinis [Order of Priests]. 1965. *Decree on the Ministry and Life of Priests, Promulgated by Pope Paul VI*. Vatican: The Vatican Archives. www.vatican.va/archive/hist_councils/ii_vatican_council/documents/vat-ii_decree_19651207_presbyterorum-ordinis_en.html.

Rockenbach, Mark. 2020. "Sexual Temptations." *SMP Videos* 3. https://scholar.csl.edu/smp2020/3.

Rohlinger, Deana A. 2007. "Primary Socialization." In *The Blackwell Encyclopedia of Sociology*, edited by Ritzer George, 590–591. https://doi.org/10.1002/9781405165518.wbeoss194.

Romeo Mateo, María Cruz. 2021. "A New Priest for a New Society? The Masculinity of the Priesthood in Liberal Spain." *Journal of Religious History* 45 (4): 540–558. https://doi.org/10.1111/1467-9809.12799.

Rovers, Martin W. 1996. *Who's in the Seminary: Roman Catholic Seminarians Today*. Ottawa: Novalis Press.

Schuth, Katarina, O. S. F. 2016. *Seminary Formation Recent History-Current Circumstances-New Directions*. Collegeville, MN: Liturgical Press.

Scott, James C. 1989. "Everyday Forms of Peasant Resistance." In *Everyday Forms of Peasant Resistance*, edited by F. D. Colburn. 1st ed. London: Routledge. https://doi.org/10.4324/9781315491455.

Scott, James C. 1992. *Domination and the Arts of Resistance: Hidden Transcripts*. New Haven and London: Yale University Press.

Sipe, A. W. Richard. 1990. *A Secret World: Sexuality and the Search for Celibacy*. 1st ed. East Sussex: Brunner-Routledge.

Sipe, A. W. Richard. 2003. *Celibacy in Crisis: A Secret World Revisited*. London: Routledge.

Sperry, Len. 2003. *Sex, Priestly Ministry, and the Church*. London: Liturgical Press.

Stanosz, Paul. 2004. "Reproducing Celibacy: A Case Study in Diocesan Seminary Formation." Fordham University ProQuest Dissertations Publishing, 3140903. www.proquest.com/openview/837656b34c4ffa9e63ac6145263e1fa7/1?pq-origsite=gscholar&cbl=18750&diss=y.

Stanosz, Paul. 2006. *The Struggle for Celibacy: The Culture of Catholic Seminary Life*. New York: Herder & Herder Book.

Sweeney, Terrance A. 1992. *A Church Divided: The Vatican Versus American Catholics*. Amherst, NY: Prometheus.

Terry, Karen J., Margaret Leland Smith, Katarina Schuth, James R. Kelly, Brenda Vollman, and Christina Massey. 2011. *The Causes and Context of Sexual Abuse of Minors by Catholic Priests in the United States, 1950–2010*. Washington, DC: USCCB. https://www.usccb.org/sites/default/files/issues-and-action/child-and-youth-protection/upload/The-Causes-andContext-of-Sexual-Abuse-of-Minors-by-Catholic-Priests-in-the-United-States-1950-2010.pdf [Accessed January 31, 2022].

The Role of Sexuality Education Within Seminaries. 2002. *The Case for Comprehensive Sexuality Education Within the Context of Seminary Human and Theological Formation: A Report of the Ford Foundation*. Wayne, PA: The Center for Sexuality and Religion.

Tirabassi, Domenick, Kelsey Porada, and Jennifer N. Fiebig. 2015. "Where Two or Three Are Gathered: Catholic Seminarians' Perspectives on Individual Versus Communal Living Arrangements of Diocesan Priests." *Pastoral Psychology* 64 (4): 469–477. https://doi.org/10.1007/s11089-015-0639-3.

USCCB (United States Conference of Catholic Bishops). 2005. *Program of Priestly Formation*. 5th ed. Washington, DC: USCCB.

Yip, Andrew K. T. 2003. "Sexuality and the Church." *Sexualities* 6 (1): 60–64. https://doi.org/10.1177/1363460703006001007.

5

CELIBATE CLERICAL FORMATION, SOCIAL RESISTANCE, AND SEXUAL ABUSE IN THE CATHOLIC CHURCH

Introduction

Social resistance by seminarians against the celibate way of life inside the Catholic seminary formation has not been sociologically explored and analyzed in the current clerical sexual abuse (CSA) research in the Roman Catholic Church (RCC). But sociologists believe that where there is imposed change and domination, there is social resistance. Resistance occurs "when the repertoire of action is imposed by force, as a means of political action, against the explicit practice of targeted population" (Even-Zohar 2002, 48). And this can be either active or passive (Scott 1989). Active or manifest resistance can easily be perceived by authorities because of its observable characteristics shown by resisters. Passive resistance, however, can be subtle and expressed in a variety of hidden everyday acts, thus difficult for powerholders to detect. In his book *Weapons of the Weak*, James C. Scott (1989) refers this type of silent protest as everyday forms of resistance that are different from the more typical forms of political resistance dominating the historiography of subordinate groups.

The imposition of mandatory clerical celibacy by the RCC on all clerics since the 11th and 12th centuries, which became the rule in the current clerical training in the Church, has created an awkward situation in Catholic priesthood where clerical celibacy, which is supposed to be a rare gift as taught by Christ, has become the universal norm for priests, while a married priesthood, which is supposed to be the universal social calling for most priests who do not have this rare gift of celibacy, has been suppressed and made rare by the Catholic hierarchy, although the RCC allowed a married clergy to flourish in Catholic Eastern churches.[1]

DOI: 10.4324/9781032722474-7

94 Celibate Clerical Training, Human Formation

The law on obligatory clerical celibacy was enacted by the RCC in the Second and Fourth Lateran Councils and maintained by the Council of Trent in the 16th century and Second Vatican Council (Vatican II) in modern and contemporary times. The obligatory clerical celibacy law that abandoned the well-entrenched custom of married priesthood in the RCC proved to be difficult to enforce after its legislation in the 12th century. Werner (2009, 3) noted a persistent social resistance among the Catholic clergy against the celibacy law, thus tough to implement:

> The enforcement of celibacy was difficult, and at the end of the twelfth century, most clerics in minor order were still married, and many priests, deacons, and subdeacons maintained public relationships with women. Church leaders repeatedly condemned priestly unchastity in local and ecumenical councils and waged a centuries-long battle to eliminate the sexual incontinence of priests.
>
> *(Werner 2009, 3)*

Miller (2014, 307) also observed that the "repetition of canons against clerical incontinence and records of ecclesiastical courts suggests a great deal of non-compliance" to the obligatory celibacy law. Finally, Waxman (2017, para. 9) noticed that "until the Reformation, parish priests frequently scandalized the faithful by taking wives, or at least keeping mistresses and concubines, as did Popes and cardinals." The priest-therapist and author A. W. Richard Sipe (1990) estimated that more than 50% of clerics are living non-celibate lives.

As a rare gift, clerical celibacy cannot be created by law or socially learned in an exclusive, all-male, and highly controlled environment of the seminary. A gift or charism is freely given by God. It is something that is personally discovered by the individual through prayer and discernment rather than acquired through spiritual and social conditioning in a closed institution like the seminary. Training future priests in what the sociologist Erving Goffman (1961) calls "total institutions" (TI) with the purpose of acquiring the gift of clerical celibacy through institutional compliance can inadvertently lead to clerical social resistance. As Witte Jr. (2006, 5) aptly argues:

> Celibacy was a gift for God to give, not a duty for the church to impose. It was for each individual, not for the church, to decide whether he or she had received this gift. By demanding monastic vows of chastity and clerical vows of celibacy, the church was seen to be intruding on Christian freedom and contradicting Scripture, nature, and common sense.

A closed organization in TI emphasizes external compliance of all members to the established rules rather than understanding the personal processes of each member who follows these rules (Goffman 1968). The RCC tacitly assumes that if seminarians are intellectually and spiritually fit and obedient to the exclusive celibate training in the seminary, they will eventually receive the rare gift of clerical celibacy during ordination. With the absence of the option for married priesthood, the celibate seminary formation only accepts eligible applicants for celibate priesthood, disregarding the fact that other aspirants may have other social calling and gender orientation and thus need a different form of clerical training.

Furthermore, owing to the scarcity of resident professional and competent counselors and experts in Catholic seminaries, regular internal processing of seminarians' psychosexual needs during formation is often neglected (Adubale and Aluede 2017). Heterosexual and gay seminarians with their strong need for intimacy and social bonding may not be fit to the celibate clerical lifestyle but are forced to silently undergo the training to become priests. This incompatibility between the gender orientation and psychosocial needs of the seminarians and the celibate lifestyle formed inside the seminary can lead to social resistance. This can also result in serious sexual repression, psychological immaturity, and covert coping resistant strategies to survive the rigid celibate seminary training just to become priests. The clerical culture of the RCC that supports the nondisclosure of emotion or emotional distress (Cozzens 2004) starts in seminary training that discourages open discussion on sexual matters.

Open talk about sexuality problems inside the seminary is prohibited. Sexual concerns can only be discussed by seminarians with their spiritual directors who are usually priests with no expertise or professional training in psychosexual issues. Thus, "priests do not and cannot talk about sex, sexual fantasies, or desires. Sexuality is censored and tabooed" (Armbruster 2021, 67) during and after the highly supervised celibate seminary training. Marie Keenan (2015) thus argues that the RCC's perfect celibate clerical masculinity has avoided and effectively denied Catholic priests of their sexuality and sexual desire. They are expected to "holy and detached" and "sexless." And this has been stressed in the celibate seminary formation that prohibits any open conversation on sexuality and gender issues.

The ideal of the perfect celibate clerical masculinity that is being imposed by formators inside the exclusive and TI environment of the seminary on all seminarians regardless of their gender socialization and sexuality often results in passive social resistance. The obligatory clerical celibacy was an imposed change by the RCC during the Medieval period owing to some major historical and sociological contingencies that required church reform, specifically prohibiting clerical marriages, which were seen as the root cause of priestly abuses, immorality, corruption, and divided loyalty of the clergy between their feudal lords and the Pope (Ballano 2023). The celibate seminary formation was also imposed by the Council of Trent in the 16th century to improve the clerical training of diocesan priests and to protect young seminarians' priestly vocation from the temptations of the city (Schuth 2016).

The mandatory clerical celibacy that commences during seminary training sidesteps human sexuality that can result in silent and hidden resistance by those seminarians who felt not having the rare gift of celibacy but called to married priesthood. Since celibacy is hostile to sexual conduct, clerics who discerned to be called to married priesthood would naturally resist this denial of human sexuality. Thus, the ecclesial campaigns to enforce clerical celibacy were at best "sporadic and often ineffective" (Brundage 2001).

Because of the fear of expulsion from seminary formation, the social resistance by heterosexual and gay seminarians against the strict celibate rules in the seminary normally takes a passive and covert form in the private sphere or what the sociologist Erving Goffman (1969) calls "the backstage" of social life. And when these seminarians become priests, this passive resistance or "hidden transcript" (Scott 1992) continues and becomes part or what the priest-therapist Richard Sipe (1990) calls the secret world of clerical sexuality. Passive social resistance against celibacy inside the seminary normally occurs in the informal or hidden curriculum, one that is parallel to the official curriculum pursued by seminary formators according to the RCC's official rules.

With the apparent lack of competent psychologists and experts who can guide seminarians for their sexuality issues, passive resistance as a covert form of noncompliance with the established seminary rules on celibacy can greatly contribute to the psychosexual immaturity and vulnerability of seminary graduates to CSA once ordained and assigned in the ministry. Seminary formators cannot cultivate healthy sexuality and human maturity when seminarians are in passive resistance. Externally, seminarians may appear obedient and compliant to the seminary celibacy and chastity rules but internally, they develop the negative feeling and attitude of resistance and opposition against these rules. Male heterosexual seminarians, for instance, who cannot conform to the rigid all-male environment with apparent absence of women are then forced to engage in secret resistant acts such as masturbation, pornography, or secret romantic relationship with women outside the seminary.

Several priests perceive the obligatory celibacy as unnecessary, unnatural, and unhealthy that is draining their passion in life (Cozzens 2006) and, thus, attract various forms of sexual misconduct as a form of social resistance. Resistance to clerical celibacy begins in the seminary and continues in clerical ministry. This "life-long practice of repressing one's sexual feelings will build up such a psychic energy that a priest could explode in inappropriate acting-out behavior" (Zullo n.d., 112). During seminary formation, once a heterosexual or gay seminarian discovers that heterosexual or homosexual married priesthood, not celibate priesthood, is his true social calling, he begins to engage in a lifelong passive resistance against celibacy and continence. He needs to survive the celibate seminary training to become a priest. Thus, in the meantime, he can externally go through the academic and spiritual formation of the seminary but engage in resistant acts privately in the hidden curriculum of sexual indiscretions and initiations.

Combining the sociological theories on symbolic interaction and social resistance as the overall theoretical framework, and drawing on secondary literature from published peer-reviewed materials and church documents as well as from the personal observation and experience of the author as a former diocesan and religious seminarian and some qualitative data from unstructured interviews with diocesan priests and former seminarians as sources of data, this chapter aims to establish the social resistance of Catholic priests against the mandatory clerical celibacy. It intends to illustrate how this resistance is expressed and initiated in the celibate seminary formation that denies seminarians the option for heterosexual or homosexual married priesthood. It ultimately aims to explore the sociological inter connections between celibate seminary formation, passive resistance, psychosexual immaturity, and weak resistance against clerical sexual abuse.

It argues that the current celibate TI structure of the diocesan seminary that lacks other social callings of Catholic priesthood and diversity in clerical training to accommodate the sexual and gender orientation of transgender candidates encourages external compliance, sexual repression, as well as passive and illicit resistant acts such as masturbation, pornography, secret visits to nightclubs, and maintaining secret romantic relationships. Passive resistance can lead to unhealthy sexuality, lack of self-control, psychosexual immaturity, and vulnerability to CSA once seminarians are ordained and exposed in the lonely life and semi-autonomous social structure of the parish. Research shows that most CSAs in the RCC are committed by immature celibate heterosexual diocesan priests (Frawley O'Dea 2004; John Jay College Report 2004), especially against adult women in parishes (de Weger 2022).

This chapter is structured into three major parts. The first part briefly establishes the theoretical orientation of the study that focuses on James Scott's theory of social resistance (19891992) and Erving Goffman's (1969) theory on the backstage of social life in his dramaturgical model of symbolic interactionism. The second part examines the initiation of seminarians into the informal and secret world of clerical resistance to celibacy. This includes an illustration and some anecdotal evidence that showed how seminarians secretly express their sexuality at the backstage of the informal sexuality curriculum of seminary formation. The last part explores how these secret sexual escapades or resistant acts can become part of the informal initiation of what A. W. Richard Sipe (1990) calls the secret world of clerical celibacy that includes CSA.

The phenomenon of clergy CSA is not something new in the RCC. Although it has been simply portrayed in the media as an "American," "Irish," or "Western" problem for the last 60 years, sexual abuses by Catholic priests have been existing since the foundation of the Church. Doyle and Rubino (2004) argue that CSA is a perennial problem in the RCC history. The entire 2,000 years of the Western Church history is characterized by church documents commenting on and sanctioning against CSA (Doyle 2006). Although "elitism" or "ecclesial pathology" (Doyle 2006) and abuse of authority and clericalism are often blamed as the root causes of CSA in the RCC (e.g., Doyle 2006; Carroll 2015; Plante 2020), some scholars, however, primarily blame the cleric-centered social structure of the RCC that is founded on celibate priesthood as weakening the Church's regulation against CSA (e.g., Frawley O'Dea 2004; Keenan 2011; Ballano 2020, 2023).

To understand the fundamental enabling structures of CSA in the RCC, sociological research and literature have apparently neglected the relationship between the persistence of sexual abuse in the RCC and the current mandatory clerical celibacy and celibate seminary training in the mainstream CSA scholarship. The exclusive and all-male seminary training that is largely seen as producing psychosexual immature priests who are vulnerable to CSA in clerical ministry could no longer be ignored as structurally contributing to the persistence of clergy sexual misconduct in the RCC (Frawley O'Dea 2004; Keenan 2015; Ballano 2023). How priests are humanly and sexually trained inside the seminary can be a primary determinant why CSA often occurs in the universal church.

Yet, most research and literature on seminary formation focuses on the historical appraisal of how ecclesiastical pronouncements on clerical formation are implemented in Catholic seminaries (Schuth 2010, 2016), its ascetical, academic, and pastoral value for clerical preparation, effectiveness of the psychological tools in screening of applicants (e.g., Sperry 2003; McGlone and Sperry 2020; Isacco et al. 2020a), and evaluating the suitability of candidates to the priesthood (e.g., Isacco et al. 2020b, 2022). Studies that explore the sociological structural connection between the current celibate seminary training and the persistent engagement of seminarians in covert sexual acts as a form of passive resistance against celibacy that can lead to CSA when ordained have been overlooked by CSA scholars.

This chapter, therefore, aims to modestly address this research gap, contending that secret sexual indiscretion and acts of unchastity of seminarians during seminary formation are a tacit passive resistance to clerical celibacy and an initiation to what the priest-therapist Richard Sipe (1990) calls the resistant secret world of clerical sexuality and sexual abuse. Sexual repression and covert resistant sexual acts done by seminarians in violation of the formal celibacy and chastity rules of the seminary calls for a serious structural analysis on what's wrong with the present social structure of Catholic seminaries.

Theoretical Orientation

Clerical Celibacy and Social Resistance

Understanding sexual deviance and sexual abuse by Catholic priests and seminarians as a form of passive and subtle social resistance to clerical celibacy has not been given attention in the current CSA and seminary formation research and literature. There is no doubt that the adoption of an exclusive and all-male celibate clerical training by the Council of Trent in 16th century has significant negative impact on male heterosexual seminarians who felt called to the priesthood but lacked charism to celibacy and maturity in their social interaction and relationship with women before entering the seminary. Thus, the adoption of an all-male celibate priesthood and clerical training can attract silent protest from this type of seminarians or what James Scott (1989) calls passive resistance.

The mandatory clerical celibacy is difficult to enforce as it opposes the long tradition of married priesthood in the RCC that continues to exist in some form from the time of the apostles up to the present times (Ballano 2023). Thus, clerical celibacy that contradicts the well-entrenched custom of the married presbyterate in the RCC is also difficult to enforce in the seminary as well as in clerical ministry without passive resistance by those who feel without the charism of celibacy. The persistence and prevalence of clerical concubinage, fornication, and illicit marital unions, especially after clerical celibacy became obligatory in the 12th century, are indicators that married presbyterate is necessary and that celibate priesthood is not suited for all priests in the RCC.

Since the implementation of clerical celibacy in the 12th century

> parish priests frequently scandalized the faithful by taking wives, or at least keeping mistresses and concubines, as did Popes and cardinals. After Protestantism rejected celibacy for the ministry as unnatural and unnecessary, the Council of Trent declared it an objectively superior state of life.
>
> *(Waxman 2017, para. 9)*

Sociologists believe that customs such as married priesthood in the RCC are "the unofficial and unenacted practices of communities" (Bederman 2010, ix).

Customs are enduring source of legal obligation even as societies move toward a firmer jurisprudential footing of legal rules and institutions. Legislating customs can strengthen any legal system (Bederman 2010). But opposing established customs can result in social resistance. Suppressing married priesthood in the 12th century and the apprenticeship clerical training in the

16th century that allowed candidates to choose married priesthood have unintendedly resulted in a persistent passive resistance culture against celibacy that commences during seminary training and continues to affect new priests after ordination. Married priesthood has existed in some form in the RCC since the time of the apostles and continues to exist up to the present, such as among married priests in Eastern Catholic churches and in the United States (Ballano 2023). Equating Catholic priesthood to celibate priesthood can indeed invite silent protest from male heterosexual priests who discerned that married priesthood is their vocation.

Passive Resistance and the Backstage

The sociologist Erving Goffman (1961, 305) observed, "Whenever worlds are laid on, underlives develop." "Although scholars have long documented the resistant practices of subordinates in social interactions, they have given these activities considerably less attention than they have to more organized challenges to power, such as revolutions, strikes, boycotts, or class-action suits" (Ewick and Silby 2003, 1329). But other scholars contend that the seemingly small acts of passive resistance by the weak can also make history since they too are "world-making" activities (Goodman *1978*).

James C. Scott's (1989) popular book *Weapons of the Weak* can be relevant as a conceptual framework to understand passive clerical resistance against celibacy and celibate seminary training. To Scott, social resistance can take two forms: active and passive. In this book, he highlights the significance of passive resistance or what he calls people's everyday resistance in contrast to active, open, and confrontational types of resistance such as revolts, insurrections, and other forms of violent political actions for social or political change. To him, passive resistance is an everyday form of popular opposition to the status quo that is distinct from political resistance that dominates the historiography of subordinate groups.

Scott (1989, 1992) argues that small acts of courageous challenges by dominated group in society to the microscopic control of behavior can give moments of dignity and self-respect for resisters. These acts can eventually grow to be powerful enough to challenge the status quo. Passive resistance can employ meanings and symbols that contest a dominant power, affirming that power can emanate from below in ways people make sense of their world (Hollander and Einwohner 2004). "Although such acts of resistance may not cumulate to produce institutional change, they may nonetheless have consequences beyond the specific social transaction" (Ewick and Silby 2003).

Passive social resistance despite consisting of small acts of protests can call the attention of powerholders for social change. For instance, the issue of the difficulties of priests in dealing with clerical celibacy often comes up in RCC's consultative bodies such as synod of bishops. Clerical sexual abuse and secret violations of celibacy have recently caused institutional crisis in the RCC that forced ecclesiastical authorities to rethink the current mandatory clerical celibacy. One of the agenda of the Synod on Synodality that is spearheaded by Pope Francis is married priesthood, owing to priest shortage in current times: The synod's working document, released June 20, asked members to prayerfully consider dozens of questions, including, "Could a reflection be opened concerning the discipline on access to the priesthood for married men, at least in some areas?" (Wooden 2023, para. 2).

Passive social resistance against obligatory clerical celibacy is not as dramatic as popular revolts because it is done behind the public eye. It is covertly committed by resisters not in the front stage of social life but at the backstage of private space. The idea of a backstage recalls the sociologist Erving Goffman's symbolic interactionist theory that metaphorically views social life as a drama with people as actors performing in front of an audience with transcripts, stage props, appropriate expressions, and attitudes that allow them to conjure up a desired self-image (Fine and Manning 2003). In his influential book *The Presentation of Self in Everyday Life* (1969), Goffman outlined the theatrical approach in analyzing social encounters in daily life.

To Goffman, the social world has both "front regions" and "back regions" or "frontstage" and "backstage" to use the elements of theatre. Performances can be done in front stage or backstage. Individuals are seen as performers who

> try to present themselves in a certain way in order to project their preferred definition of the situation, whereas they as "audience" attempt to accommodate the projected images of others to facilitate interaction rituals. Importantly, what comes out through such interaction is not a genuine agreement but a "veneer of consensus" to which everyone present feels obliged to give lip service in order to maintain working relationships in the front stage.
>
> *(Joo 2010, 279)*

Since the backstage is hidden from public life, it becomes the perfect place for covert passive social resistance for people who silently oppose the status quo. Passive resistance is discreetly committed in everyday life by the powerless away from public eye to avoid surveillance and sanctions from powerholders. In the RCC, clerical passive resistance against the mandatory clerical celibacy and at its demand for sexual continence is done at the backstage of clerical life away from the gaze of the Catholic hierarchy. This is the hidden region that the priest-therapist Richard Sipe (1990) calls the secret world of clerical sexuality, where sexual indiscretions and sexual abuse become resistant acts against the imposed clerical celibacy and celibate seminary training.

102 Celibate Clerical Training, Human Formation

Finally, people engaging in covert or passive resistance may not be aware that they are opposing the status quo (Scott 1989). Passive social resistance of seminarians and clerics who resist the demands of clerical celibacy is done at the backstage of clerical life or the silent world of clerical sexuality (Sipe 1990). Since discussing sexuality that can lead to marriage is a taboo in celibate seminary training, heterosexual seminarians express their repressed sexuality and resistant acts against the established celibacy rule of the seminary in the hidden private life of the seminary.

Passive Resistance and Seminary Formation

Clerical passive resistance against celibacy does not commence after ordination. It structurally begins during the seminary formation, which only accepts the calling to celibacy. Research suggests that more than 50% of vowed celibates or seminary graduates who professed the vow of celibacy after ordination live noncelibate lifestyles in either long-term, committed partnerships, or short-term relationships (Sipe 1995). Also, "the staggering incidences of child sexual abuse by priests in North America have brought the relevance of celibacy into question and have led to a decline in its endorsement" (Gregoire and Jungers 2010, 72).

The appropriateness of imposing the perfect celibate clerical masculinity on seminarians in an exclusive total institution of the seminary (Goffman 1968) regardless of their sexual orientation and social calling to the priesthood has started to be noticed by some scholars who saw the seminary as largely producing immature heterosexual priests who became the main cohort of sexual offenders in the RCC (Frawley O'Dea 2004; John Jay College Report 2004; Keenan 2015; Ballano 2023).

The institutional life of a same-sex environment of Catholic seminaries brackets the social and sexual development of individuals in society. In the RCC, new priests are usually in their mid- to late twenties. They may be considered intellectually and physically adults, but emotionally underdeveloped (Cravatts 2007). During seminary formation, the seminarians' normal psychosexual development in society is suspended for several years during philosophical and theological training. Seminarians become powerlessness in dealing with "a structured, autocratic culture of men in which they are not treated like fully developed adults" (Cravatts 2007, para six).

A study by Patrick McDevitt (2012) involving Catholic priests, for instance, indicated a strong need for early intervention and education during seminary formation, as well as ongoing education after ordination, and psychotherapy support for their sexual and intimacy health. With the current shortage of experts and competent psychologists in Catholic seminaries, this need for early intervention and education for the sexuality and intimacy problems of seminarians remains largely unaddressed during formation, much more after ordination where priests are presumed to be mature and are largely unsupervised by their co-priests and bishops in the parish and diocese.

As a total institution (Goffman 1968) for celibate priesthood, the seminary strictly prohibits sexual matters that can lead to romantic and marital relationships. Seminarians who have unresolved sexual issues before seminary formation and who attempt to resolve them through secret romantic relationship risk expulsion from the seminary. Thus, for fear of sanction, seminarians learn to hide their sexual concerns at the backstage of seminary life or at the hidden informal seminary curriculum. This informal curriculum on clerical sexuality secretly contravenes the established seminary rules on celibacy and chastity and can include "sexcapades" without the knowledge of seminary rectors and formators. In moral terms, these can constitute sinful temptations of the flesh and acts of unchastity, which are not properly handled in seminary formation for lack of competent counselors and professional psychologists.

The overall assumption behind the seminary training in a TI structure is to make all clerical candidates become celibate priests in a controlled environment, regardless of their personal and sexual issues and social calling, whether they are called to celibate or married priesthood. If seminarians willingly comply with the seminary rules and rational plan, it is assumed that they can become spiritually celibate priests. As *Optatam Totius* (para. 10) suggests, seminarians are to be educated in the tradition of celibacy and are to see it as a "gift to which, inspired by the Holy Spirit and helped by the divine grace, they must freely and generously respond" (Pope Paul VI 1965).

With the controlled seminary environment under the supervision of formators, as well as spiritual practices that simulate Christ's celibate life and ministry, it is expected that seminary graduates can receive the charism of clerical celibacy. But this assumption is empirically unsustainable. "From this theological perspective, celibacy is understood as a gift that is voluntarily and generously received; nevertheless, it is often considered a 'forced lifestyle' imposed on Catholic priests" in the current TI celibate seminary structure (Bauman et al. 2019, 606). This assumption is contrary to the nature of clerical celibacy as a charism that is freely chosen by the individual after discernment rather than being imposed on him by an institution through the internal rules of the seminary.

Informal Seminary Socialization

Training is crucial for an organization to form the commitment of members to organizational values. But organizational formators are aware that elements of socialization, especially the informal ones, are largely outside their control (Fielding 2023). While formal and informal influences undoubtedly operate, the situation is complicated by the individuals' attempt to their own sense of their experiences. Socialization is a process of identity transformation. Social conflicts are normally resolved by attempting to reconcile the procedures taught in formal socialization and those derived from informal sources (Fielding 2023).

In the seminary organization, informal elements that exist vis-à-vis the formal rules can also influence the behavior of seminarians during clerical training. Seminary education, like in any other institution of learning, has two curricula: the formal and informal. The formal curriculum refers to the courses prescribed by the RCC's official documents on seminary formation, while the informal curriculum refers to the informal learning seminarians acquire inside and outside the seminary customs. This is a type of learning, if it is connected to sexuality, is largely banned in ordinary seminary conversation. It is usually done in secret meetings among seminarians and their social networks outside the seminary.

In the seminary, candidates face moral temptations that can lead to spiritual failure and feelings of guilt and shame (Coe 2008). Seminary temptations include the drive to access pornography and engage with sexual partners (Rockenbach 2020), selfishness (Oakley 2017), and trivializing the importance of disagreement (Cordell Bontrager 2017). Seminarians are expected to surpass these temptations to complete their seminary training to be ordained as priests. This is one reason why seminaries are isolated from the community to protect priestly vocation (Oberdorf 2021).

Suppressing one's sexuality and finding means to overcome temptations of the flesh can oftentimes lead to conflict with the seminary's organizational ideals on celibacy and chastity. One negative unintended consequence of the strict TI priestly formation in the seminary is social resistance. The imposition of seminary rules and emphasis on compliance can result in covert social resistance in seminarians' life and informal learning from the hidden curriculum of the seminary.

Social resistance in seminary formation can be expressed in terms of temptations to deviate from the normal seminary structure. Some seminarians, for instance, expressed difficulties in dealing with the structured seminary formation and engage in everyday passive resistance:

> They experienced temptations to deviate from the structure. This temptation includes going out at night, drinking, struggling for independence, craving more food, laziness, and not exerting effort in studying. Some seminarians got bored with the structured life in the seminary and thus found ways to go out of the seminary at night without the knowledge of the seminary rectors.
>
> *(Naparan et al. 2022, 22–23)*

Major Passive Resistant Acts During Formation

Living Double Lives

One significant form of passive social resistance against clerical celibacy, which starts with seminary formation, is living double lives. Living a double life is a consequence of the incompatibility of the seminarian's chosen vocation and their sexual orientation that conflicts with the celibate seminary formation. This results in artificiality and a life of hypocrisy where the person projects a public image that does not reflect his or her inner life. The RCC's culture of secrecy and nondisclosure of sexuality and emotional distress contribute greatly to living double lives. Living a double life is passive resistance against the strict celibacy rule that denies priests sexual intimacy, family life, and companionship that are offered by married priesthood for heterosexuals and homosexuals if same-sex marriage is allowed in the RCC.

Structurally, the current celibate seminary training encourages the resistant lifestyle of living double lives. Heterosexual seminarians, for instance, who do not have the rare gift of celibacy will be constrained to undergo the celibate way of life inside the seminary, which they are not called for. Consequently, their normal gender socialization as heterosexuals is suppressed in TI environment of the celibate seminary. As a coping mechanism for their repressed sexual needs without violating the celibacy rule, some engage in covert indecent sexual acts in private life to appear conforming publicly to the expected celibate lifestyle in the seminary.

Thus, the celibate seminary formation encourages double lives because of its lack of alternative training appropriate for heterosexual seminarians with a sacred calling to married priesthood. To pursue priesthood, these seminarians need to "pretend" to possess the gift of celibacy and undergo the usual spiritual, academic, and human formation intended for celibate priesthood. In fact, an apprenticeship clerical training that allows candidates to live their normal lives to pursue married priesthood is more suitable for this type of seminarians. Subtle coercion of forcing heterosexual seminarians to become celibates can lead to passive or covert resistance to living double lives that commences during seminary training and continues in clerical ministry.

This is also the case for homosexual candidates. With the current policy of the RCC of prohibiting homosexual men to enter seminary formation to become priests, gay applicants are forced to declare themselves as heterosexual and enter the celibate clerical training that is not appropriate for their gender orientation. Like heterosexual men, they have also a strong need for intimate relationship and companionship. But the heterosexual orientation of celibate seminary training encourages them to live a double life inside the seminary, appearing as heterosexual when in fact they are not, although the all-male seminary environment is conducive for same-sex attraction and preference.

106 Celibate Clerical Training, Human Formation

In the seminary, gays could not just openly develop relationships with fellow seminarians with the panoptic surveillance of seminary fathers and the present policy of the RCC that expels any homosexual activity during formation (Congregation for Catholic Education 2005).

The current exclusive seminary training is also a structurally inappropriate clerical training that results in passive resistant acts and double lives for gay candidates. Homosexual seminarians with no gift to clerical celibacy are also constrained to become celibate priests when, in fact, their appropriate social calling is homosexual married priesthood, and this can also be truly realized in an apprenticeship style of priestly training with the RCC allowing same-sex marriage for clerics. Aware of the contributory cause of clerical celibacy to sexual abuse, German bishops are pushing for this type of priesthood for gay priests.

It is probably the proper time for the RCC under its Synod on Synodality to recognize the existence of gays as a separate gender identity and who are not naturally disordered and may be genuinely called to the priesthood. Gay priests are attracted to adolescent and adult men but not to children. Like heterosexual diocesan priests, they are also lonely in the parish with no male spouses who can restrain them to commit CSA. Not recognizing their gender identity and their need for homosexual marriage can lead to passive resistance and double lives for gays inside the seminary and in the ministry.

Living a double life starts in the seminary, as manifested in the resistant acts of some seminarians who maintain romantic relationships after acceptance in the seminary or establish new intimate relationships with women outside the seminary premises while in priestly formation. Another example of double lives inside the seminary formation is when seminarians appear holy and chaste inside the seminary while secretly visiting nightclubs and viewing strip shows, as well as engaging in compulsive masturbation or addictive online pornography. These resistant sexual acts can continue once problematic seminarians become priests and assigned in the autonomous structure of the parish where panoptic surveillance of the seminary formators is absent with clerical celibacy giving them absolute personal privacy. Thus, diocesan clerics can appear as "holy celibates" during sacramental celebration of the Eucharist to the parishioners but maintain concubines and lovers, sexually abusing children, adolescents, adult women, and nuns (Pullella 2022), as well as visiting brothels and massage parlors for sex (Day 2015).

Because of the culture of silence on sexuality among Catholic clerics that starts in seminary formation (Sipe 1990), seminarians who become priests can live double lives in the parish, engaging in the most reprehensible acts of sexual abuse against innocent children, adolescents, and adults under their pastoral care and still maintaining the good image in public life as venerable celibates. The covert resistant act of CSA remains unnoticed by the public and parishioners. Some bishops who are equally guilty of CSA like their priests tend to cover-up CSA cases and just transfer abusive priests to new parishes or incardinate them to new dioceses.

It appears that sexually abusive Catholic clerics tend to treat double lives in what sociologists call the reactivist definition of deviance. Under this definition, deviance, or any rule-breaking behavior such as CSA, requires both discovery of the act and public condemnation; otherwise, there is no crime or deviance (Goode 2019). If the deviant act of CSA has no public discovery and is kept secret due to the lack of witness with the silence of both the priest offender and victim, then the criminal and sinful act, although consummated, is not considered deviance or a crime due to the lack of negative public reaction or condemnation.

The Catholic hierarchy also tends to adopt this kind of definition in viewing sexual abuses in the RCC. Some bishops exhaust all means to hide CSA to avoid public discovery and scandals, trying to settle amicably cases with the clause that victims would not about the case publicly. "For years, the Church used confidential settlements to silence abuse victims. Although these agreements protected the identity of the victim, they also concealed the identities of the priests who often continued to serve at their parishes or other ministries" (Philp 2003, 845). Thus, if these abusive priests were transferred by bishops to other parishes or dioceses, parishioners would not consider them deviants or sex offenders. They would not be forewarned of the danger that these priests might commit the same sexual abuses in their parish.

The model of perfect celibate clerical masculinity that is initiated in seminary formation to form future priests as celibate and sexless beings encourages resistance and double lives. Clerical celibacy in Catholic priesthood, which was considered a rare gift, has been made obligatory and universal by the Second and Fourth Lateral Councils in the 11th and 12th centuries, and married priesthood, which was supposed to be the dominant social calling for Catholic priests, was suppressed. It created a structural problem in Catholic priesthood and encouraging heterosexual and gay priests to engage in secret resistant sexual acts and live immoral clerical lives. Living a celibate and chaste life for priests who do not possess the rare charism of celibacy is a tough life to follow and a form of silent martyrdom.

The best-selling book by Frederic Martel (2019), which was based on actual interviews of 1,500 Catholic clerics entitled *In the Closet of the Vatican*, claimed that 80% of Vatican priests are homosexual and several of them engaged in active homosexual acts and relationships despite vocally advocating clerical celibacy and continence. This is an example of the passive resistance of living double lives. The more disturbing account in the book was the revelation that even some top clerics such as cardinals also engaged in covert homosexual acts and relationships, living double lives and yet actively promoting clerical celibacy and chastity.

Pornography

"Pornography is a generic term that encompasses all sexually oriented material intended to arouse the reader, viewer, or listener. Internet pornography specifically refers to sexually explicit material available to consumers on the Internet" (Cleaveland 2004). Pornography is considered as one of the most serious challenges to clerical celibacy and celibate seminary formation in the 21st century. The secret access and use of online pornography by seminarians is part of the hidden informal sexual curriculum that parallels the official celibate curriculum.

The convergence of technologies and the invention of the smartphone have allowed people to express and experience sexuality online. With the growing penetration of Internet around the world and the popularity of digital gadgets, it is expected that most people will have an Internet connection on their mobile phones to communicate and transact personal and business matters online, as well as to pursue and develop online sexual relationships and access pornographic materials. Seminarians during formation can have smartphones that can easily access pornographic sites. Thus, heterosexual seminarians who have no strong disposition to celibacy and chastity will encounter serious sexuality problems and will find resistant acts such as pornography and masturbation to silently oppose the celibate rules of the seminary.

The frequent consumption of online pornography can be an addictive behavior for seminarians. There is a correlation between online pornography and addictive behavior. Research on mental health showed a direct relationship between addictive behavior and engagement in Internet pornography (Weber 2008). In an exploratory research, Kimberly Young (1997), who classified 396 cases of dependent Internet users, suggested that the use of chat rooms is highly addictive and can result in finding companionship to engage in deviant sexual activities, sexual excitement, and alter identities. The American Catholic bishops have already warned the faithful in a pastoral letter entitled "Create in Me a Clean Heart: A Pastoral Response to Pornography" about the negative effects of pornography on Christians, such as objectification, exploitation, and degradation of human dignity and unhealthy social relationships (USCCB 2015).

The pornography industry is earning more than $1 billion yearly. It is projected to increase to around $5 billion to $7 billion for the forthcoming years (Cleaveland 2004). With the astronomic rise of pornographic sites on the Internet, it is now easier to access online pornography through smartphones and other gadgets. And many Christians, including priests, pastors, and seminarians, became prey to this type of sin and sexual deviance. Recent research revealed that one in five smartphone searches is connected to pornography.

There is no comprehensive and updated data on priests and seminarians' use of and addiction to online pornography. However, research on Internet pornography based on interviews with some priests, seminarians, and religious revealed that there is an inordinate use and attachment to electronic media and Internet pornography among religious people in the Church, urgent issues that the RCC needs to immediately address (Weber 2008). Generally, the use of smartphones is prohibited in college seminaries but not in theologates.

Thus, access to online pornography is easier for theological seminarians nearing the priesthood compared to college seminarians. However, college seminarians can circumvent this rule on the use of smartphones. According to some informants[2] in one college seminary, some seminarians would bring in mobile phones secretly to the seminary from the outside during weekly break or pastoral exposure and hide them in their lockers. These phones have Internet connection that can allow them to watch pornographic materials online.

In other cases, some seminarians would watch porn in the seminary computer room with Internet, usually late at night, according to key informants. They usually make the physical arrangement in such a way that they can hide their activity from formators and other seminarians. They have lookouts to ensure that they are not caught by the seminary fathers or by other seminarians who might report them to the Prefect of Discipline. Others covertly watch porn with their laptops using discs or USBs, which they brought to the seminary from outside during weekly breaks. According to the informants, confiscation of smartphones and pornographic materials and a warning are the usual sanction when caught by seminary formators. But expulsion from the seminary is the most serious punishment for repeat offenders.

Compulsive Masturbation

> The most reliable population-based surveys indicate that masturbation is neither particularly rare nor particularly universal as a practice . . . studies suggest that masturbation occurs at a fairly high frequency for unmarried young people . . . Smaller scale surveys suggest that masturbation is common among male college students.
>
> (Kwee and Hoover 2008, 259–260)

Celibacy is rare since it takes a certain form of socialization during childhood and adolescence, which makes some individuals more disposed to live perpetual continence in religious calling without encountering serious sexuality problems. Certain saints in the Catholic Church, for instance, have shown that celibate priesthood and holiness can be achieved. However, this is rare, and the culture and historical period of these saints are totally different from the contemporary world characterized by digital technology, cyberspace, and

110 Celibate Clerical Training, Human Formation

telepresence or technology-mediated communication where sexual matters and pornographic materials are readily available online.

The easy access and use of pornographic sites can often lead to masturbation, another covert resistant act to celibacy and chastity. It is a common knowledge among seminarians that masturbation is the most popular sexual sin inside the all-male seminary. In one seminary in the Philippines, for instance, a separate "express lane" was created to accommodate several seminarians with the sin of masturbation. This is confirmed by the priest-therapist Richard Sipe (1990), who acknowledged that masturbation is commonly practiced inside the seminary. Indeed, candidates who do not possess the gift of celibacy and thus not humanly disposed to celibate lifestyle oftentimes engage in compulsive masturbatory acts, a form of covert and passive resistance that is contrary to clerical celibacy and continence taught by the RCC.

Occasional masturbation may be tolerated as a normal transgression in an exclusive and all-male seminary environment, although allowing wet dreams to release pent-up sexual energies and urges without masturbation is a more appropriate and natural way without committing a sin in the RCC. However, compulsive or habitual masturbation is a different matter. Seminary formators usually interpret this as a strong sign that the candidate has no vocation to the priesthood but to marriage and would usually advise him to leave the seminary. Compulsive masturbation is a serious psychological and moral problem that cannot be resolved in the exclusive and all-male organization of the seminary.

Compulsive masturbation despite its deviancy and sinfulness cannot however be interpreted altogether as absence of priestly vocation. It can instead be seen as a form of passive social resistance against the celibate clerical training that does not allow married priesthood. It is part of the hidden transcript (Scott 1989) or informal sexual formation that silently contravenes the rigid celibacy and chastity rules of the seminary that bans all forms of open discussion on sexual matters. So, it is probable that heterosexual seminarians, who have serious difficulties in dealing with sexuality and engage in compulsive masturbation, are called to married priesthood. But with the suppression of this type of priesthood, seminary fathers usually misinterpret compulsive masturbation as a sign of absence of calling altogether to Catholic priesthood.

Night Life and Secret Romance

Some research had shown that celibate priests with active sexual life often visited brothels and engaged in clerical fornication. Despite the absence of comprehensive data, one can still associate the practice of visiting nightclubs as part of the hidden curriculum of seminary formation. There is a lack of comprehensive study on seminarians' nightlife during seminary formation, but there is anecdotal evidence that suggests that some seminarians in certain seminaries secretly visit nightclubs and watch lewd shows during free time, especially during nighttime, semestral breaks, or pastoral exposures outside the seminary. According to some key informants, senior seminarians with active sex life usually take the lead in inviting and initiating new seminarians to join them in this type of hidden and informal sexuality curriculum without the knowledge of seminary formators.

According to key informants, some seminarians in one seminary, for example, usually escaped the seminary premises before midnight by covertly climbing the back fence of the compound to go to the city and watch strip shows in nightclubs. The security guard is stationed only at the entrance of the seminary. One of the seminarians who has a relative operating a nightclub in the city recruited others to watch indecent shows. A few out of curiosity also joined this group. They normally returned to the seminary at dawn by climbing the back fence again. In other cases, some seminarians visited nightclubs during pastoral exposures, where they are usually assigned to parishes outside the seminary. Normally, seminarians who had experienced visiting nightclubs would covertly recruit others to join them in their sexcapades.

Visiting nightclubs and watching strip shows would be easier for theological seminarians whose daily schedule is more relaxed than college seminarians according to informants. Following the principle of gradualism, the RCC expects that seminarians in theological formation would be more mature and responsible compared to college seminarians who require more supervision by formators. "In short, the closer the program is to priestly ordination, the greater the applicant's development of the requisite qualities ought to be" (USCCB 2005, #35). Formators assume that seminarians in the theological formation who are closer to ordination have already internalized self-discipline and priestly formation. Thus, theological seminaries tend to be more relax in seminary structure and observation of curfews compared to college seminaries.

In one theological seminary in a Catholic country, there is no curfew for seminarians as long they attend the morning praise and perform well in their academic studies. In one instance, a group of senior theological seminarians secretly brought new seminarians to a certain nightclub to watch strip shows for the entire night as a form of "initiation" and informal welcoming to the secret curriculum of celibate seminary formation.[3] In another seminary, the curfew starts before midnight. This gives sexually active theological seminarians ample time to visit nightclubs before they return to the seminary according to the experience of one former priest.

In another instance, the lay formator appointed by seminary formators to guide theological seminarians' exposures or "trials" during their pastoral year brought seminarians to indecent shows in fun houses during exposure breaks.[4] Being a former owner of a nightclub, this lay formator argued that bringing seminarians to lie indecent shows is part of the informal sex education for celibate seminarians.

This covert deviant practice of visiting fun houses and brothels can be an initiation to the real secret sexual life of priests, which can persist after ordination, especially when assigned in the lonely life of the parish. Historical research has suggested a persistent pattern of diocesan priests visiting brothels and engaging in clerical fornication in contradiction to their vow to clerical celibacy and continence. Secretly visiting brothels or prostitution houses seemed to have a long history in Catholic clerical life.

Although there is little empirical evidence on the sexuality of clerics during the Medieval church, historians Ruth Karras (2011) and Jeremy Goldberg (2019), for example, claimed that were brothels in England that specifically catered to the needs of the clergy. In France, there were also several municipal ordinances to prevent clerics from visiting urban prostitution houses, showing that priests are regular customers of brothels.

Visiting brothels can even be easier for priests in urban parishes because of social alienation and anonymity in the city. With the nonwearing of religious cassock for priests outside the church after Vatican II, secular priests with active sexual life can easily visit nightclubs and prostitution houses or bring their partners or victims in motels unnoticed by the laity. One senior cleric and a president of a Catholic college in the Philippines, for instance, was apprehended by the police because of a tip for attempting to bring a 13-year-old girl to a nearby motel without the knowledge of the parishioners (Agoncillo 2017).

Lastly, some heterosexual seminarians with the strong need for romantic relationship secretly establish or maintain intimate relationship with women outside the seminary – another form of passive resistance against clerical celibacy during priestly formation. Despite the strict surveillance of seminary fathers, some seminarians can develop intimate relationships with women during seminary training, such as during pastoral exposures or seminary breaks, and covertly maintain them during their formation years. Maintaining a girlfriend for a seminarian with a vocation to celibate priesthood constitutes a major crisis. One seminarian in a qualitative study confessed of having a girlfriend while in the seminary: "We did not have a closure of our relationship and ordination is fast approaching. I am pressured and I am in a crisis" (Bala and Bance 2022, para. 33).

In some instances, seminarians with girlfriends kept the romantic relationship secret for fear of expulsion from the seminary. They would decide before ordination either to marry their girlfriends or to abandon the relationship to become priests. Anecdotal evidence and stories abound, some of which are even shared in the social media, where seminarians maintain girlfriends while they are in seminary formation only to break with them before ordination.

There are also instances that the priest himself solemnized the marriage of his former girlfriend (Kaonga 2021).

Maintaining romantic relationships during seminary formation is part of the informal hidden curriculum, which is strictly prohibited and punished by expulsion under official seminary rules. Several seminarians who enter the seminary at a young age normally have no prior experience with dating and romantic relationships, and the celibate seminary formation that forbids this type of experience further prolongs their lack of normal adult socialization with women, making them immature in dealing with the opposite sex.

Indeed, watching online pornography, indecent shows in nightclubs, and secretly forming and maintaining romantic relationships with women outside the seminary are part of the resistant informal curriculum that provides gender socialization and sex education to seminarians. This is a resistant and hidden curriculum that opposes the official seminary curriculum, which teaches celibacy and chastity and views sexuality as a matter to be processed in the context of spiritual direction. The exclusive and secluded celibate seminary formation aims to form a detached and "sexless" perfect celibate clerical masculinity (Keenan 2015); thus, it encourages passive resistant sexual activities of this kind as coping strategies for heterosexual seminarians who may be called to married priesthood.

Summary and Conclusion

This chapter has argued that passive social resistance through small and every acts by the powerless against the status quo may not be as dramatic as active resistance in popular revolts and revolutions that manifestly alter the course of history. Nevertheless, small acts of resistance can get the attention of powerholders for social change. In the RCC, the mandatory clerical celibacy, which became the foundation of celibate seminary training, has generated passive social resistance. For fear of sanction from the Catholic hierarchy, clerics silently oppose the imposition of clerical celibacy and the celibate priesthood as the only social calling of Catholic priesthood at the backstage of seminary formation and clerical life.

Passive clerical resistance acts against celibacy start during seminary formation, which occurs in the informal and hidden sexuality curriculum parallels with the official celibate seminary curriculum. Seminary rules prohibit open discussion on sexuality, sexual activities, and intimate relationships with women that contravene the ideal celibate clerical masculinity. These resistant acts include living double lives for heterosexual and homosexual seminarians whose gender and sexual orientation are suppressed by celibate seminary structure. Thus, seminarians may appear publicly in the seminary as chaste but privately engage in sexual deviance that opposes this image.

114 Celibate Clerical Training, Human Formation

Living double lives can continue after ordination for priests with serious problems in dealing with celibacy and chastity.

Engaging in covert online pornography and compulsive masturbation are also a form of covert resistant acts that serve as coping mechanism for heterosexuals with a strong need for intimacy and romantic relationships, which are denied by the seminary formation. Lastly, visiting nightclubs with indecent shows and interacting with prostitutes are further examples of resistant acts in the hidden curriculum of seminary formation. All these resistant acts and relationships with the opposite or same sex, which are prohibited by the official seminary curriculum, can persist after ordination where new priests found new freedom or absolute privacy in the lonely autonomous life of the parish without effective guardians.

Notes

1 For more detailed discussion on the imposition of mandatory clerical celibacy in the Catholic Church, please refer Ballano 2023. *In Defense of Married Priesthood: A Sociotheological Investigation of Catholic Clerical celibacy.* London and New York: Routledge.
2 The key informants here include one former seminarian, priest, and one active priest, an instructor, and seminary professor. All of them are product of this same seminary who shared this information to the author in a recent unstructured interview.
3 This is based on the personal experience of the author as a new theological seminarian of this seminary.
4 This anecdotal evidence is based on the experience of one seminarian who had undergone this exposure and experienced watching indecent shows, as well as the author's personal experience and knowledge as a former diocesan seminarian who assisted this lay formator who is also the president of the alumni association of the seminary.

References

Adubale, Andrew A., and Oyaziwo Aluede. 2017. "A Survey of Counselling Needs of Seminarians in Catholic Major Seminaries in Nigeria." *Asia Pacific Journal of Counselling and Psychotherapy* 8 (1): 29–40. https://doi.org/10.1080/21507686. 2016.1260610.
Agoncillo, Jodee A. 2017. "Priest Nabbed 'En Route to Motel' with 13-Year-Old Girl." *Inquirer.Net*, July 29, 2017. https://newsinfo.inquirer.net/918633/priest-arrested-for-trafficking-minor-in-marikina.
Armbruster, Andre. 2021. "On the Undisclosed Transfer of Abusive Catholic Priests: A Field Theoretical Analysis of the Sexual Repression Within the Catholic Church and the Use of Legitimate Language." *Critical Research on Religion* 10 (1): 61–77.
Bala, Jesus Cirilo R., and Lucila O. Bance. 2022. "Crisis on Discernment of Vocation among Selected Seminarians." *Seminary Journal.* https://seminaryjournal.com/crisis-on-discernment/.
Ballano, Vivencio O. 2023. *In Defense of Married Priesthood: A Sociotheological Investigation of Catholic Clerical Celibacy.* London and New York: Routledge.
Cleaveland, Raymond. 2004. "Pornography and Priestly Vocations." *Homiletic and Pastoral Review* 18–26. www.catholicculture.org/culture/library/view.cfm?id=6182&repos=1&subrepos=0&searchid=465613.

Bauman, Klaus, Eckhard Fricj, Chrsitoph Jacobs, and Arndt Bussing. 2019. "Spiritual Dryness and Celibacy of Priests – Discernment of Ongoing Spiritual Journeys from Relational and Psychosocial Immaturities." *Pastoral Psychology* 68: 605–617. https://doi.org/10.1007/s11089-019-00886-1.

Bederman, David J. 2010. *Custom as a Source of Law*. Cambridge: Cambridge University Press.

Brundage, James. 2001. "Sin, Crime, and the Pleasures of the Flesh: The Medieval Church Judges Sexual Offences." In *The Medieval World*, edited by P. Linehan, 294–307. London: Routledge.

Coe, John. 2008. "Resisting the Temptation of Moral Formation: Opening to Spiritual Formation in the Cross and the Spirit." *Journal of Spiritual Formation and Soul Care* 1 (1): 54–78. https://doi.org/10.1177%2F193979090800100105.

Congregation for Catholic Education. 2005. "Instruction Concerning the Criteria for the Discernment of Vocations With Regard to Persons With Homosexual Tendencies in View of their Admission to the Seminary and to Holy Orders." *L'Osservatore Romano* (Weekly Edition in English), December 7, p. 3.

Cordella-Bontrager, M. 2017. "Matt's Declassified Seminary Survival Guide." *Vision: A Journal for Church and Theology* 18 (2): 69–75. https://press.palni.org/ojs/index.php/vision/article/view/61.

Cozzens, Donald. 2004. *Sacred Silence: Denial and the Crisis in the Church*. 1st ed. Collegeville, MN: Liturgical Press.

Cozzens, Donald. 2006. *Freeing Celibacy*. Collegeville, MN: Liturgical Press.

Cravatts, Richard. 2007. "L.A. Sex Abuse Settlement Leaves Troubling Questions Unanswered." *The State Journal-Register*, July 25, 2007. www.sj-r.com/story/news/2007/07/25/l-sex-abuse-settlement-leaves/47782055007/.

Day, Michael. 2015. "Vatileaks Scandal: Vatican Properties Used as Brothels and Massage Parlors Where Priests Pay for Sex,' Claims Report." *Independent*, November 10, 2015. www.independent.co.uk/news/world/europe/vatileaks-scandal-vatican-properties-used-as-brothels-and-massage-parlours-where-priests-pay-for-sex-claims-report-a6729251.html.

de Weger, Stephen Edward. 2022. "Unchaste Celibates: Clergy Sexual Misconduct Against Adults – Expressions, Definitions, and Harms." *Religions* 13 (5): 1–27. https://doi.org/10.3390/rel13050393.

Doyle, Thomas. 2006. "Clericalism: Enabler of Clergy Sexual Abuse." *P astoral Psychology* 54 (3):189–213.

Doyle, Thomas P., and Stephen C. Rubino. 2004. "Catholic Clergy Sexual Abuse Meets the Civil Law." *Fordham Urban Law Journal* 31: 549–615. https://ir.lawnet.fordham.edu/ulj/vol31/iss2/6.

Even-Zohar, Itamar. 2002. "Cultural Planning and Cultural Resistance in the Making and Maintaining of Entities." *Sun Yat-Sen Journal of Humanities* 14: 45–52.

Ewick, Patricia, and Susan Silby. 2003. "Narrating Social Structure: Stories of Resistance to Legal Authority." *American Journal of Sociology* 108 (6): 1328–1372.

Fielding, Nigel G. 2023. *Joining Forces: Police Training, Socialization and Occupational Competence. Routledge Library Editions: Police and Policing*. London: Routledge.

Fine, Gary Alan, and Philip Manning. 2003. "Erving Goffman." In *The Blackwell Companion to Major Contemporary Social Theorists*, edited by Ritzer George, 34–62. Oxford: Blackwell Publishing.

Frawley O'Dea, M. G. 2004. "Psychological Anatomy of the Catholic Sexual Abuse Scandal." *Studies in Gender and Sexuality* 5 (2): 121–137. https://doi.org/10.1080/15240650509349244.

Goffman, Erving. 1961. *Asylums: Essays on the Social Situation of Mental Patients and Other Inmates*. New York: Anchor Books.

Goffman, Erving. 1968. *Asylums: Essays on the Social Situation of Mental Patients and Other Inmates*. 1st ed. New York, NY: Anchor Books.

Goffman, Erving. 1969. *The Presentation of Self in Everyday Life*. Harmondsworth: Penguin Books.

Goldberg, Jeremy. 2019. "The Priest of Nottingham and the Holy Household of Ousegate: Telling Tales in Court." In *Town Courts and Urban Society in Late Medieval England, 1250–1500*, edited by R. Goddard, and T. Philip, 60–76. Woodbridge: Boydell & Brewer.

Goode, Erich. 2019. *Deviant Behavior*. 12th ed. London: Routledge.

Goodman, Nelson. 1978. *Ways of Worldmaking*. Indianapolis: Hackett Publishing.

Gregoire, Jocelyn, and Crissy Jungers. 2010. "Sexual Addiction and Compulsivity Among Clergy: How Spiritual Directors Can Help in the Context of Seminary Formation." *Sexual Addiction & Compulsivity* 11 (1–2): 71–81. https://doi.org/10.1080/10720160490458256.

Hollander, Jocelyn E., and Einwohner, A. 2004. "Conceptualizing Resistance." *Sociological Forum* 19 (4): C2004. https://doi.org/10.1007/s11206-004-0694-5.

Isacco, Anthony Ingram, Paul B. Finn, Katie Dimoff, John D. Gebler, Brendan. 2020a. "A Novel Approach to Examining Personality Risk Factors of Sexual Offending in Clergy Applicants." *Spirituality in Clinical Practice* 7 (4): 246–261. https://doi.org/10.1037/scp0000224.

Isacco, A., K. Finn, D. Tirabassi, K. A. Meade, and T. G. Plante. 2020b. "An Examination of the Psychological Health of Applicants to the Catholic Priesthood and Diaconate." *Spirituality in Clinical Practice* 7 (4): 230–245. https://doi.org/10.1037/scp0000229.

Isacco, Anthony, David G. Songy, and Thomas G. Plante. 2022. "Psychological Evaluations of Clergy Applicants in the Catholic Church: Answering Frequently Asked Questions." *Spirituality in Clinical Practice* 9 (2): 127–139. https://doi.org/10.1037/scp0000294.

John Jay College Report. 2004. *The Nature and Scope of Sexual Abuse of Minors by Catholic Priests and Deacons in the United States 1950–2002*. USCCB. http://www.bishop-accountability.org/reports/2004_02_27_JohnJay/.

Joo, Hyung-min. 2010. "Hidden Transcripts . . . Shared? Passive Resistance in the Soviet Case." *The Korean Journal of International Studies* 8–2: 277–298.

Kaonga, Gerrard. 2021. "Video of Priest Officiating Wedding of His Ex-Girlfriend Goes Viral." *Newsweek*, December 15, 2021. www.newsweek.com/wedding-video-priest-marriage-ex-girlfriend-roniel-sulits-viral-1659624.

Karras, Ruth M. 2011. "The Regulation of Sexuality in the Late Middle Ages: England and France." *Speculum* 86 (4): 1010–1039. www.jstor.org/stable/41409206.

Keenan, Marie. 2011. *Child Sexual Abuse and the Catholic Church: Gender, Power, and Organizational Culture*. 1st ed. London and New York: Oxford University Press.

Keenan, Marie. 2015. "Masculinity, Relationships and Context: Child Sexual Abuse and the Catholic Church Catholic Church." *Irish Journal of Applied Social Studies* 15 (2): 64–77.

Kwee, Alex W., and David C. Hoover. 2008. "Theologically-Informed Education About Masturbation: A Male Sexual Health Perspective." *Journal of Psychology and Theology* 36 (4): 258–269.

Martel, Frederic. 2019. *In the Closet of the Vatican: Power, Homosexuality, Hypocrisy*. London: Bloomsbury Continuum.

McDevitt, Patrick J. 2012. "Sexual and Intimacy Health of Roman Catholic Priests." *Journal of Prevention & Intervention in the Community* 40 (3): 208–218. https://doi.org/10.1080/10852352.2012.680413.

McGlone, G., and L. Sperry. 2020. "Psychological Evaluation of Catholic Seminary Candidates: Strengths, Shortcomings, and an Innovative Plan." *Spirituality in Clinical Practice* 7 (4): 262–277. https://doi.org/10.1037/scp0000240.

Miller, Maureen C. 2014. "Reform, Clerical Culture, and Politics." In *The Oxford Handbook of Medieval Christianity*, edited by, John H. Arnold. Oxford: Oxford University Press.

Naparan, Genesis, Mike R. Canoy, Foelan Degie Mahinay, and Jan Elbe Villaflor. 2022. "Walking on Hot Coals: A Phenomenological Study on Dealing With Temptations in the Seminary." *Millah: Journal of Religious Studies* 21 (3): 613–638. https://doi.org/10.20885/millah.vol21.iss3.art1.

Oakley, D. 2017. "Seminary Education and Formation: The Challenges and Some Ideas About Future Developments." *International Studies in Catholic Education* 9 (2): 223–235. https://doi.org/10.1080/19422539.2017.1360613.

Oberdorf, Andreas. 2021. "The American College of St Maurice at Münster, 1867–1879: The Formation of Catholic Clergy for the United States between Seminary Education and Academic Studies." *Paedagogica Historica* 1–19. https://doi.org/10.1080/00309230.2021.1987936.

Philp, Ryan M. 2003. "Silence at Our Expense: Balancing Safety and Secrecy in Non-Disclosure Agreements." *Seton Hall Law Review* 33: 845–880.

Pope Paul VI. 1965. *Optatam Totius* [Decree on Priestly Formation]. Vatican: Vatican Archives. www.vatican.va/archive/hist_councils/ii_vatican_council/documents/vat-ii_decree_19651028_optatam-totius_en.html.

Pullella, Philip. 2022. "Prominent Jesuit Priest and Artist Disciplined After Abuse Allegations." *Rueters*, December 6, 2022. www.reuters.com/world/europe/prominent-jesuit-priest-artist-disciplined-after-abuse-allegations-2022-12-05/#:~:text=The%20Jesuits%20issued%20a%20statement,at%20a%20convent%20in%20Slovenia.

Rockenbach, Mark. 2020. "Sexual Temptations." *SMP Videos*, p. 3. https://scholar.csl.edu/smp2020/3.

Schuth, Katrina OSF. 1999. *Seminaries, Theologates, and the Future of Church Ministry: An Analysis of Trends and Transitions*. Wilmington, Delaware: Michael Glazier Books.

Schuth, Katarina. 2016. *Seminary Formation: Recent History-Current Circumstances-New Directions*. Collegeville, MN: Liturgical Press.

Scott, James C. 1989. "Everyday Forms of Peasant Resistance." In *Everyday Forms of Peasant Resistance*, edited by F. D. Colburn. 1st ed. London: Routledge. https://doi.org/10.4324/9781315491455.

Scott, James C. 1992. *Domination and the Arts of Resistance: Hidden Transcripts*. New Haven and London: Yale University Press.

Sipe, A. W. Richard. 1990. *A Secret World: Celibacy and the Search for Celibacy*. New York: Brunner/Mazel.

Sipe, A. W. Richard. 1995. *Sex, Priests, and Power: Anatomy of a Crisis*. New York: Brunner/Mazel.

Sperry, Len. 2003. *Sex, Priestly Ministry, and the Church. Collegeville*, Minnesota: Liturgical Press.

USCCB (United States Conference of Catholic Bishops). 2005. *Program of Priestly Formation, Fifth Edition*. Washington, DC: USCCB.

USCCB (United States Conference of Catholic Bishops). 2015. *Create in Me a Clean Heart: A Pastoral Response to Pornography*. Washington, DC: USCCB.

Waxman, Olivia B. 2017. "Pope Francis Might Consider Ordaining Married Priests. Here's Why That's Not Already a Thing." *Time*, March 10, 2017. https://time.com/4698125/pope-francis-married-priests-history/.

Weber, Sister Marysia. 2008. "Pornography, Electronic Media, and Priestly Formation." *Homiletic and Pastoral Review*, April 1, 2008. www.hprweb.com/2008/04/pornography-electronic-media-and-priestly-formation/.

Werner, Janelle. 2009. "Just as the Priest Have Their Wives: Priests an Concubines in England, 1375–1549." Dissertation Submitted to the Department of History, University of South Carolina at Chapel Hill. https://core.ac.uk/download/pdf/210598143.pdf.

Witte, John Jr. 2006. "The Perils of Celibacy: Clerical Celibacy and Marriage in Early Protestant Perspective." In *Sexuality in the Catholic Tradition*, edited by Cahill Lisa, and Garvey John, 107–119. Chicago, IL: Crossroad Publishers.

Wooden, Cindy. 2023. "Reflection on Married Priests at Synods Past and Present." *UCA News*, June 22, 2023. www.ucanews.com/news/reflection-on-married-priests-at-synods-past-and-present/101730.

Young, Kimberly. 1997. "What Makes the Internet Addictive: Potential Explanations for Pathological Internet Use." *Paper presented at the 105th annual conference of the American Psychological Association*, August 15, 1997. Chicago, IL. www.healthyplace.com/addictions/center-for-internet-addiction-recovery/what-makes-the-internet-addictive-potencial.

Zullo, James R. n.d. "Freeing Celibacy: Review." *Seminary Journal* 110–112. www.drawnbylove.com/seminary_journal/17SJV13N1Spr07-cozzens%20zullo.pdf.

PART III

Major Forms of Clerical Sexual Abuse and Seminary Formation

6

HETEROSEXUAL CLERICAL SEXUAL ABUSE AND SEMINARY FORMATION

Introduction

The mainstream research and literature on clerical sexual abuse (CSA) in the Roman Catholic Church (RCC) has neglected to sociologically associate the persistence of clergy sexual misconduct committed by male heterosexual priests, specifically by diocesan clerics, with the current celibate seminary formation in the Church. The highly publicized sexual abuse by pedophile priests in the United States against children has created a public hysteria that downplayed the impact of sexual abuse committed by male heterosexual priests in the RCC against children, adolescents, or adults. Yet, most studies and investigations on CSA in the RCC point to heterosexual clerics as the main cohort of sexual offenders who do not consider the gender orientation of their victims (e.g., Keenan 2011; Terry et al. 2011; Frawley O'Dea and Goldner 2016; De Weger 2022).

The priest-therapist and popular CSA author Richard Sipe (1990) calculated that heterosexual priests committed the highest incidence of CSA in the RCC, between 20% and 40% of all cases, while pedophile priests committed only 2% against children, and gay priests about 4% against adolescents and adults. He claimed (1994, 134) that "four times as many priests involve themselves sexually with adult women, and twice the number with adult men, as priests who involve themselves sexually with children." Marie Keenan's early research in Ireland (2011) also revealed the same pattern – that those who abused both girls and boys, aside from adult women, tend to be heterosexually oriented, debunking the myth that CSA is related to sexual orientation and mostly committed by gay and pedophile priests in the RCC. As Gartner (1999) argues, when heterosexual clerics molested minors, they

DOI: 10.4324/9781032722474-9

tend to be blind to their victims' gender orientation and choose their victims based on their availability.

Most CSA reports in the RCC tend to focus on boys, while abuse against girls and adults is underreported. In one RCC-commissioned research (John Jay College Report 2004), it was revealed that 64% of the priest offenders were heterosexuals who abused males only, 22.6% abused females only, 3.6% against both genders, and remaining 10% against victims with unknown genders (John Jay College Report 2004). It also revealed that 33% of the victims of heterosexual priests have one allegation of abuse against women compared to 19% of victims of all priests (Terry 2008). And most priests with allegations of CSA were diocesan priests (69%), followed by religious priests (22%) (Terry 2008). Frawley O'Dea and Goldner (2016, 22) also revealed that most CSA victims by heterosexual priests were not only males but also pubescent or adolescents.

Aside from minors and adolescents of both genders, male heterosexual priests were also singled out by several research as the primary group of sexual offenders in the RCC who targeted adult women (e.g., Loftus and Camargo 1993; De Weger 2022). Despite the media hype on CSA by pedophile and homosexual priests, the fact remains that the gender orientation of most Catholic priests committing CSA in the RCC is heterosexuality, directed against adult women. An early study involving a larger clinical sample of 1,322 priests and brothers revealed that 27.8% of the priest respondents acknowledged that they had sexual relationship with adult women, while only 8.4% engaged in sexual misconduct against a minor (Loftus and Camargo 1993).

Thomas Plante (2002) also estimated that CSA committed by Catholic priests against children and minors is relatively lower compared to adults. He estimated that only about 2% to 5% of priests have had a sexual experience with a minor. New research by De Weger (2022) confirmed that the clergy sexual misconduct against adult women constitutes the largest cases of CSA in the RCC, much higher than those committed by gay and pedophile priests against children and minors. He calculated that the number of victims/survivors of clergy sexual abuse against adults over the last half century had probably reached into the early millions, causing several personal, relational, and practical harms. Thus, he concluded that the most popular type of CSA in the RCC with the largest number of cases is done by heterosexual priests that is not directed against children and adolescents but against vulnerable adult women or what is technically called by scholars as clergy sexual misconduct against adults (CMMA).

In addition, research findings of Doris Reisinger (2022) showed that most serious cases of CMMA are committed by diocesan priests against adult women or what she characterizes as reproductive abuse. Under this type of CSA, heterosexual priests impregnated adult women and forced them into

Heterosexual Clerical Sexual Abuse and Seminary Formation **123**

hiding, abortion, or adoption. As a matter of statistical probability, most victims of this type of CSA are adult women. "Catholic priests who impregnated their victims usually put their own reputation above the victim's bodily autonomy and health and sometimes even above the life of their victim and their (unborn) child" (Reisinger 2022, 5). Thus, many abusers tried to end or conceal the pregnancy of their victims at all costs regardless of will and need of the abused women (Reisinger 2018).

To account why CSA persists in the RCC, several theories were conceived by scholars. They can be generally categorized into two: single-cause explanation and the multiple-cause account of why heterosexual priests commit most of the CSA cases in the RCC. A single-cause explanation primarily focuses on a single primary factor such as homosexuality (Pope Benedict XVI and Seewald 2010), psychosexual immaturity (e.g., Frawley O'Dea 2004; Frawley O'Dea and Goldner 2016), hierarchalism (e.g., Keenan 2018; Hogan 2021), "elitism" or "ecclesial pathology" (Cozzens 2002; Doyle 2006), lack of moral leadership (Keenan 2018; Hogan 2021; Mescher 2023), or clericalism (e.g., Doyle 2003; Neuhaus 2008; Wilson 2008; Plante 2020; Ormerod 2022).

A multiple-cause explanation of CSA sees a combination of societal factors that cause CSA such as power, traditional gender role, mandatory celibacy, cleric-centered social structure, and absence of lay participation in formal ecclesial governance (e.g., Keenan 2011; Ballano 2019, 2020, 2023). Furthermore, most of these explanations tend to focus on the micro level, which uses psychological, psychiatric, and theological perspectives, largely blaming the exaggerated role of priests in RCC or what is popularly called clericalism.

Surprisingly, Catholic research and literature on the causes of CSA have not included the current seminary training as a major factor that structurally contributes to clergy sexual abuse in the RCC. The celibate clerical formation in the exclusive and all-male seminary structure rarely surfaces in CSA research for producing humanly and sexually immature heterosexual seminarians who would later turn into sexually abusive priests after being assigned in the autonomous social structure of the parish with the absence of effective guardians. Explanations on the persistence of Catholic CSA continue to disregard the structural connections between the celibate seminary training that separates future priests from the normal socialization in society and prevalence of immature heterosexual priests who are largely responsible for most CSA cases in the RCC.

Looking for structural explanation of CSA, Sands (2003, 79) argues that the

> Church's sins against women and its abuse of children are founded in the priesthood's male-only character, its conceptualization as cultic and sacramental, its sexual asceticism, and its celibacy rule. The male-only

character of the priesthood sets the foundation for the abuse of women by excluding women from power and idolizing the image of God as male.

Yip (2003, 60) also contends that the endurance of clergy sexual misconduct by celibate priests reflects the "culture of repression and secrecy" within the RCC, where open discussion about sexuality and relationship with women are generally prohibited. And Catholic seminaries as the primary institution for the formation of celibate priests in the RCC share this ineptitude and culture of repression and secrecy in dealing with sexuality issues.

Thus, CSA committed by Catholic clergy reflects the problematic sexuality development and sexual repression of future priests inside the exclusive, all-male, semi-monastic, and highly regulated social and spiritual environment of Catholic seminaries. Although case studies and research on sexual abuse against adults by Catholic priests are still relatively limited (Chibnall, Wolf, and Duckro 1998; Sands 2003; Plante and Aldridge 2005; De Weger and Death 2017; Reisinger 2018; Haslbeck et al. 2020), existing studies have already shown a strong indication that CSA by Catholic priests is mostly committed, not by pedophile or gay priests but by immature and sexually repressed heterosexual priests (Frawley O'Dea 2004; John Jay College Final Report 2004; Terry et al. 2011). They spent much of their late adolescent and early adult life inside the exclusive all-male seminary formation.

All male heterosexual Catholic priests accused and found guilty of CSA underwent the same human formation and gender role socialization in the celibate seminary formation set by the RCC for all candidates to Catholic priesthood. In the 11th and 12th centuries, the Second and Fourth Lateran Councils decreed the mandatory clerical celibacy for all Catholic clerics, resulting in the abandonment of the long tradition of the clerical training by apprenticeship and the adoption of celibate seminary training as the only method of clerical formation. The apprenticeship clerical training allows the option for married priesthood and the continuation of normal socialization of clerical candidates in society while undergoing clerical training. But the secluded and all-male clerical seminary training, which is ideal for religious and monastic priests with the rare gift of celibacy, is separated from the real world.

A sociological analysis is needed to analyze whether this shift of the method of clerical training and human socialization that led to the suspension of the normal gender socialization of heterosexual seminarians is structurally connected to the formation of immature Catholic celibate priests as well as the persistence of CSA by heterosexual priests, especially by diocesan clergy, in the ministerial priesthood. The current seminary system only provides seminarians with celibate clerical training and with the RCC's traditional teaching on gender and sexuality, regardless of their sexual orientation and chosen social calling to the priesthood.

Thus, one wonders: Is the gender socialization of heterosexual seminarians inside the exclusive seminary environment a structural enabler of CSA in the RCC? Does the current celibate seminary structure contribute to the formation of immature heterosexual seminarians who would later constitute the main cohort of clergy sexual abusers in the RCC? What is structurally wrong with the current celibate clerical training that it fundamentally produces potential sexual predators in the RCC?

The primary objective of this chapter is to explore the sociological links between the exclusive and all-male social environment of the celibate seminary formation and the psychosexual immaturity of priests as reflected in the gender socialization and sexuality training that basically reflects the RCC's traditional teaching on gender and gender socialization. It examines the structural flaws of the gender role socialization of male heterosexual seminarians inside the seminary training. The seminary provides a spiritualized gender socialization of a "third gender" for celibate priests, viewing gender as ahistorical and immutable, contrary to the social sciences' perspectives that see it as an historical and evolving social construct in society.

This chapter assumes that social deviance and crime such as CSA by heterosexual priests is not just a product of human decision but also the result of a structural conditioning. Sociologists believe that a social structure influences human action. What happens in the micro level of social interaction reflects the nature of the social structure in the macro level. As Marie Keenan (2011, xviii) contends

> when results of micro level research . . . are interpreted in the larger context, it becomes obvious that there are noticeable links between what happens on the grand scale of things and on the local level, and that the individual, the organization, and the institutional dimensions are actually influencing each other and bound together in particular dynamic relations.

The sociologist C. Wright Mills (2000) sees the inseparability between the micro and macro levels of social reality in a holistic thinking called "sociological imagination": What happens at the micro level is related to the macro; what occurs in biography is connected to history; and what takes place in human action is linked to social structure. Thus, applying sociological imagination, the RCC's traditional teaching on gender and gender socialization in priestly training can be seen as structurally conditioning the psychosexual life of seminarians at the micro level. If many heterosexual priests, who are products of celibate seminary formation, are generally immature and prone to commit CSA in the RCC, then one needs to sociologically inquire how the social structure of the seminary training facilitates human and sexual immaturity that can lead to weak social control against CSA.

To illustrate this structural connection, this chapter is divided into three major parts. The first part provides the basic theoretical orientation of the study. It discusses the importance of socialization in the formation of mature heterosexuals as well as the need of a conducive and appropriate social

126 Major Forms of Clerical Sexual Abuse and Seminary Formation

environment rooted in genuine human experience for male heterosexuals to develop appropriate gender role socialization. The second part investigates the RCC's concept of gender for celibate Catholic priests and how this is applied in the current clerical seminary formation. The third part examines the gender role socialization of seminarians inside the seminary and its limitations and negative consequences to the ability of male heterosexual priests to deal with CSA in the parish.

In general, it argues that the persistence of CSA in the RCC is sociological connected to the Church's traditional and ahistorical view of gender and gender socialization that greatly influenced the celibate seminary formation. With the imposition of mandatory clerical celibacy, which became the foundation of celibate clerical training, and the replacement of apprenticeship clerical training that allows married priesthood, the typical socialization of heterosexual seminarians in society is suspended and their sexuality repressed, resulting in the psychosexual immaturity when they become ordained Catholic diocesan priests. Diocesan clerics are found in most CSA research as the most vulnerable type of priests to commit CSA in the RCC.

Theoretical Foundation

Socialization, Sex, and Gender in Society

"Socialization is the process whereby individuals learn and internalize the attitudes, values, and behaviors appropriate to people living in any given society" (Wunder 2007, 589).

> The concept of socialization is among the most important in sociology because it attempts to illustrate and explain the tremendous impact living in society has on shaping the individual. The individual becomes a human being through socialization, and what it means to be an individual evolves over the life course.
>
> *(Kotarba 2007, 589)*

"Human societies use the dynamic process of socialization to produce a desired gender" (Hopkins 2008). Gender differs from sex. Sex refers to the biological aspect of the person, which is determined by nature or genitalia, while gender refers to all manifestations of masculinity or femininity, which is determined by social learning and culture (Blank 2012).

> By expecting different behaviors from people because they are male or female, society nudges boys and girls in separate directions from an early age, and this foundation carries over into adulthood. Parents begin the process; researchers have concluded that in our society, mothers

unconsciously reward their female children for being passive and dependent and their male children for being active and independent. The mass media reinforce society's expectations of gender in many ways.

(Cooley et al. 2010, 4–5)

"The family, thus, remains the basic unit for modeling male and female genders. Other factors of influence are schools, sports, visual and audio entertainment, sex roles, jobs and professions, churches and other faith institutions, news media, languages, myths, rituals, laws, and race" (Hopkins 2008, 577). "Human beings make other human beings into specific male and female genders, and the family remains the main modeling for male heterosexuality (Hopkins 2008, 576). To shape the individual's gender according to society's expectations, gender socialization is normally introduced in the family.

Gender socialization generally refers to "the ways in which society sets children onto different courses in life because they are male or female. From the time of their birth, children are constantly presented with cultural messages that teach them how to act masculine or feminine based on their sex" (Cooley et al. 2010, 2). It is the "process through which boys and girls learn sex appropriate behavior, dress, personality characteristics, and demeanor" (Rohlinger 2007, 590). Males and females learn what it means to be boys and girls and, later, men and women through this process of gender socialization.

Gender socialization includes teaching males and females on the expected mannerisms, proper ways of dress and grooming, societal roles, speech patterns, and other conventions about masculinity and femininity in society (Blank 2012). It is a lifelong process that is gradually influenced by factors such as the "family, school, group of friends, work, religion, mass media, etc." (Crisogen 2015, 290). How a person becomes a mature male or female is determined by various societal factors such as "child-rearing and parenting models, peer pressure and positive examples, movies and other media, educational institutions and training organizations, and biblical interpretation and faith communities" (Blank 2012).

RCC Teaching and Seminary Gender Socialization

People usually learn how to actualize their gender according to the expectations of their cultures and subcultures to appear "gender typical." This implies that they should conform to the gender socialization according to society's cultural and institutional expectations of what masculine males and feminine females must be like (Blank 2012). In the RCC, the Catholic hierarchy expects Catholics to actualize their gender socialization according to the official teachings of the Church.

For the formation of its future priests, the RCC expects seminary formators to socialize seminarians according with Church's orthodox teachings on gender, sexuality, and celibate heterosexuality. Thus, the gender training in the seminary only reflects the institutional expectation and teaching of the RCC. Currently, the Church still follows the traditional gender role and socialization and rejects the emerging theories on gender and gender ideology in contemporary society (Bracke and Paternotte 2016; Case 2016).

Although there are attempts by some Catholic theologians to adopt a more sex positive views on gender, these efforts are still done within the context of the RCC's traditional doctrine and theology of the body (Barnes 2022). The RCC still dismisses the social sciences' perspectives that view gender and gender differences as products of historical and cultural forces (see Congregation for Catholic Education 2019). Instead, it sees them as something immutable and ahistorical. As Szwed and Zielińska (2016, 120–121) explain:

> The Church also very seldom refers to the cultural or historical transformations of gender constructions. If it is to speak about any changeability, then the statements rather concern a partial transformation of the social and religious roles played by women and men, but not the essence on which their identity is based – that remains unchangeable. . . . The Roman Catholic Church condemns the very notion of gender as ontologically impossible. The bishops reject the cultural fabric of gender because they perceive it predominantly in terms of the categories of nature and biology. They declare an "integral" approach to gender, encompassing carnality, spirituality, and psyche, and emphasize that man's sexuality determines human identity and shapes the whole of man's life.

Conversely, the Catholic traditional conception of gender only reflected the 19th-century view that saw gender as complementarity (Ruether 2008). The RCC believes in gender equality but relates it to the differences between sexes, although it upholds their complementarity. To the Catholic hierarchy, "transgressing the assigned identities means denial of the 'natural' role, that is, given by God" (Szwed and Zielińska 2016, 121). The RCC further views heterosexuality as natural and closely related to male and female bodies.

Under the RCC's overall view, gender, gender equality, gender complementarity, and the naturalness of gender identities are designed and assigned by God. The seminary as a Catholic institution is expected to uphold this ecclesial view for gender socialization of seminarians. In clerical training, the RCC expects seminary formators to spiritually form seminarians according to its official teachings on celibate priesthood and the perfect celibate masculinity (Keenan 2015). Although Christ originally taught optional celibacy and married priesthood has been existing in the Western Church in some form since the time of the apostles up to the present, the RCC imposed clerical celibacy in the 11th and 12th centuries that only allowed celibate priesthood as ideal model for Catholic priesthood (Ballano 2023). This adoption of celibate priesthood as the only recognized universal calling for Catholic priesthood has shifted the gender socialization for priestly candidates in Catholic seminaries in favor of candidates who are able to live chaste and celibate heterosexual life like Christ.

Third Order Gender for Celibate Priests

Catholic seminaries aim to form new celibate priests to be "Another Christ" (*Alter Christus*). To actualize this, seminary formators need to train seminarians according to the RCC's conception of "third order" gender orientation created by the mandatory clerical celibacy. Under this spiritualized gender construction, the celibate priest is different from ordinary men who is pure and clean from sexual and marital impurities and whose primary role is to celebrate the Eucharist, the summit of Christian life. Celibate priests are unambiguously real mean but different from ordinary men and lay people in the RCC (Miller 2003).

Priests belong to a higher order: "Their life of celibacy sets them apart as being true Christians since marriage is really only a concession to man's weakness and results from sin" (Frazee 1972, 155). Under this type of masculinity, sexual intercourse for celibate clerics would make them spiritually unclean and unworthy of the clerical ministry.

[The] priest is seen as a male whose role was to give orientation and spiritual guidance to other men and women, and whose influence depended, beyond the obvious powers conferred upon him by the church, on his personal authority, based on his own ability to relate to the social circumstances around him, which did not exclude considerations of his gender.
(Romeo Mateo 2021, 542)

Indeed, this notion of "third order" in gender construction, that is, between lay and monastic vocation, only reflects the Gregorian reform movement that idealized celibate masculinity to defend clerical celibacy. The RCC's understanding of the gender socialization of heterosexual celibate clerics as immutable is a product of a theological interpretation based on natural law theory that tends to disregard the normal gender socialization of ordinary men in society. However, the theological dictum that "grace builds on nature" requires that the normal socialization and human experience in society be recognized before theologizing. God also speaks in human experience. Bracketing it in favor of a highly spiritual and theological conception of gender and gender socialization can lead to several negative unintended consequences to clerical training.

This spiritualized gender construction of the celibate clergy as "third order" ignores the nature of masculinity and heterosexuality as historical and cultural as pointed out by sociologists and social scientists. "Masculinity is a sequence of changing meanings and practices, a fact that demolishes any pretensions of immutability" (Romeo Mateo 2021, 542). Spiritually projecting the gender of celibate priest as spiritually strong, sexually pure, and celibate like Christ could not be sustained in human experience and empirical reality.

Despite the spiritual formation in the seminary and ordination, priests remain human and vulnerable to commit human abuses such as CSA as a compensatory behavior (Doyle 2006). Repressing clerical sexuality and heterosexuality in favor of a spiritualized view of gender for celibate priests as a sign of true manhood for Christ can result in resistant acts such as clerical concubinage, sexual abuse, and other covert sexual perversion since not all seminarians and priests possess the rare charism of celibacy (Ballano 2023).

Gender Socialization in the Seminary as a Total Institution (TI)

The RCC stressed the importance of human formation for Catholic priests. In the document for seminary formation entitled "The Gift of Priestly Vocation" (*Ratio Fundamentalis Sacerdotalis*), it states that

> Human formation, being the foundation of all priestly formation, promotes the integral growth of the person and allows the integration of all its dimensions. . . . Psychologically it focuses on the constitution of a stable personality, characterized by emotional balance, self-control, and a well-integrated sexuality.
>
> *(Congregation for the Clergy 2016, n. 94)*

This teaching is indeed desirable and ideal for celibate priests with formidable task in the ministry. However, one wonders: How can this goal of integral human formation be realized if seminarians are trained in a spiritualized gender socialization inside the exclusive all-male environment without the significant social interaction with agents of socialization such as women?

When seminarians are required to enter a special and exclusive organization such as the Catholic seminary for gender resocialization to change their identity to be like Christ, their normal human formation and gender orientation in society are largely interrupted. The seminary as a TI (Goffman 1968), like exclusive organizations such as boot camps, prisons, and mental institutions, does not train people according to their usual human experience and gender formation but according to a set of institutional rules implemented by officials who are in-charge of the institution to alter the identity of the members. A TI is an umbrella term for an environment where individuals are secluded from society and controlled by administrative staff (Macionis 2012).

In a TI, residing members are prepared for the outside world whenever they are discharged, hence, the term resocialization. Resocialization can be understood as the process of forming personality traits that will eventually contribute to the redevelopment of broken relationships and social ties (Timofeeva 2019). A TI such as the seminary is "a place where people are cut off from the rest of society and are almost totally controlled by the officials in charge" (Cooley et al. 2010, 2). It is an exclusive organization that aims to change seminarians' normal gender socialization to be become another celibate Christ. The Catholic seminary, which was instituted by the Council of Trent in the 16th century for the formation of diocesan priests, intends to change altogether the normal dynamics of gender socialization for Catholic priests to internalize the ideal "third gender."

New priests are expected to assume the third gender of Catholic celibate priesthood. With the imposition of the mandatory practice of clerical celibacy in the 12th century, the method of priestly training shifted from apprenticeship to exclusive seminary training that had substantially spiritualized the process of gender socialization for priests. With its emphasis on spiritual training for future priests inside the exclusive all-male environment, it bans open discussion on sexuality, and sexuality problems of seminarians are only processed in spiritual direction. Thus, the current seminary system generally offers no genuine gender socialization comparable to heterosexuality of ordinary men in society.

Although the Council of Trent institutionalized the seminary to improve the moral and educational training of diocesan priests, its structure is primarily focused on the academic, spiritual, and pastoral training, which unintendedly neglected the normal heterosexual socialization in the outside world. The seminary's basic social structure is only ideal for religious and monastic priests who live religious communities and presumably possess the rare gift of clerical celibacy. This mode of training is, however, unsuitable for diocesan priests who normally live in the secular world of the parish and are expected to be normal heterosexual men despite being religious ministers when they deal with their parishioners.

The apprenticeship clerical training that allows normal gender socialization in society and married priesthood could have been an appropriate clerical training for diocesan clergy. Without the social bonding of an intimate social group such as the family in married priesthood or an intimate religious community in monastic life to inhibit sexual deviance, diocesan priests are highly vulnerable to the serious temptations of CSA in the parish owing to their lack of human maturity in personality and sexuality and their lack of effective guardians to monitor their behavior. The parish clergy, who are denied normal gender socialization in seminary training, usually live alone in the parish without effective supervision by their bishops and fellow priests to check for possible sexual deviance, thus facing CSA without safety nets.

Celibate Seminary Training and Psychosexual Immaturity

Research has shown that most clerical sexual offenders in the RCC are male heterosexual priests with problematic human and gender socialization (e.g., Sipe 2003; Frawley O'Dea 2004; De Weger 2022). Following the fundamental structure of monastic and religious life structure, the current TI seminary formation is generally seen as fleeing from the world, shielding young candidates for the priesthood from the temptations of the city (Schuth 2016) and problems associated with secular gender socialization. With the seminary exclusivity, seminarians are denied of the normal interaction with sociocultural agents of socialization such as the family, friends, relatives, and women, which is crucial for genuine human maturity.

With the TI structure of the seminary, heterosexual seminarians are also deprived of the real opportunities for actual heterosexual growth such as dating, building intimate relationships with the opposite or same sex, and interacting with people with various age, sexual orientation, and gender for in-depth social learning and human maturity. Conversely, "many diocesan seminarians are in the stage of emerging adulthood. This developmental level is characterized by five features: age of identity exploration, possibilities, self-focus, instability, and a feeling of being in-between" (Abano and Bedoria 2023, 315). Unfortunately, with the social isolation of the seminary, young seminarians are largely prevented to achieve psychosexual maturity. Because of a spiritualized gender orientation, they tend to view "any sexual desire as an evil and in need of suppression rather than as something integrated into a healthy male image and masculinity" (Cozzens 2004, 12).

Some studies have shown that many seminarians struggled in the seminary formation because of the celibate training and the temptation to engage in an intimate relationship with ladies, which can be considered disrupted of their religious vocation (Stanosz 2004; Naparan et al. 2022). In the seminary, seminarians are expected to interact only with their male formators and instructors. Female teachers are rare. Exposures of seminarians to women during pastoral exposures and trials are also limited that discourage meaningful and healthy interaction.

Thus, heterosexual seminarians are not normally exposed to women and socialized as mature heterosexual individuals comparable to their counterparts in society during seminary training. They are instead encouraged by their formators to socialize with their biological mothers and the Virgin Mary as their spiritual mother. Interacting with the opposite sex and informal talks about sexuality are prohibited inside the seminary. Sexual matters are discussed secretly with spiritual directors (Stanosz 2004).

Moreover, since the seminary training is intended for celibate priesthood, women are inadvertently seen as temptation and obstacle to the seminarian's vocation, a perception that can intensify their fear with women and psychosexual immaturity:

> Psychologists are of the opinion that a majority reason for the sexual abuse by Catholic priests is that these men are grossly unaware of their sexuality and very immature and that the Catholic church does a poor job of educating seminarians about how to cope with sexual feelings. Clergy have been found to have more sexual-identity confusion problems than non-clerical offenders.
>
> *(Matthias 2020, 444)*

Seminarians who have not experienced dating or having romantic relationships with women would find the all-male seminary a serious hindrance to their genuine heterosexual maturity. With the strong supervision of seminary formators who are always on lookout for any breach of seminary rules on celibacy and chastity, addressing unresolved issues during seminary training would expose seminarians to expulsion from the seminary. To the priest-sociologist Andrew Greely (1986), most priests are heterosexual but around 40% of these priests have never dated a girl in high school, even once (Greely 1972). Thus, when they entered the seminary, the chance of resolving this issue is slim and may imply breaking the vow of celibacy (Adams 2011). If they become priests, resolving their unmet needs with women would also imply sexual deviance and acts of unchastity.

As Cravatts (2007, para. 5) contends, for

> some men, the institutional life in the same-sex environment may have served to further postpone social and sexual development. For these men, at the age of their ordination in their mid- to late twenties, they were intellectually and physically adults, but emotionally they remained far younger.

Thus, in the case of heterosexual priests abusing children and teen, predator priests consider their young victims, regardless of gender, as their peers, owing to their immaturity (Gartner 1999).

Repression and difficulty in dealing with sexuality, especially for heterosexual seminarians, may resort to covert and unhealthy sexual acts such as masturbation and online pornography inside the seminary, which can greatly contribute to their psychosexual immaturity. Sexual repression in the seminary can later translate into actual cases of CSA after ordination as compensatory behavior in the absence of effective guardians in the parish. Lastly, a few of these heterosexual seminarians can be regressive pedophiles whose attraction to women was not developed in the celibate formation

134 Major Forms of Clerical Sexual Abuse and Seminary Formation

due to strict policy against women and romantic relationships. When deviant opportunities come after ordination, these regressive pedophile priests would prey on innocent children and commit pedophile clerical sexual abuse in the RCC.

CSA by Immature Heterosexual Priests

Instead of examining the negative unintended consequences of the abnormal social environment of the seminary as a TI, the Catholic hierarchy blames homosexual priests for largely causing sexual scandals in the RCC. The priest-therapist, Dr. Leslie Lothstein, for instance, insisted that the sexually active gay priests he treated had sex with age-appropriate men and that even priests who abused minor males were, in fact, mostly heterosexual priests (Frawley O'Dea and Goldner 2007).

One universal trait revealed in several CSA research related to both sexual misconduct and abuse is that most offenders were male heterosexuals (Francis and Baldo 1998; Friberg and Laaser 1998; Thoburn and Whitman 2004; Chaves and Garland 2009; Garland and Argueta 2010). The RCC-commissioned research by John Jay College (2004) also showed that most cases of CSA in the Church is committed by male heterosexual priests against adults (Terry et al. 2011). De Weger's research (2022) also confirmed this finding by claiming that the majority of CSA cases in the RCC are targeted against adult women, which is much higher than CSA committed by gay and pedophile priests.

Frawley O'Dea (2004) specifically argues that the psychosexual immaturity of priests is the core of the cohort of sexual abusers in the RCC. She noted that many of these priests entered seminaries when they were as young as 14 years old. And the seminary formation trains them to avoid or talk and think about sex of any kind with no guidance for authentic manhood and appreciation of celibacy as a free choice. Therefore, the exclusive all-male celibate seminary training is largely responsible for nurturing psychosexual immature seminarians who would later become diocesan priests and commit CSA in the ministry.

An institutional life with a same-sex environment such as the seminary, which is away from actual social life, can inevitably delay the human and sexual development of individuals. "In the RCC, newly priests are usually in their mid- to late twenties. They may be considered intellectually and physically adults, but emotionally underdeveloped" (Cravatts 2007, para. 5). Seminarians usually enter the TI environment of the seminary at a young age for the highly spiritualized clerical formation that cuts short their normal human growth in society. As a TI for celibate priesthood, the seminary prohibits sexual matters that can lead to romantic and marital relationships and expels seminarians who violate the celibacy rule.

To avoid sanction such as expulsion, seminarians tend to circumvent the rules and express their sexual concerns and needs covertly. This includes going out secretly at night without the knowledge of the seminary rectors (Naparan et al. 2022, 22–23). Visiting nightclubs with strip shows during semestral breaks, online pornography, and masturbation as among the secret sexual activities by done by heterosexual seminarians to cope with the sexually repressed environment of the seminary. The sexually repressive, all-male, and celibate seminary clerical training, therefore, facilitates unhealthy sexual practices that can lead to psychosexual immaturity.

Last, male heterosexual seminarians whose vocation is married priesthood should be trained not inside the TI environment of the seminary but in the real world under an apprenticeship clerical training that exposes them to the normal adult socialization. Heterosexual males who are called to married presbyterate could not grow maturely in the highly spiritualized gender formation in the all-male structure of the seminary, which structurally intended for religious and monastic seminarians with gift of celibacy. Thus, an alternative clerical training in an apprenticeship system, which continues the normal adult socialization of candidates who may be called to married diocesan priesthood, is necessary to prevent the ordination of immature heterosexual priests who can commit serious CSA in the RCC.

Unless structural reforms in the current clerical training are done to reestablish the apprenticeship method of clerical training that allows married priesthood, the psychosexual immaturity and vulnerability of diocesan priests to commit CSA will continue to bring more sexual scandals in the Church that can undermine the moral credibility of the Catholic hierarchy.

Conclusion

This chapter has attempted to show the sociological and structural connections between CSA and the RCC's traditional teaching on gender and gender socialization and the seminary's adoption of this teaching in a highly spiritualized gender socialization inside its TI social structure that bans women and open discussion on sexuality matters. The TI environment of the seminary cuts short the normal human and gender socialization of heterosexual seminarians who are denied of the choice for married priesthood with the imposition of clerical celibacy in the 11th and 12th centuries and the adoption of celibate seminary formation by the Council of Trent in the 16th century as the only method of clerical training. The exclusive and highly spiritualized all-male seminary formation that aims to form seminarians into another Christ facilitates psychosexual immaturity that makes heterosexual seminarians vulnerable to commit CSA once assigned in the parish with no effective guardianship by an intimate social group such as the family if married priesthood is allowed.

136 Major Forms of Clerical Sexual Abuse and Seminary Formation

This chapter recommends the reestablishment of the traditional apprenticeship style of clerical training adapted to contemporary times that allows married priesthood for diocesan priests and the continuation of the normal adult gender socialization of heterosexual clerical candidates in society during priestly formation for greater human and sexual maturity and inhibition of CSA in the RCC.

References

Abano, John Dave A., and Chris John C. Bedoria. 2023. "Assessing Grit of Emerging Adult Diocesan Seminarians in Negros Island, Philippines." *Technium Social Science Journal* 43: 314–326.

Adams, Kenneth. 2011. "Clergy Sexual Abuse: A Commentary on Celibacy." *Sexual Addiction & Compulsivity: The Journal of Treatment & Prevention* 10 (2–3): 91–92. https://doi.org/10.1080/107201 6039 0230 583.

Ballano, Vivencio O. 2019. *Sociological Perspectives on Clerical Sexual Abuse in the Catholic Hierarchy An Exploratory Structural Analysis of Social Disorganisation.* Singapore: Springer Nature.

Ballano, Vivencio O. 2020. "The Catholic Laity, Clerical Sexual Abuse, and Married Priesthood: A Sociological Analysis of Vatican II's Lay Empowerment." *Cogent Social Sciences* 6 (1): 1–17. https://doi.org/10.1080/23311886.2020.1813438.

Ballano, Vivencio O. 2023. *In Defense of Married Priesthood: A Sociotheological Investigation of Catholic Clerical Celibacy.* London: Routledge.

Barnes, Medora W. 2022. "Catholic Seminarians on 'Real Men', Sexuality, and Essential Male Inclusivity." *Religions* 13 (352): 1–14. https://doi.org/10.3390/rel13040352.

Blank, Hanne. 2012. *Straight: The Surprisingly Short History of Heterosexuality.* Boston: Beacon Press.

Bracke, Sarah, and David Paternotte. 2016. "Unpacking the Sin of Gender." *Religion and Gender* 6 (2): 143–154.

Case, Mary Anne. 2016. "The Role of the Popes in the Invention of Complementarity and the Vatican's Anathematization of Gender." *Religion and Gender* 6 (2): 155–172.

Chaves, Mark, and Garland Diana. 2009. "The Prevalence of Clergy Sexual Advances Toward Adults in Their Congregations." *Journal for the Scientific Study of Religion* 48: 817–824.

Chibnall, John T., Wolf Ann, and Paul N. Duckro. 1998. "A National Survey of the Sexual Trauma Experiences of Catholic Nuns." *Review of Religious Research* 40: 142–167.

Congregation for Catholic Education. 2019. "Male and Female He Created Them: Towards a Path of Dialogue on the Question of Gender Theory in Education." *Vatican City.* https://efaidnbmnnnibpcajpcglclefindmkaj/www.newwaysministry.org/wp-content/uploads/2019/06/Male-and-Female-Document-June-10-2019.pdf.

Congregation for the Clergy. 2016. *The Gift of the Priestly Vocation: Ratio Institutionis Fundamentalis.* Vatican City: L' Observatore Romano.

Cooley, Charles Horton, George H. Mead, Jean Piaget, Lawrence Kohlberg, and Carol Gilligan. 2010. "Socialization." In *Cooley Studies the Development of the Self, Coining the Term "the Looking-Glass Self,* 2–39. www.csun.edu/~hbsoc126/soc1/chapter%203%20outline.pdf.

Cozzens, Donald. 2004. "The Clerical Culture: Set for the Ages." In *Clerical Culture: Contradiction and Transformation,* edited by Michael L. Papesh. Collegeville, MN: Liturgical Press.

Cozzens, Donald. 2002. *Sacred Silence: Denial and the Crisis in the Church*. Collegeville, MN: Liturgical Press.

Cravatts, Richard. 2007. "L.A. Sex Abuse Settlement Leaves Troubling Questions Unanswered." *The State Journal-Register*, July 25, 2007. www.sj-r.com/story/news/2007/07/25/l-sex-abuse-settlement-leaves/47782055007/.

Crisogen, Disca Tiberiu. 2015. "Types of Socialization and Their Importance in Understanding the Phenomena of Socialization." *European Journal of Social Sciences Education and Research* 2 (4): 288–293.

de Weger, Stephen E., and Death Jodi. 2017. "Clergy Sexual Misconduct Against Adults in the Roman Catholic Church: The Misuse of Professional and Spiritual Power in the Sexual Abuse of Adults." *Journal for the Academic Study of Religion* 30: 129–159.

de Weger, Stephen Edward. 2022. "Unchaste Celibates: Clergy Sexual Misconduct Against Adults – Expressions, Definitions, and Harms" *Religions* 13 (5): 1–27. https://doi.org/10.3390/rel13050393.

Doyle, Thomas P. 2003. "Roman Catholic Clericalism, Religious Duress, and Clergy Sexual Abuse." *Pastoral Psychology* 51:189–231. https://doi.org/10.1023/A:1021301407104.

Doyle, Thomas P. 2006. "Clericalism: Enabler of Clergy Sexual Abuse." *Pastoral Psychology* 54 (3): 189–213. https://doi.org/10.1007/s11089-006-6323-x.

Francis, Perry C., and Tracy D. Baldo. 1998. "Narcissistic Measures of Lutheran Clergy Who Self- Reported Committing Sexual Misconduct." *Pastoral Psychology* 47: 81–96.

Frawley O'Dea, Mary Gail. 2004. "Psychosocial Anatomy of the Catholic Sexual Abuse Scandal." *Studies in Gender and Sexuality* 5 (2): 121–137. https://doi.org/10.1080/15240650509349244.

Frawley-O'Dea, Mary Gail, and Virginia Goldner, eds. 2007. *Predatory Priests, Silenced Victims: The Sexual Abuse Crisis and the Catholic Church*. London: Routledge.

Frawley O'Dea, Mary Gail, and Virginia Goldner. 2016. "Abusive Priests: Who They Were and Were Not." In *Predatory Priests, Silenced Victims: The Sexual Abuse Crisis and the Catholic Church*, edited by Frawley O'Dea, Mary Gail, and Goldner, Virginia. London and New York: Routledge.

Frazee, Charles A. 1972. "The Origins of Clerical Celibacy in the Western Church." *Church History* 41 (02): 149. https://doi.org/:10.2307/3164156.

Friberg, N. C., and M. R. Laaser. 1998. *Before the Fall: Preventing Pastoral Sexual Abuse*. Collegeville: Liturgical Press.

Garland, Diana R., and Christen Argueta. 2010. "How Clergy Sexual Misconduct Happens: A Qualitative Study of First- Hand Accounts." *Social Work & Christianity* 37: 1–27.

Gartner, R. B. 1999. *Betrayed as Boys*. New York: Guilford Press.

Goffman, Erving. 1968. *Asylums: Essays on the Social Situation of Mental Patients and Other Inmates*. 1st ed. New York, NY: Anchor Books.

Greeley, Andrew M. 1972. *The Catholic Priest in the United States: Sociological Investigations*. Washington, DC: United States Catholic Conference.

Greeley, Andrew M. 1986. *Confessions of a Parish Priest: An Autobiography*. New York: Pocket Books.

Haslbeck, Barbara, Heyder Regina, Leimgruber Ute, and Sandherr-Klemp Dorothee. 2020. *Erzählen als Widerstand*. Münster: Aschendorff.

Hogan, Linda. 2021. "Moral Leadership: A Challenge and a Celebration." *Theological Studies* 82 (1): 138–155. https://doi.org/10.1177/0040563921993456.

Hopkins, D. N. 2008. "Toward a Positive Black Male Heterosexuality." *Anglican Theological Review* 90 (3): 575–581.

John Jay College Report. 2004. "The Nature and Scope of Sexual Abuse of Minors by Catholic Priests and Deacons in the United States 1950–2002." *USCCB*. www.bishop-accountability.org/reports/2004_02_27_JohnJay/.

Keenan, James F. 2018. "Vulnerability and Hierarchicalism." *Melita Theologica: Journal of the Faculty of Theology University of Malta* 68 (2): 129–142.

Keenan, Marie. 2011. *Child Sexual Abuse and the Catholic Church: Gender, Power, and Organizational Culture*.1st ed. London and New York: Oxford University Press.

Keenan, Marie. 2011. *Sexual Abuse and the Catholic Church: Gender, Power, and Organizational Culture*. Oxford: Oxford University Press.

Keenan, Marie. 2015. "Masculinity, Relationships and Context: Child Sexual Abuse and the Catholic Church Catholic Church." *Irish Journal of Applied Social Studies* 15 (2): 64-77.

Kotarba, Joseph A. 2007. "Adult Socialization." In *The Blackwell Encyclopedia of Sociology*, edited by G. Ritzer, 589. https://doi.org/10.1002/9781405165518.wbeoss194.

Loftus, J. A., and R. J. Camargo. 1993. "Treating the Clergy." *Annals of Sex Research* 6: 287–303.

Macionis, J. 2012. *Sociology*. 14th ed. London: Pearson.

Matthias, Gabriel, O. F. M. 2020. "Sexual Abuse Scandal and Its Implications for Seminary Formation." *Asian Horizons* 14 (2): 443–458.

Mescher, Marcus. 2023. "Clergy Sexual Abuse as Moral Injury: Confronting a Wounded and Wounding Church." In *Responding to the Sexual Abuse Crisis in the Catholic Church: Perspectives from Theology and Theological Ethics*, edited by Daniel J. Fleming, James F. Keenan, SJ, and Hans Zollner. Eugene, OR: Wipf and Stock.

Miller, Maureen C. 2003. "Masculinity, Reform, and Clerical Culture: Narratives of Episcopal Holiness in the Gregorian Era." *Church History* 72 (1): 25–5.

Mills, C. Wright. 2000. *The Sociological Imagination*. New York, NY: Oxford University Press.

Naparan, G., M. Canoy, F. D. Mahinay, and J. E. Villaflor. 2022. "Walking on Hot Coals: A Phenomenological Study on Dealing With Temptations in the Seminary." *Millah: Jurnal Studi Agama*. https://doi.org/10.20885/millah.vol21.iss3.art1.

Neuhaus, Ricard John. 2008. "Clerical Scandal and the Scandal of Clericalism." *First Things*, March 2008. www.firstthings.com/article/2008/03/clerical-scandal-and-the-scandal-of-clericalism.

Ormerod, Neil. 2022. "The Parable of the Good Samaritan, Clericalism, and the Sexual Abuse Crisis in the Australian Context." *Revista Iberoamericana de Teología*, XVIII (34): 35–56.

Plante, Thomas G. 2002. "Celibacy and the Child Sexual Abuse Crisis." *Clio's Psyche: Understanding the 'Why' of Culture, Current Events, History, and Society* 9: 110–112.

Plante, Thomas G. 2020. "Clergy Sexual Abuse in the Roman Catholic Church: Dispelling Eleven Myths and Separating Facts from Fiction." *Spirituality in Clinical Practice* 7 (4): 220–229. https://doi.org/10.1037/scp0000209.

Plante, Thomas G., and Ariana Aldridge. 2005. "Psychological Patterns Among Roman Catholic Clergy Accused of Sexual Misconduct." *Pastoral Psychology* 54 (1): 73–80. https://doi.org/10.1007/s11089-005-6184-8.

Pope Benedict XVI, and Peter Seewald. 2010. *Light of The World: A Conversation With Peter Seewald*. San Francisco, CA: St. Ignatius Press.

Reisinger, Doris. 2018. "#NunsToo: Sexueller Missbrauch an Ordensfrauen- Fakten und Fragen." *Stimmen Der Zeit* 236: 374–384. www.herder.de/stz/hefte/archiv/143-2018/6-2018/nunstoo-sexueller-missbrauch-an-ordensfrauen-fakten-und-fragen/.

Reisinger, Doris. 2022. "Reproductive Abuse in the Context of Clergy Sexual Abuse in the Catholic Church." *Religions* 13 (3): 198. https://doi.org/10.3390/rel13030198.

Rohlinger, Deana A. 2007. "Primary Socialization." In *The Blackwell Encyclopedia of Sociology*, edited by G. Ritzer, 590–591. https://doi.org/10.1002/9781405165518.wbeoss194.

Romeo Mateo, Maria Cruz. 2021. "A New Priest for a New Society? The Masculinity of the Priesthood in Liberal Spain." *Journal of Religious History* 45 (4): 540–558. https://doi.org/10.1111/1467–9809.12799.

Ruether, Rosemary Radford. 2008. *Catholic Does Not Equal the Vatican: A Vision for Progressive Catholicism*. New York: New Press.

Sands, Kathleen M. 2003. "Speaking Out: Clergy Sexual Abuse: Where Are the Women?" *Journal of Feminist Studies in Religion* 19 (2): 79–83. www.jstor.org/stable/25002477.

Schuth, Katarina, O. S. F. 2016. *Seminary Formation Recent History-Current Circumstances-New Directions*. Collegeville, MN: Liturgical Press.

Sipe, A. W. Richard. 1990. *A Secret World: Sexuality and The Search for Celibacy*. 1st ed. East Sussex: Brunner-Routledge.

Sipe, A. W. Richard. 2003. *Celibacy in Crisis: A Secret World Revisited*. New York: Brunner- Routledge.

Stanosz, Paul. 2004. "Reproducing Celibacy: A Case Study in Diocesan Seminary Formation." *ETD Collection for Fordham University* AAI3140903. https://research.library.fordham.edu/dissertations/AAI3140903.

Szwed, Anna, and Katarzyna Zielińska. 2016. "A War on Gender? The Roman Catholic Church's Discourse on Gender in Poland. Religion, Politics, and Values in Poland." In *Religion, Politics, and Values in Poland* (Palgrave Studies in Religion, Politics, and Policy), edited by S. Ramet, and I. Borowik. New York: Palgrave Macmillan. https://doi.org/10.1057/978-1-137-43751-8_6.

Terry, Karen J. 2008. "Stained Glass: The Nature and Scope of Child Sexual Abuse in the Catholic Church." *Criminal Justice and Behavior* 35: 549–569.

Terry, Karen J., Smith Margaret Leland, Schuth Katarina, James R. Kelly, Vollman Brenda, and Massey Christina. 2011. *The Causes and Context of Sexual Abuse of Minors by Catholic Priests in the United States, 1950–2010*. Washington, DC: USCCB. www.usccb.org/sites/default/files/issues-and-action/child-and-youth-protection/upload/The-Causes-and Context-of-Sexual-Abuse-of-Minors-by-Catho lic- Prie sts-in-the-United-States-1950–2010.pdf.

Timofeeva, E. 2019. "Foreign Prison Experience Resocialization of Prisoners." *SHS Web of Conferences* 62: 1–4. https://doi.org/10.1051/shsconf/20196212004.

Thoburn, John, and Whitman D. Mitchell. 2004. "Clergy Affairs: Emotional Investment, Longevity of Relationship and Affair Partners." *Pastoral Psychology* 52: 491–506.

Wilson, G. 2008. *Clericalism: The Death of Priesthood*. Collegeville, MN: Liturgical Press.

Wunder, Dolores F. 2007. "Socialization, Agents of." In *The Blackwell Encyclopedia of Sociology*, edited by G. Ritzer, 59–590. https://doi.org/10.1002/9781405165518.wbeoss194.

Yip, Andrew K. T. 2003. "Sexuality and the Church." *Sexualities* 6 (1): 60–64. https://doi.org/10.1177/1363460703006001007.

7

HOMOSEXUAL CLERICAL SEXUAL ABUSE AND SEMINARY FORMATION

Introduction

One of the most controversial types of clerical sexual abuse (CSA) in the Roman Catholic Church (RCC) is one that is committed by homosexual priests. Aside from CSA by pedophile priests against innocent children, the second most popular form of clerical sexual abuse (CSA) in the RCC is homosexual clerical sexual abuse. Homosexuality has been a polarizing issue in Christianity and Catholicism. The RCC's official teachings are basically against homosexuality, which considers it as intrinsically disordered (Mounwe 2021). With this prevailing ecclesial belief, several top church officials blamed homosexual clerics for the sexual scandals in the RCC.

Cardinal Gerhard Müller, the former Prefect of the Dicastery of the Doctrine of the Faith, for instance, believed that homosexuality is the primary enabler of the clergy sexual abuse scandal in the Church. To him, the root cause of Catholic CSA is the depraved personality of the gay priest offender, which, to him, is unrelated to clerical office (Pongratz-Lippitt 2019). In his book *The Changing Face of Catholic Priesthood*, Donald Cozzens (2000) cited studies from 1989 revealing that 48.5% of Catholic priests and 55.1% of seminarians were gay. He then concluded that gay profession would prevent heterosexual men from becoming priests.

The popular Catholic sociologist, Father Andrew Greeley, also published an article in 1989, sounding this alarm that a gay subculture of homosexual priests existed in most Catholic dioceses (Boisvert and Goss 2005). The perception of the growing dominance of gay priests and the existence of gay culture in the RCC have inadvertently increased homophobia among Catholic bishops who connected gay priesthood to the growing sexual scandals

DOI: 10.4324/9781032722474-10

in the RCC. Thus, Cardinal Brandmüller (2019) remarked that 80% of cases of abuse in the church environment only affected male adolescents, not children. To him, there is a causal link between homosexuality and Catholic CSA.

Apparently, the lack of updated scientific knowledge on the true nature homosexuality and CSA among Catholic bishops and Catholic authors has magnified homophobia in the RCC and unfair blaming of homosexual priests as the primary culprit for most CSA cases in the RCC. Fr. Donald Cozzens (2000), for instance, magnified this homophobia by claiming that American Catholic seminaries were attracting larger and larger number of gays. To him, Catholic priesthood in the 21st century is predominantly a gay profession, implying that having more homosexual priests in the RCC is itself a serious problem.

This lack of scientific knowledge on the sociological connection between homosexuality and CSA in the RCC has misled many bishops on the role of homosexual priests in the current clergy sexual scandals in the Church. The Catholic hierarchy sees gay priests as largely responsible of the current sexual abuses in the RCC; thus, it bans gay applicants and seminarians with homosexual attraction from seminary formation as well as the priesthood. The Catechism of the Catholic Church (2003) defines homosexual attraction as "an exclusive or predominant sexual attraction toward persons of the same sex, (#2357)," which is considered "objectively disordered" (#2358) and is a sign of affective immaturity. Here, the RCC inaccurately equates homosexual attraction as a sign of immaturity.

Thus, several bishops wrongly see the prohibition of gay men to the priesthood as the primary solution to the prevent CSA crisis in the universal church. Individuals with deep-seated homosexual tendencies who join seminary formation or who support "gay culture are considered potential contributors to the sexual scandals in the Church" (Instruction from the Congregation for Catholic Education 2005, para. 2). The RCC sees a big difference between heterosexual and homosexual candidates to the priesthood. As Cardinal Anthony Bevilacqua of Philadelphia argues:

> There is a big difference between a heterosexual and homosexual candidate for the priesthood. A heterosexual candidate is taking on a good thing, becoming a priest, and giving up a good thing, the desire to have a family. A gay seminarian, even a chaste one, by his orientation is not a suitable candidate for the priesthood, even if he did not commit an act of [of gay sex]. He is giving up what the church considers an abomination.
>
> *(Talbot 2002, 18)*

To ban homosexuals from Catholic priesthood, the RCC approved the Instruction Concerning the Criteria for the Discernment of Vocations with

142 Major Forms of Clerical Sexual Abuse and Seminary Formation

Regard to Persons with Homosexual Tendencies in View of Their Admission to the Seminary and to Holy Orders by the Congregation for Catholic Education in 2005 to prevent homosexuals from joining seminary formation and the presbyterate:

> [T]his Dicastery, in accord with the Congregation for Divine Worship and the Discipline of the Sacraments, believes it necessary to state clearly that the Church, while profoundly respecting the persons in question, cannot admit to the seminary or to holy orders those who practice homosexuality, present deep-seated homosexual tendencies or support the so-called "gay culture."
>
> *(Congregation for Catholic Education 2005, 3)*

The position of the RCC on homosexuality and seminary formation is clearly reflected by this instruction: "[M]en who are sexually attracted to other men do not possess those qualities necessary to be icons of Christ and spiritual fathers. They find themselves in a situation that gravely hinders them from relating correctly to men and women" (Congregation for Catholic Education 2005, 3). This prohibition of homosexuals to the priesthood is primarily seen by the RCC as the ultimate solution to the persistent CSA in the RCC, allegedly committed by ordained gay priests. Thus, one wonders: Is homosexuality largely the cause of the growing and enduring clerical sexual abuse scandals in the RCC? Do gay priests constitute the primary cohort of sexual abusers in the RCC? Does the current celibate seminary training contribute significantly to the growing clergy sexual scandals by gay priests?

The primary aim of this chapter is to sociologically investigate whether homosexual priests are mainly responsible for the persistent CSA in the RCC and whether the current celibate seminary training is nurturing homosexual tendencies among gay seminarians that can translate into serious cases of sexual abuse against children after their ordination. The current research and investigation on CSA generally ignore the role of seminary formation in Catholic clergy sexual misconduct, specifically on how the human and sexual formation of gay seminarians are structurally linked to the current sexual scandals in the RCC.

To achieve this objective, this chapter is structured into four main sections. The first section clarifies the misconception of the RCC on homosexual CSA and its relation to seminary formation and Catholic priesthood, arguing that homosexual priests are not the primary cohort of sexual abusers in the RCC. The second section examines the implications of blaming homosexuals for the CSA scandals in the RCC and its consequences to clerical formation and mental health of gay seminarians and priests.

The last section recommends a separate and specialized training and pastoral care for gay candidates as well as apprenticeship style of clerical training that allows same-sex marriage for homosexual diocesan priests who are obligated to live and work alone most of the time in the parish. It argues that, like heterosexual priests, gay clerics are also giving up their need for intimacy and capacity to enter a same-sex marriage in order to become priests. Similar to the situation of heterosexual diocesan clergy, gay priests also experience loneliness and absence of intimate social bonding offered by same-sex marriage, which can provide social control and guardianship against CSA in the ministry.

Many CSA studies involving gay priests are micro and quantitative studies using the psychological and psychiatric perspectives and rarely the qualitative research method and sociological approach that relate the homosexual CSA to seminary formation. The exclusive, all-male, and celibate seminary social structure is the breeding ground for Catholic priests. Thus, examining its formation and socialization processes are crucial in understanding how homosexual individuals are screened and trained in the exclusive environment of the seminary before ordination, whether the seminary formation facilitates or hinders sexual abuses by gay priests in the RCC.

Misconceptions on Homosexual CSA

CSA by gay priests is among the most misunderstood type of clerical sexual abuses in the RCC. Homosexual priests are often associated with child sexual abuse, a type of CSA that has resulted in intense media mileage and public hysteria. Although child sexual abuse by Catholic pedophile clergy constitutes only the smallest percentage of the total CSA in the RCC (Sipe 1990; John Jay College Report 2004), it nevertheless caused lot of public condemnation and media hype that led to an inaccurate portrayal that child sexual abuse by homosexual priests is the greatest form of clerical sexual scandal in the history of the RCC (Sipe 1990; John Jay College Report 2004, Freiburger 2010).

But recent research has revealed that classic pedophilia, which involves molesting prepubescent children or those minors with age below 13 years, is mostly committed by pedophile clerics and not by gay priests. The sexual abuse of pubescent minors or adolescents is not pedophilia but as ephebophilia (Freiburger 2010). Many studies on CSA of minors in the RCC have shown that most victims are not children or prepubescent minors but adolescents, that is, pubescent or postpubescent boys – thus, not a case of pedophilia but ephebophilia (Kraschl 2020).

Ephebophilia or sexual abuse of adolescents can be an appropriate category for most gay priests but not pedophilia. One must not unscrupulously accuse gay priests of child sexual abuse and blame them for most CSA in the RCC. Richard Sipe's early estimate (1990), for instance, indicated that probably only 2% of all priests commit sexual abuse against children or pedophilia, 4% against adolescent boys or girls (ephebophilia), but a high

144 Major Forms of Clerical Sexual Abuse and Seminary Formation

20% to 40% of CSA cases are committed by heterosexual priests not only against adolescents and adult women but also against children. Heterosexual priests, who have infantile human and sexual maturity, abuse people in the RCC based on the victims' availability rather based on gender and age (e.g., Frawley O'Dea 2004; De Weger 2022).

Early studies such as those by Camargo and Loftus (1992), Lothstein (2004), and Robinson (1994) had already established that most priests who abused minors aged 13 years and older are ephebophiles. The study of the Royal Commission into Institutional Responses to Child Clerical Sexual Abuse (2017) also revealed the dominance of sexual abuse against adolescents rather than children. It reported that only 7% of all Catholic priests committed child sexual abuse; the rest are committed against adolescents and adults by heterosexual priests.

Furthermore, recent research has shown that the perpetrators of sexual abuse against boys and girls are much more likely to be heterosexual men rather than gays across all settings (e.g., Dowling et al. 2021; McPhillips et al. 2022). Findings of public inquiries on CSA in Australia, Ireland, the United Kingdom, and the United States further revealed that offenders of boys and girls are male heterosexual clerics rather than gay priests. The psychologist Thomas Plante (2018), who has done several research on CSA, also debunks the idea that sexual abuse in the RCC is largely committed by homosexual priests, thus he aptly explains:

> Since about 80 percent of the victims of clergy sexual abuse are male, many wish to blame the clergy abuse problem in the Church on homosexual priests. While research does suggest that the percentage of Catholic priests who are homosexual is much higher than found in the general population, we know that sexual orientation is not a risk factor for pedophilia. Homosexual men may be sexually attracted to other men but not to children. Research has found that most of the sexual abuse perpetrators didn't consider themselves homosexual at all but were "situational generalists" (i.e., they abused whoever they had access to and control over, boys or girls).

Despite the research pattern that shows that most CSA cases in the RCC are not committed by homosexual clergy but by male heterosexual clerics and "situational generalists," still some authors and members of the Catholic hierarchy blame gay priests as the primary culprit for all clergy sexual abuses in the Church. Bill Donahue, for instance, asserts that almost all clerics who molest children are gays (Lavictoire 2011). Groeschel (2002) also claims that child CSA in the RCC is all about homosexuality. And some Catholic officials such as Cardinal Brandmüller (2019) estimated that 80% of all cases of CSA in the Church are committed by gay priests, asserting that there is a causal link between CSA and homosexuality.

Blaming Homosexuals for CSA and the Priesthood

With the misconception on the relationship between homosexuality and CSA, the Catholic hierarchy tends to blame all homosexual priests for all the sexual scandals in the RCC. Two senior Catholic cardinals such as Raymond Burke and Walter Brandmüller view CSA as "the plague of the homosexual agenda [that] has been spread within the Church" (Gledhill 2019, para. 5). Because of this misleading perception, the RCC bans individuals with homosexual tendencies to enter seminary formation and the priesthood (Congregation for Catholic Education 2005) to prevent sexual scandals in the RCC. It views heterosexual candidates as fit for the priesthood but not homosexuals since they are incapable of giving up marriage.

As Cardinal Anthony Bevilacqua of Philadelphia argues:

> There is a big difference between a heterosexual and homosexual candidate for the priesthood. A heterosexual candidate is taking on a good thing, becoming a priest, an giving up a good thing, the desire to have a family. A gay seminarian, even a chaste one, by his orientation is not a suitable candidate for the priesthood, even if he did not commit an act of [of gay sex]. He is giving up what the church considers an abomination.
>
> *(Talbot 2002, 18)*

Since official Church teachings only view gender as male or female in accordance with the Scriptures, the RCC generally considers homosexuals as deviants and "abomination" in the Church and homosexuality as intrinsically disordered (Mounwe 2021). Because of the indiscriminate blaming of gay priests for the current sexual scandals in the Church, especially child sexual abuse, the RCC has been criticized by some scholars. Barnes (2022, 9), for instance, argues,

> The Church . . . has been rightly criticized for drawing false connections between homosexuality and sexual or child abuse. This is especially salient, as the majority of sexual misconduct by Catholic priests involves adult and female victims, although this type of abuse is under discussed and less studied.

The current sexual abuse panic in the RCC wrongly magnifies the connection between homosexuality and pedophilia that "persecuted" good gay priests and seminarians in the Church.

The psychologist Thomas Plante (2002) clarifies that an increasing number of gay priests in the RCC does not necessary lead to higher risks of CSA against children. Generally, sexual orientation does not predict child CSA. Heterosexual men are more likely to commit sexual abuse with children and adolescents compared to gays. To Feierman (2020), the correlation between homosexuality and child abuse is not that simple as "child" or "children" will always mean prepubertal, "adolescent," or peri-pubertal with ages between 11 and 14 years to just postpubertal (ages 15–17). But gays committing CSA involve adolescents and adults rather than prepubescent children. There is also no evidence that gay priests change their gender and age preference in choosing their victims through time.

Thus, Boisvert and Goss (2005) dismissed accusations against gay priests for being the primary cohort of all clerical sexual abusers in the RCC as highly inaccurate and could lead to further discrimination against homosexuals in the Church. They argued that there is solid scientific evidence that heterosexual priests rather gay priests are more prone to commit child sexual abuse and other forms of CSA in the RCC. To them, blaming homosexual priests for the plague of sexual scandals in the RCC is only a scapegoat by Catholic bishops to hide the inability of the RCC as an institution to stop CSA and defend victims:

> Although social scientific research has demonstrated that heterosexuals are the predominant perpetrators of sexual abuse of minors, the Catholic bishops ignore the scientific research in much the same way as they ignored clerical predators in the past. They zero in on sexual abuse of young boys and fail to pay much attention to the abuse of young girls or vulnerable women.
>
> *(Boisvert and Goss 2005).*

Even though there is a secret history of same-sex relationships in the Church (Boswell 1980), the official Catholic teachings remain anti-homosexual that view homosexuality as morally and intrinsically disordered (Mounwe 2021). With their attraction to men that contravenes heterosexuality, gays are generally discriminated in the RCC, specifically in Catholic priesthood. This accusation against homosexual priests as causing the sexual scandals in the RCC is an added psychological burden for Catholic homosexuals to bear that can lead to negative unintended consequences to their mental life.

Thus, Dr. Leslie Lothstein (2004) cautions against indiscriminate blaming of homosexuals for the current CSA scandals in the Church, which can result in serious negative impact on their mental health.

> [For] homosexual priests to survive in their Church, they may have to adopt a "don't tell" attitude and maintain a secret self at the expense of their mental health . . . [M]aintaining a false self and keeping secrets can only lead to emotional trouble, especially in the Catholic priesthood, which depends on a virtuous and celibate priesthood.
>
> *(Lothstein 2004, 169)*

Church Stand on Homosexuality and Seminary Formation

> [The RCC] believes that homosexual orientation could be innate, learned, or developed as one matures through life. CDF (1975) differentiates temporary or curable orientations from innate or incurable ones. Temporary or curable orientations may be traced to wrong education, derailed sexual development, habit or bad example.
>
> *(Mounwe 2021, 101)*

The church sees homosexual orientation as an "objective moral disorder" ordained toward "an intrinsic moral evil" and as harboring a tendency that is so strong that can lead people away from God (Congregation for the Doctrine of the Faith 1986).

To the RCC,

> to be disordered means that homosexuality does not follow the normal, natural order of things, and is opposed to the end to which normal, natural order of sexual relations lead – unity of man and woman in marriage and procreation. It is, therefore, not homosexually inclined person that is described as being objectively disordered, but his or her sexual inclination or orientation.
>
> *(Mounwe 2021, 101)*

Sociological literature, however, clarifies that homosexuality is a socially learned phenomenon rather than an innate trait of persons. Since most candidates enter the seminary with an age of 14 years and older, they are presumed to have undergone their primary socialization and established their basic gender identity whether as heterosexual or gay. Homosexual candidates who therefore enter the seminary at this stage and age range have already undergone the transformation from heterosexuality to homosexuality (Cass 1984). Thus, the gender heterosexual orientation of priestly formation could not change the already established gay identity of homosexual seminarians before they enter in the seminary.

The fear of the RCC that homosexuals entering the exclusive all-male seminary formation could make them "incurable" gay priests and future primary sexual offenders in the Church is unfounded. The strict surveillance of the seminary as a total institution (Goffman 1968) by formators prohibits open discussion on sexuality and homosexual activity. Rectors and prefects of discipline in the seminary normally enforce the stringent seminary rules on chastity – although in some rare cases, covert intimate relationships may be developed between gay formators and heterosexual seminarians.

Besides, gay seminarians generally constitute only a small minority inside the seminary. Thus, homosexual seminarians could not just develop intimate

148 Major Forms of Clerical Sexual Abuse and Seminary Formation

and gay relationships nor cultivate a gay culture inside the seminary – as feared by ecclesiastics with homophobia – because of this panoptic surveillance of seminary formators. Expulsion is the most common penalty for those who violate seminary norms on sexuality and chastity.

The seminary as a total institution (Goffman 1968) can have a significant impact on the formative years of adolescent and young adult candidates to the priesthood. Any abnormality in human development during this formative period can result in maldevelopment or underdevelopment of the sexual life of seminarians, which can continue after ordination. Structurally speaking, the current seminary system is originally intended for male heterosexual priests who can give up the heterosexual Christian marriage for celibate priesthood in the Church. Thus, those priestly candidates with homosexual gender orientation could not be accommodated and properly trained under this system. At present, there is no pastoral care and psychological counseling for gay seminarians inside the seminary.

An early statement from Rome revealed that the RCC is reluctant to allow gay individuals to enter the priesthood. As early as 1961, the Church warned the faithful through the Sacred Congregation for the Religious in a document entitled "On the Careful Selection and Training of Candidates for the States of Perfection and Sacred Orders" that the "advancement to religious vows and ordination should be barred to those who are afflicted with evil tendencies to homosexuality or pederasty, since for them the common life and the priestly ministry would constitute serious dangers" (Fernandes 2011, 313).

Several Catholic bishops seem unaware of the true nature of homosexuality and CSA; thus, they tend to magnify homophobia in the RCC and intensify the campaign against homosexuals entering the seminary and Catholic priesthood. Official Church teachings resist accepting homosexuals into seminary formation given the heterosexual standard of the RCC on priesthood and marriage as well as its rejection of same-sex marriage. Furthermore, well-known Catholic scholars and theologians also contribute to the homophobia and campaign against homosexual priests and seminarians in the RCC.

The popular Catholic priest and sociologist Fr. Andrew Greeley (1989), for instance, cautioned the Church that a gay subculture is existing and developing in Catholic priesthood that can paralyze the Catholic hierarchy. Fr. Donald Cozzens (2000) further magnified this alarm against homosexuals by claiming in his book that American Catholic seminaries were attracting larger and larger number of gays that discourages heterosexuals to join seminary training to enter the priesthood. Pursuing the celibate priesthood model since the 12th century with the imposition of clerical celibacy and rejection of married priesthood, the RCC expects male heterosexuals to flock the seminary instead of homosexuals. But the all-male celibate seminary organization turned out to be attractive for gays whose sexual orientation is toward heterosexual men. Thus, seminary formators are strictly screening applicants with homosexual tendencies and remove gay seminarians from formation.

The RCC views the seminary training as a supreme sacrifice of manhood for heterosexual priests by bravely giving up marriage for the sake of Christ and undivided service for the Church. Thus, Pope Benedict XVI saw the incompatibility between homosexuality and priestly vocation. To him,

> homosexuality is incompatible with the priestly vocation. Otherwise, celibacy itself would lose its meaning as a renunciation. It would be extremely dangerous if celibacy became a sort of pretext for bringing people into the priesthood who don't want to get married anyway. For in the end, their attitude toward man or woman is somehow distorted, off-center, and, in any case, is not within the direction of creation of which we have spoken.
>
> *(Pope Benedict XVI and Seewald 2010, 151–152)*

To Benedict XVI, accepting homosexuals to the priesthood could be a refuge for those who would not desire marriage. This is the logical conclusion if the celibate priesthood model is seen as only sacrificing heterosexual marriage and not homosexual marriage if same-sex marriage is allowed in the RCC. The current clerical celibacy supports the idea that heterosexuals give up marriage for the sake of imitating Christ's celibate life and ministry. It does not contemplate the possibility that homosexual individuals who become priests are also sacrificing marriage if same-sex union is officially recognized by the Church.

Celibate homosexual priests can also be lonely and tempted to commit CSA in the parish just like heterosexual priests. Married priesthood for diocesan homosexual and heterosexual priests can provide the necessary intimacy and direct social control to clerical behavior to prevent CSA and other forms of sexual deviance. It is undeniable that currently there are covert homosexual and heterosexual relationships among diocesan clergy as a form of passive resistance to mandatory clerical celibacy (Ballano 2023).

Implications of Blaming Gay Priests for CSA

Because of the wide publicity against child sexual abuse in the RCC by mass media, most CSA cases is blamed on homosexual and pedophile priests. Specifically, the blaming of gay priests as causing CSA in the RCC has resulted in social discrimination in clerical formation and ministry. Thus, gay priests and seminarians are forced to keep silent and suffer mental health problems. This unjustified CSA accusation against gays in the Church is however contrary to the mainstream research on clergy sexual misconduct in the RCC, which points to the immature male heterosexual priests as the primary cohort responsible for most clergy sexual abuses in the Church, including sexual molestations against children, adolescents, and adults.

CSA by homosexual priests constitutes only a small fraction compared to CSA committed by heterosexual priests. The priest-therapist and popular CSA author Richard Sipe (1994, 134) estimates that "four times as many priests involve themselves sexually with adult women, and twice the number with adult men, as priests who involve themselves sexually with children." One universal trait revealed in several CSA research related to both sexual misconduct and abuse is that most offenders were male and homosexual (Francis and Baldo 1998; Friberg and Laaser 1998; Thoburn and Whitman 2004; Chaves and Garland 2009; Garland and Argueta 2010). This trait would be expected as most Christian denominations (88%) only allow males to be leaders in their churches (Cooperative Congregations Studies Partnership 2010).

The final report of the John Jay College (2004) entitled "Causes and Context of Sexual Abuse of Minors" also supports the conclusion that most CSA cases in the RCC are committed by male heterosexual priests, especially against adults, and not by gay priests (Terry et al. 2011). And more recent research by De Weger (2022) also confirmed that the majority of CSA cases in the RCC are committed against adult women that is constituting as the number one form of clergy sexual misconduct in the RCC with a frequency that is much higher than those committed by gay and pedophile priests.

Even though current research has revealed that heterosexual priests are the predominant perpetrators of CSA against minors, the RCC tends to disregard scientific findings: The main perpetrators of CSA in the RCC are not gays but male heterosexual priests with infantile sexual maturity who molest vulnerable children, adolescents, and adults to resolve their personal and sexual issues that were not properly addressed during and after seminary training because of the celibacy rule (Adams 2011). In this regard, Catholic bishops who blame homosexuals for the CSA crisis can be seen as barking at the wrong tree, scapegoating gay priests for their failure to effectively address CSA in the Church (Boisvert and Goss 2005).

If the number one group that committed CSA in the RCC, whether against children, adolescents, and adults, are male heterosexual priests, then blaming homosexuals for the CSA crisis in the Church and banning them from seminary formation and Catholic priesthood can be seen as another form of persecution against gays in the Church in addition to existing the antihomosexual teachings in the RCC. Research reveals that gay priests mostly establish sexual relationship with adolescent or adult males, which does normally convert to attraction to children. To survive this unjust accusation and mental persecution for being responsible for child sexual abuses in the RCC, Dr. Lothstein (2004) claims that homosexual priests adopt a "don't tell" strategy and maintain a secret self at the expense of their mental health.

In the United States, for example, homosexual priests are often ignored and largely blamed for CSA crisis in the RCC. Despite current data suggesting pedophile and immature male heterosexual priests as the primary culprits of child sexual abuse in the RCC, the media and Catholic bishops still blame homosexual priests resulting in their persecution and marginalization in the Catholic priesthood. Garland Thomas (2005) aptly describes the predicament of gay Catholic priests as voiceless in the Church:

> Many bishops and religious superiors, who either embarrassed by the presence of gay priests under their jurisdiction or who deny their existence, are understandably skittish about conducting research that would confirm the presence of homosexual priests in the church. . . . In addition to the lack of data, a strict code of silence concerning homosexual priests has been imposed. Bishops and religious superiors have forbidden many priests from speaking, writing, or preaching about their homosexuality. . . . Voiceless, the gay priest cannot defend himself within the church. Stereotyped, he cannot escape the suspicions of society at large.

The Need for Specialized Formation for Gays

To avoid unjust blaming homosexual seminarians and priests as creating a gay culture in the Church and responsible for the CSAs in the RCC, a specialized or separate seminary formation or pastoral care is necessary to deal with gays and individuals with homosexual tendencies. Owing to the lack of diversity of clerical formation in the RCC that can appropriately deal with homosexual individuals, applicants to clerical training are forced to join the all-male and exclusive priestly training. The pastoral exhortation *Pastores Dabo Vobis* (1992) ["I Shall Give You Shepherds"] by Pope John Paul II stressed the human aspect of priestly formation and recommended a specialized clerical training for seminarians with peculiar needs. It provided some guidelines and stressed that "the training of normal men in mind, since candidates for the priesthood ought to be normal. In cases of more or less abnormal persons, a more specialized kind of work has to be undertaken" (*Pastores Dabo Vobis* 1992, n. 5).

But this recommendation to provide a specialized training to seminary candidates with peculiar needs, such as homosexual men, seems unattainable given the lack of human resources, programs, and experts in Catholic seminaries who can deal with homosexual issues during clerical training. The Catholic hierarchy prohibits homosexuals in seminary formation altogether, but loopholes in the screening process for applicants enable gays to join clerical formation and become priests. It rationalizes this prohibition of gays in clerical training based on a moral teaching that homosexuality is intrinsically

152 Major Forms of Clerical Sexual Abuse and Seminary Formation

disordered and that homosexuals are not giving up heterosexual marriage when they become priests.

The reason why gays are prohibited in seminary training is grounded on a shaky empirical foundation. Indeed, homosexual priests are not giving up marriage under the current standard of Catholic heterosexual marriage. But they can be seen as giving up marriage like the heterosexual priests if the RCC recognizes the existence of gay priests and their need for same-sex marriage in the Church. The RCC needs to relax its rigid view on gender as immutable and ahistorical and see that homosexuals are indeed empirically existing and constituting a separate gender identity and category in society. Like heterosexual priests, they also experience loneliness, lack of intimate companionship due to celibacy, and the temptation to commit CSA as a compensatory behavior for their repressed sexuality.

Gay priests, especially diocesan clerics, can also experience clerical spiritual dryness owing to the absence of a strong social bonding and communal spirituality in the parish. When the RCC adopted the celibate priesthood model during the Council of Trent in the 16th century, it presumed that candidates to the priesthood were all male heterosexuals who should give up marriage for the sake of Christ and ministerial priesthood. Historically, the semi-monastic seminary training is primarily intended for male heterosexual candidates who would become celibate religious or monastic priests but not for secular priests who are homosexual.

Married priesthood, which should also recognize same-sex clerical marriage, is appropriate for secular priests in an apprenticeship style of clerical formation. But this is not available in the current seminary formation as taught by ecclesial documents. The Catholic hierarchy had not foreseen the entry of homosexuals in seminary formation when the Council of Trent instituted the seminary and retained currently by the RCC.

Thus, Catholic clerical training does not generally advance special interventions or a separate seminary formation for candidates with peculiar needs such as gay seminarians as recommended by the pastoral exhortation *Pastores Dabo Vobis*. Since almost all aspirants claim that they are heterosexuals and the psychological examinations are not totally reliable to stop the entry of homosexuals, gay seminarians were able to participate in the celibate seminary training but without the necessary psychological and human interventions by experts and social scientists. They instead only receive spiritual guidance from the seminary's spiritual directors – who are mostly trained in philosophy, spirituality, and theology but not in the social sciences, which specialize in the study of gender and sexuality.

It is then necessary for the RCC to recognize that homosexuality constitutes a separate gender identity and that good gay priests, like heterosexual priests, also suffer loneliness and temptation to commit CSA in the parish. To form and strengthen their human and spiritual sexual resistance against

Homosexual Clerical Sexual Abuse and Seminary Formation 153

CSA, a specialized seminary program, pastoral care, or intervention for homosexual candidates is important. The RCC should also start allowing same-sex marriage for diocesan priests as some German bishops are advocating.

Without these structural changes, the RCC and conservative bishops will continue to unjustly hinder homosexuals to enter clerical formation and the priesthood as well as blame them for causing sexual scandals in the RCC. Official church teaching has already judged homosexuality as intrinsically disordered (Mounwe 2021). Banning them in seminary formation and imputing them with guilt for the CSA in the RCC can increase homophobia and result in more mental anguish (Lothstein 2004) and "persecution" of gay priests and seminarians in the RCC (Boisvert and Goss 2005).

Conclusion

This chapter has shown that most sexual scandals and CSA cases in the RCC are committed by heterosexual priests rather than by gay priests. The lack of knowledge of some conservative bishops of the Catholic hierarchy on the true nature of homosexuality and its sociological connections to CSA has resulted in the indiscriminate banning of homosexual individuals from the celibate seminary training and Catholic priesthood. This action has further intensified homophobia and mental anguish that stigmatized gays whose homosexual orientation has already been unjustly judged by official Catholic teachings as intrinsically disordered. Gays are then seen as unworthy of the priesthood since they are not capable of giving up manhood and heterosexual marriage for Christ and his Church.

Homosexuals who enter the seminary have already acquired their homosexual identity and thus cannot develop homosexual tendencies inside the seminary. With the strict panoptic surveillance of seminary formators, they cannot just establish gay relationship and culture inside the seminary. Gay seminarians usually undergo celibate clerical formation without the appropriate professional intervention and program to take care of their peculiar human and sexual needs, as recognized by Pope John Paul II's papal exhortation, *Pastores Dabo Vobis*. The RCC should also start considering same-sex marriage for gay diocesan priests to provide them with greater social control against CSA. Like heterosexual secular priests, they also experience loneliness and lack of social support and personal intimacy in the parish and, thus, can strongly be tempted to commit CSA when deviant opportunities come during their ministry.

Finally, this chapter recommends an apprenticeship style of clerical training aside from seminary formation where those who intend to join the diocesan and married priesthood are allowed to continue their normal gender socialization in society while undergoing academic and spiritual formation under the supervision of veteran diocesan priests or bishops. This method of clerical training also allows a specialized spiritual and psychosexual pastoral care for homosexual candidates to the priesthood.

References

Adams, Kenneth. 2011. "Clergy Sexual Abuse: A Commentary on Celibacy." *Sexual Addiction & Compulsivity: The Journal of Treatment & Prevention* 10 (2–3): 91–92. https://doi.org/10.1080/107201 6039 0230 583.

Ballano, Vivencio O. 2023. *In Defense of Married Priesthood: A Sociotheological Investigation of Catholic Clerical Celibacy*. London and New York: Routledge.

Barnes, Medora W. 2022. "Catholic Seminarians on 'Real Men', Sexuality, and Essential Male Inclusivity." *Religions* 13: 352. https://doi.org/10.3390/rel13040352.

Benedict XVI, and Seewald Peter. 2010. *Light of the World: The Pope, the Church, and the Signs of the Times*. San Francisco: Ignatius Press.

Boisvert, Donald, and Goss Robert. 2005. *Gay Catholic Priests and Clerical Sexual Misconduct: Breaking the Silence*. London: Routledge.

Boswell, John E. 1980. *Christianity, Social Tolerance, and Homosexuality: Gay People in Western Europe from the Beginning of the Christian Era to the Fourteenth Century*. Chicago: University of Chicago Press.

Brandmuller, Cardinal Walter. 2019. "*Der Spiegel* online, Cardinal Calls Outrage over Abuse in the Church Hypocrisy." [Google translation from the German], January 4, 2019. www.spiegel.de/panorama/gesellschaft/walter-brandmueller-kardinal-nennt-empoerung-ueber-missbrauch-in-der-kirche-heuchelei-a-1246364.html'.

Camargo, Robert J., and John Allan Loftus. 1992. "Child Sexual Abuse Among Troubled Clergy: A Descriptive Summary." *Paper Presented at 100th Annual Convention of the American Psychological Association*, Washington, DC., August 1992, Toronto, Canada.

Cass, Vivienne C. 1984. "Homosexual Identity Formation: Testing a Theoretical Model." *The Journal of Sex Research* 20 (2): 143–167.

Catechism of the Catholic Church. 2003. Vatican: Libreria Editrice Vaticana www.vatican.va/archive/ENG0015/_INDEX.HTM.

CDF (Congregation for the doctrine of the Faith). 1975. *Persona Humana: Declaration on Certain Questions Concerning Sexual Ethics*. Vatican: The Roman Curia. https://www.vatican.va/roman_curia/congregations/cfaith/documents/rc_con_cfaith_doc_19751229_persona-humana_en.html.

Chaves, Mark, and Garland Diana. 2009. "The Prevalence of Clergy Sexual Advances toward Adults in Their Congregations." *Journal for the Scientific Study of Religion* 48: 817–824.

Congregation for the Doctrine of the Faith. 1986. "Letter to the Bishops of the Catholic Church on the Pastoral Care of Homosexual Persons." Vatican: Roman Curia. www.vatican.va/roman_curia/congregations/cfaith/documents/rc_con_cfaith_doc_19861001_homosexual-persons_en.html.

Congregation for Catholic Education. 2005. "Instruction Concerning the Criteria for the Discernment of Vocations With Regard to Persons With Homosexual Tendencies in View of their Admission to the Seminary and to Holy Orders." *L'Osservatore Romano* (Weekly Edition in English), December 7, p. 3.

Cooperative Congregations Studies Partnership. 2010. "Faith Communities Today: 2010 National Survey of Congregants." Hartford, CT, USA. http://faithcommunitiestoday.org/sites/faithcommunitiestoday.org/files/2010FrequenciesV1.pdf.

Cozzens, Donald B. 2000. *The Changing Face of the Priesthood: A Reflection on the Priest's Crisis of Soul*. Collegeville, MN: Liturgical Press.

de Weger, Stephen Edward. 2022. "Unchaste Celibates: Clergy Sexual Misconduct Against Adults – Expressions, Definitions, and Harms." *Religions* 13 (5): 1–27. https://doi.org/10.3390/rel13050393.

Dowling, Christopher, Hayley Boxall, Kamarah Pooley, Cameron Long, and Christie Franks. 2021. "Patterns and Predictors of Reoffending Among Child Sexual Offenders: A Rapid Evidence Assessment." *Trends & Issues in Crime and Criminal Justice No.* 632. Canberra: Australian Institute of Criminology. https://doi.org/10.52922/ti78306.

Feierman, Jay. 2020. "Sexual Abuse of Young Boys in the Roman Catholic Church: An Insider Clinician Academic Perspective." In *The Abuse of Minors in the Catholic Church*, edited by Par A. Blasi et L. Oviedo, 7–47. New York, NY: Routledge.

Fernandes, Fr. Earl. 2011. "Seminary Formation and Homosexuality: Changing Sexual Morality and the Church's Response." *The Linacre Quarterly* 78 (3): 306–329. https://doi.org/10.1179/002436311803888249.

Francis, P. C., and T. D. Baldo. 1998. "Narcissistic Measure of Lutheran Clergy Who Self-Reported Committing Clergy Sexual Misconduct." *Pastoral Psychology* 47 (2): 81–96.

Friberg, Nils C., and Mark R. Laaser. 1998. *Before the Fall: Preventing Pastoral Sexual Abuse*. Collegeville: The Liturgical Press.

Frawley O'Dea, Mary Gail. 2004. "Psychosocial Anatomy of the Catholic Sexual Abuse Scandal." *Studies in Gender and Sexuality* 5 (2): 121–137. https://doi.org/10.1080/15240650509349244.

Freiburger, Dr. James. 2010. *Clergy Pedophiles: A Study of Sexually Abusive Clergy and Their Victims*. Bloomington, ID: Author House.

Garland, D. R., and C. Argueta. 2010. "How Clergy Sexual Misconduct Happens: A Qualitative Study of First-Hand Accounts." *Social Work & Christianity* 37 (1): 1–27.

Gledhill, Ruth. 2019. "Dubia cardinals condemn "Plague" of Gay Agenda." *The Tablet*, February 20, 2019. www.thetablet.co.uk/news/11395/dubia-cardinals-condemn-plagueof-gay-agenda.

Goffman, Erving. 1968. *Asylums: Essays on the Social Situation of Mental Patients and Other Inmates*. 1st ed. New York, NY: Anchor Books.

Greeley, Fr. Andrew. 1989. "Bishops Paralyzed Over Heavy Gay Priesthood." *National Catholic Reporter*, November 10, 1989.

Groeschel, B. J. 2002. *From Scandal to Hope*. Huntington, IN: Our Sunday Visitor Publishing.

John Jay College Report. 2004. *The Nature and Scope of Sexual Abuse of Minors by Catholic Priests and Deacons in the United States 1950–2002*. Washington, DC: USCCB. www.bishop-accountability.org/reports/2004_02_27_JohnJay/.

Kraschl, Dominikus. 2020. "Sexual Abuse of Minors and Clerical Homosexuality: Comments on a Puzzling Correlation." In *The Abuse of Minors in the Catholic Church: dismantling the Culture of Cover-Ups*, edited by Anthony Blasi, and Luis Oviedo. London: Routledge.

Lavictoire, Bridgette P. 2011. "Bill Donohue Blames the Victims, Gays for Catholic Sex Abuse Scandal Once Again." *Lez Get Real*, April 11, 2011. www.bishop-accountability.org/news2011/03_04/2011_04_11_Lavictoire_BillDonohue.htm.

Lothstein, Leslie M. 2004. "Men of the Flesh: The Evaluation and Treatment of Sexually Abusing Priests." *Studies in Gender and Sexuality* 5 (2): 167–195. https://doi.org/10.1080/15240650509349246.

McPhillips, Kathleen, McEwan Tracy, Death Jodi, and Richards Kelly. 2022. "Does Gender Matter? An Analysis of the Role and Contribution of Religious Socialization Practices in the Sexual Abuse of Boys and Girls in the Catholic Church." *Religion and Gender* 12: 52–57.

Mounwe, Micheal. 2021. "Homosexuality Debate and Prospects for Anglican-Catholic Ecumenical Relations." *OWIJOPPA* 5 (1): 98–114.

Pastores Dabo Vobis [I Shall Give You Shepherds]. 1992. *A Post-Synodal Apostolic Exhortation on the Formation of Priests in the Circumstances of the Present Day.* Vatican: Vatican Archives. www.vatican.va/content/john-paul-ii/en/apost_exhortations/documents/hf_jp-ii_exh_25031992_pastores-dabo-vobis.html.

Plante, Thomas G. 2002. "Celibacy and the Child Sexual Abuse Crisis. Clio's Psyche: Understanding the 'Why' of Culture." *Current Events, History, and Society* 9: 110–112.

Plante, Thomas G. 2018. "Separating Facts About Clergy Abuse from Fiction." *Illuminate*, August 30, 2018 (Santa Clara University). www.scu.edu/illuminate/thought-leaders/thomas-plante/separating-facts-about-clergy-abuse-from-fiction.html.

Pongratz-Lippitt, Christa. 2019. "Pope Surrounded by Sycophants and Church Run according to Jesuit Order"s Rules." *The Tablet*, 18 February 2019. www.thetablet.co.uk/news/11382/pope-surrounded-by-sycophants-and-church-run-according-to-jesuit-order-s-rules-says-mller-.

Robinson, T. 1994. "Shadows of the Lantern Bearers: A Study of Sexually Troubled Clergy." *Paper presented at the 23rd International Congress of Applied Psychology*, July 1994, Madrid, Spain.

Royal Commission into the Institutional Responses to Child Sexual Abuse. 2017. "Catholic Church." In *Royal Commission into the Institutional Responses to Child Sexual Abuse Final Report, Religious Institution*. Vol. 16, Book 2. Australia: Commonwealth of Australia.

Sipe, A. W. Richard. 1990. *A Secret World: Sexuality and the Search for Celibacy.* 1st ed. East Sussex, UK: Brunner-Routledge.

Sipe, A. W. Richard. 1994. "The Problem with Sexual Trauma and Addiction in the Catholic Church." *Sexual Addiction & Compulsivity* 1 (2): 130–137. https://doi.org/10.1080/10720169408400036.

Talbot, Jack. 2002. "Calling all Gay Priests." *The Gay & Lesbian Review Worldwide* 9 (4). https://link.gale.com/apps/doc/A88128690/AONE?u=anon~5f28a157&sid=googleScholar&xid=dcee8857.

Terry, Karen J., Smith Margaret Leland, Schuth Katarina, James R. Kelly, Vollman Brenda, and Massey Christina. 2011. *The Causes and Context of Sexual Abuse of Minors by Catholic Priests in the United States, 1950–2010*. Washington, DC: USCCB. www.usccb.org/sites/default/files/issues-and-action/child-and-youth-protection/upload/The-Causes-and Context-of-Sexual-Abuse-of-Minors-by-Catholic-Priests-in-the-United-States-1950–2010.pdf.

Thomas, Garland. 2005. "A Gay Speaks Out: The Vatican, Homosexuals, and Holy Orders." *Commonweal Magazine* 132 (2): 14–16.

Thoburn, John, and Whitman D. Mitchell. 2004. "Clergy Affairs: Emotional Investment, Longevity of Relationship and Affair Partners." *Pastoral Psychology* 52: 491–506.

8

CHILD CLERICAL SEXUAL ABUSE, PEDOPHILIA, AND SEMINARY FORMATION

Introduction

Pedophile Clerical Sexual Abuse in the Catholic Church

One of the most difficult types of clerical sexual abuse (CSA) in the Roman Catholic Church (RCC) to detect and prevent is child sexual abuse committed by priests against prepubescent children. Covert deviant behavior such as child clerical sexual abuse by Catholic clerics is difficult to track down, especially in religious institutions that are secretive on the sexual life of their priests such as the RCC. Sociology views deviance and rule-breaking behavior such as child clerical sexual abuse (cCSA) as social and cultural in origin rather than biological. It is not an inborn trait but a socially learned disposition that is acquired by people through the process of socialization in society.

By its very nature, child abuse scandals generally cause public hysteria, much more when committed religious ministers such as Catholic priests. However, almost all reported cases of CSA in the RCC involved pubescent boys or adolescents rather than prepubescent children. Thus, most CSA in the RCC is technically not a case of pedophilia but rather a case of ephebophilia or pederasty. The *Diagnostic and Statistical Manual of Mental Disorders* describes ephebophilia as molestation of pubescent minors or adolescents. It is committed by priests with "recurrent, intense, sexually arousing fantasies about adolescents" (Terry 2008, 561).

Those who insist that pedophilia cannot be associated with "gay" men defined pedophile as a primary and exclusive sexual attraction to prepubescent children. Although the majority of pedophiles prefer one sex or

DOI: 10.4324/9781032722474-11

the other, those, who define pedophilia in this way, view the sex of the child as irrelevant.

(Fitzgibbons and O'Leary 2011, 256)

Experts insist that what matters to a true pedophile is the age of the child not the sex. Thus, the RCC-commissioned research on CSA in the United States by the John Jay College (2004) concluded that only 96 of the 4,329 priest offenders were considered as true pedophiles.

Pedophilia involves sexual abuse of all minor children below 13 years of age. It is usually applied to abusers of all children before puberty, while ephebophilia involves abuse of adolescents (Freiburger 2010). Although cCSA by pedophile Catholic priests has generated intense public condemnation, resulting in its portrayal as the greatest scandal in the history of RCC, empirical research shows that it only constitutes the smallest percentage of the total CSA cases in the RCC (Sipe 1990; John Jay College Report 2004, Freiburger 2010).

The real pedophile priests who abuse innocent children in the RCC represent only about 20% of all sexually abusive Catholic clerics. The majority of CSA involves adolescents and adults who were abused mostly by heterosexual priests (e.g., Frawley O'Dea 2004; Cozzens 2006; Doyle 2006; Garland and Argueta 2010; de Weger 2022). Early studies by Camargo and Loftus (1992), Lothstein (1995), and Robinson (1994) also revealed that most priests who abused minors are ephebophiles, that is, people who abused adolescents or pubescent and postpubescent minors older than 13 years.

Furthermore, a study released by the Royal Commission into Institutional Responses to Child Clerical Sexual Abuse also suggested that only 7% of all Catholic priests were alleged perpetrators of child sexual abuse against preteen children (Royal Commission, Final Report 2017). The priest-therapist and popular CSA author, A. W. Richard Sipe (1990), estimated in an earlier study that only 2% of priests committed pedophiliac behavior, 4% with adolescent boys or girls, but a high 20% to 40% of heterosexual priests engaged in sexual misconduct of various kind. Thus, one wonders: Why is pedophile CSA became prominent in clergy sexual scandals in the RCC if it constitutes only the smallest percentage of the total CSA cases in the Church?

To account this magnification of pedophile CSA in the RCC, Philip Jenkins (1996) offers an interesting assessment. To him, the current drama of cCSA by Catholic pedophile priests is largely a product of social construction because of a shift in media coverage during the 1980s with the "framing" by women's movements and growing awareness of child sexual abuse. To substantiate this, Jenkins claimed that between 1960 and 1992, there were about 150,000 Catholic priests in the United States. But out of this number, only around 400 priests in the 1980s were found to have committed cCSA, representing only less than 1%, hardly sufficient to constitute CSA by pedophile

Child Clerical Sexual Abuse, Pedophilia, & Seminary Formation   **159**

priests as the greatest crisis of the RCC in contemporary times. To him, the media socially constructed cCSA in the RCC and created the image of the "pedophile priest" (Jenkins 1996).

Karen J. Terry (2008) also claimed that child sexual abuse by Catholic pedophile priests has been specifically projected out of proportions by the media since 2002 with the sensational case of Fr. John Geoghan of Boston Archdiocese who was accused, defrocked, and imprisoned for abusing more than 130 children in three decades. Although this case is hardly the typical form of CSA in the RCC, it nevertheless resulted in intense media attention and hype. Other forms of CSA were then overlooked, portraying pedophile CSA as the primary scourge of the RCC in the current age.

Understanding the Structural Causes of Pedophile cCSA

To understand the persistence of cCSA by pedophile priests in the RCC, several explanations and proposals are advanced to address this issue. They include blaming homosexuality, mandatory celibacy, lack of lay empowerment, and infidelity to Church teachings (Frawley O'Dea 2008). Historically speaking, cCSA is not a new phenomenon in the RCC. It did not begin only with the media reports of the Boston Globe in the United States in the 1980s.

"The delayed and inadequate response of the Catholic Church leaders to allegations of sexual abuse against clergy has led many to believe that this is a contemporary phenomenon or one that historically was dealt with in a similarly ineffective manner" (Dale and Alpert 2007, 61). But Rashid and Barron (2018) argued that cCSA in the RCC is structural in nature, expanding from the 1st century to 19th century. Thus, to understand the institutional roots of pedophile CSA, investigations should include the social and power structures of the RCC as creating a climate for cCSA by Catholic priests (e.g., Sipe 1990; Frawley O'Dea 2004; Doyle 2006; Keenan 2011; Ballano 2019).

The RCC is organized as a male monarchial institution. Within this structure, clerics, especially bishops, are accountable only to the Supreme Pontiff or the Pope (Kennedy 2001; Wills 2001; Cozzens 2002; Ballano 2019). To the canon lawyer Fr. Thomas Doyle, the Church's pervasive power as a self-governing institution that controls its parishioners' lives was fundamentally responsible for creating a social environment where abuse could be sustained. Child sexual abuse has been occurring in the RCC for nearly 2,000 years (Dale and Alpert 2007). Ecclesiastical pronouncements on CSA throughout RCC's history are indicators that sexual abuse by Catholic clergy is connected to the Church's social structure, especially to its weak system of monitoring and sanctioning abusive clerical behavior.

Benkert and Doyle (2009) also argue that the RCC's theological construction of celibate priests as men set apart from others with awesome spiritual powers that enable abusers to be near potential victims for centuries is

160 Major Forms of Clerical Sexual Abuse and Seminary Formation

blamed for the recurring CSA in the Church. To the Catholic hierarchy, the celibate priest is special and joined to Christ, making him completely different from ordinary men and the laity by divine action. To authors such as Sipe (1990, 2010), Wills (2000), and Scheper-Hughes and Devine (2003), the mandatory clerical celibacy is the primary enabler of CSA in the RCC, which serves as a "halo" that provides abusive priests with spiritual powers to access their potential victims. Thus, Doyle and Rubino (2004, 615) aptly argue that the persistence of CSA such as cCSA by pedophile priests in the RCC is not something isolated from the Church's social structure that greatly empowers celibate priests.

Pedophile CSA in the RCC has systemic roots that are directly connected to the Church's institutional structure as a sacerdotal church, that is, a religious institution that is totally dependent on the social functions of priests. The RCC is governed solely by ordained celibate clerics called the Catholic hierarchy led by the Pope. And Anderson (2004) specifically noted that cCSA happened periodically in the Western Church's history, especially during the 11th, 12th, 14th, and 15th centuries when the mandatory practice of clerical celibacy had just been imposed by the RCC during the late Medieval period (Ballano 2023). By imposing and supporting clerical celibacy, the RCC is creating an ecclesial environment and culture that encourage the suppression of sexuality, making priests more prone to less healthy and immature incorporation of sexuality into their daily lives such as in the case of cCSA by pedophile priests (Gorrell 2006).

Despite the growing literature that connects the mandatory clerical celibacy to cCSA, there is no emerging research that sociologically links it to the current celibate seminary formation – the training ground for celibate priests – to the persistence of child abuse in the RCC. But according to the popular CSA author and priest-therapist A. W. Richard Sipe (1990), who tried to trace the structural foundation of CSA in the RCC, the inquiry into cCSA scandals in the Church should begin with the celibate seminary clerical training.

Chapter's Research Objectives and Main Arguments

The primary objective of this chapter is to sociologically examine how the current exclusive celibate seminary training for Catholic priests facilitates, rather than prevents, pedophile CSA in the RCC. It explores how the total institution (TI) social structure of the seminary, specifically the effectivity of its method in screening pedophile candidates and programs that can detect and treat seminarians with regressive and fixated pedophile tendencies. Since pedophilia is a socially acquired behavior and difficult to treat, it is necessary to structurally investigate how the exclusive, semi-monastic, and exclusive institution of the seminary addresses it during clerical training to prevent child sexual abuse scandals in the ministry when seminarians become priests.

Child Clerical Sexual Abuse, Pedophilia, & Seminary Formation **161**

It primarily applies the sociological theories on socialization and TI as well as utilizes secondary qualitative data from published articles, books, media reports, and church documents to achieve research objectives and formulate its main argument. It is structured into four major sections. The first section provides the methodology and theoretical foundation of the chapter. The second section clarifies the nature of pedophilia in general and pedophile CSA in the RCC. The third section discusses the limitations of the current celibate seminary formation in preventing and curing individuals with pedophilia. The last section gives some recommendations on how to address pedophile CSA in seminary formation and priestly ministry.

Generally, it argues that celibacy and celibate seminary training inadvertently hide individuals with pedophile tendencies from public suspicion and detection during seminary formation and after ordination. With clerical celibacy, blending abilities of pedophiles, and seminary structural defects such as the lack of effective screening methods, programs for detection and treatment of pedophile seminarians, and experts on pedophilia, the seminary formation then becomes an incubation period that represses and heightens pedophilic tendencies of pedophile seminarians that can readily translate into serious cases of cCSA once ordained and exposed to enabling environment in the parish, largely due to loneliness and lack of effective guardians as a consequence of celibate priesthood.

Jason Berry's (1992) book *Lead Us Not Into Temptation: Catholic Priests and Sexual Abuse of Children* blames the celibate social structure of the RCC. To him, the political and theological model of mandatory celibacy is a failure that has been promoted by an ecclesiastic, pedophile-harboring power structure of the hierarchy that fears the loss of power. The mandatory practice of clerical celibacy also erodes seminary formation and gay behavior patterns in rectories and religious communities that cause CSA controversies.

Clerical celibacy can serve as a cloak that hides pedophile priests from public suspicion and detection during seminary formation and after ordination. With inadequate screening system for seminary applicants, absence of in-house experts and effective interventions against pedophilia, as well as the banning of open conversation on sexuality inside the seminary, the celibate clerical training can be a cover that represses and intensifies pedophile tendencies that can become actual cases of cCSA if pedophile seminarians get ordained and assigned in the semi-autonomous social structure of the parish.

Theoretical Foundation

Socialization Theory

Peoples' human and sexual maturity largely depends on their exposure to the type of social structure and social norms offered to them by an institution or society. Strengthening human resolve against rule-breaking behavior such as sexual abuse would depend on their social upbringing or what sociologists call the process of socialization (Guhin, Calarco, and Miller-Idriss 2021). Hoy and Woolfolk (1990, 283) define socialization as "the learning process that deals with the acquisition of the necessary orientations for satisfactory functioning in a role."

Socialization is a lifelong process that starts from birth and ends in death. Sociologists usually classify socialization into two major stages: primary and secondary. The primary socialization occurs during the early life of the person, from birth to early adolescence, which is considered the crucial formative years for his or her personality and sexuality. Secondary socialization happens during the late adolescence to adulthood where the person learns more social norms through formal education and interaction with sociocultural agents to achieve human maturity in society (Henslin 2013).

The secondary socialization of individuals, however, can be supplanted by another type of socialization called resocialization, that is, "the process of learning a different set of norms, values, attitudes, and behaviors in a separate or exclusive institution to assume a new identity" (Jenness and Gerlinger 2020). This happens when individuals enter a unique, closed, and exclusive organization called by the sociologist Erving Goffman (1968) "total institutions" (TI) such as prisons, hospitals, military barracks, and boarding schools. People under a TI are generally "cut off from the rest of society and are under almost total control of agents of the institution" (Henslin 2013, 3).

A TI environment that is isolated from the real world does not offer a natural environment for authentic human growth. With the strong behavioral control of TI's authorities, members are being forced to undergo human resocialization process that is often contrary to their personal and gender preferences (Scott 2011). To Erving Goffman, a TI always operates in accordance with established internal rules that directly and indirectly organize the sex life of its members in which sexual relations are often limited, banned, and even sanctioned (Giami 2020).

Catholic seminaries are TIs where open discussion of sexuality is prohibited. With the prohibition of the universal married priesthood and imposition of the mandatory practice of clerical celibacy in the 11th and 12th centuries, the celibate seminary training, which was institutionalized by the RCC's Council of Trent in the 16th century, became the only mode and social locus for priestly training, abandoning the long tradition of apprenticeship clerical training that allowed both celibate and married priesthood in the RCC.

Thus, the exclusive, abnormal, and all-male socialization process for clerical training that is separated from the normal socialization in society became the only option for clerical human formation and spiritual training for Catholic priests. It is, therefore, appropriate to examine how the seminary social structure deals with individuals with pedophile conditions before and during seminary formation. Although pedophilia is labeled by the WHO as a mental disorder, crime, and deviance, sociologists believe that any rule-breaking behavior such as cCSA is a social behavior learned through the process called socialization and resocialization rather than inherited as an inborn or biological trait.

The Seminary as a TI

Although not all elements of a TI conceived by Erving Goffman (1968) can be applied to Catholic seminaries, its primary components, however, can still be found in these organizations. The four elements of a TI such as "members living in the same place and under the same authority, batch living, rigid timetabling and scheduling of activities and an institutional goal of resocialization" (Scott 2010, 215) are apparent in Catholic seminaries. Furthermore, a TI's emphasis on external compliance of its members to the established rules rather than on their personal processes is also found in seminaries.

A TI as a same-sex environment in Catholic seminaries can delay the normal social and sexual development of individuals. In the RCC, new priests are usually in their mid- to late twenties. They may be considered intellectually and physically abled adults, but emotionally underdeveloped persons (Cravatts 2007, para. 5). During seminary formation, priests' emotional and sexual development is usually stunted in the exclusive and semi-monastic organization of a TI. They are powerlessness in dealing "a structured, autocratic culture of men in which they are not treated like fully developed adults" (Cravatts 2007, para. 6).

The current celibate seminary training in the RCC normally screens seminary applicants with a battery of psychological tests and interviews to choose only those who are intellectually, spiritually, and humanly fit for celibate priesthood training. However, owing to the scarcity of professional and competent counselors in Catholic seminaries, regular internal processes for seminarians' life are usually neglected (Adubale and Aluede 2017). Seminary applicants and seminarians with pedophilic orientation often evade seminary screening and detection for lack of experts in the seminary who can identify signs of pedophilia and prevent pedophile seminarians to become priests.

"Pedophilia is a significant public health problem. Despite its cost to society, little effort has been directed toward understanding idiographic differences in the development and maintenance of pedophilia. Extant literature emphasizes biological underpinnings and predictors of re-offense" (Swaminath, Simmons, and Hatwan 2023, 1). *The Diagnostic and Statistical Manual for Mental Disorders* (DSM-IV-TR) specifically characterizes sexual activity with a prepubescent child 13 years old or younger as pedophilia (Freiburger 2010).

With the complexity of pedophilia and lack of investment by the RCC to hire experts such as psychiatrists and psychologists with specialization on pedophilia, pedophile individuals are often undetected before and during seminary formation and become ordained priests. Pedophile CSA, although constituting only the smallest percentage of all CSAs in the RCC, generates the greatest public hysteria and condemnation for the Catholic hierarchy. Therefore, detecting and expelling seminarians with pedophilic tendencies is a proactive move rather than allowing these seminarians to be ordained and inflict the RCC with shameful sexual scandals that victimized innocent children.

Celibate Seminary Formation and Pedophile CSA

Authors Dale and Alpert (2007) blame celibacy as a strong factor in the cCSA. By promoting clerical celibacy in the RCC, Catholic bishops created a social environment that makes the crime of CSA against children easy and safe to commit. In the parish or ministry, priests act as spiritual parents or fathers to children. Thus, parents become confident that with priests, their children will foster good character and grow in self-confidence, moral and spiritual values, and mental health. But the RCC's secrecy in dealing with its pedophile clerics has kept parents ignorant about the actual situation of their children (Dale and Alpert 2007).

Yip (2003, 60) further views the sexual abuse in the church as a sad reminder of the ineptitude of the RCC as an institution in dealing with sexuality issues. Scheper-Hughes and Devine (2003) believe that until the RCC becomes comfortable with human sexuality and prevents an enabling climate that allows psychologically immature men to be with boys, the risk situation for cCSAn continues. "Church officials, by continuing to promote celibacy, created a place where it was safe to commit crimes on innocent children" (Dale and Alpert 2007, 67).

The promotion of mandatory practice of clerical celibacy starts in the exclusive and semi-monastic clerical seminary training in a TI social environment. With the imposition of the obligatory clerical celibacy law in the 11th and 12th centuries, the current clerical training only offers celibate formation primarily for heterosexual individuals who are ready to give up marriage for the sake of Christ. Those candidates with homosexual and pedophilic tendencies have no choice but join the celibate training in the absence of apprenticeship clerical formation that allows married priesthood and normal socialization process in society.

Richard Sipe (1990) strongly believes that there is a structural connection between the celibate seminary formation and the persistence of child abuse by Catholic clerics in the RCC. To Sipe (1994, 4), the celibacy system is "based on a false understanding of the nature of human sexuality and primary Christian experience" and that "the maintenance of this system develops, fosters, and protects sexual abuse and violence." Pedophile men would not have been ordained in the RCC and allowed to commit cCSA if the current celibate seminary formation is effective and efficient in preventing and eliminating pedophile individuals to become priests rather than allowing them to get ordained and assigned in the autonomous social structure of the parish, which lacks behavioral monitoring and intervention against pedophilia. Although constituting only the lowest percentage of all CSA cases in the RCC, cCSA inflicts the greatest harm on innocent children and to the religious image of the Church.

Thus, the RCC needs to invest more in terms of resources, training, and the hiring of competent personnel to improve the seminary screening and detection system to weed out pedophile candidates before they become priests and commit CSA to avoid sexual scandals that can tarnish the institutional image of the Church. Pedophiles are known to blend well with the social environment. They usually appear normal, educated, and heterosexual in public life. Celibacy can enhance the spiritual status of pedophile priests, which can further enhance this blending ability when applying, participating in seminary formation, or doing clerical ministry.

cCSA poses the greatest threat to the moral credibility and spiritual mission of the RCC. Although constituting only as the fewest number of all CSA cases in the RCC, it nevertheless causes grave moral, social, and spiritual harm to victims and society, as well as to the Church's institutional image that preferentially protects the poor, the weak, and the innocent. To speak of a "pedophile priest implies that the victims are younger and more defenseless than they are and that the offenders are severely compulsive and virtually incurable" (Jenkins 1996, 7).

This chapter contends that the RCC should prioritize the strengthening of the institutional apparatus of the current celibate seminary training to prevent the ordination of pedophile priests rather than allowing them to escape the seminary screening process that can result in actual cases of cCSA, higher costs of treatment for pedophile priests, explosive sexual scandals for the faithful, cover-ups by bishops, and greater injustice to victims. It primarily illustrates how the celibate seminary formation in a TI structure with the structural limitations in terms of resources, programs, and personnel freely allows pedophile individuals to join seminary formation and get ordained to the priesthood, leading to a host of serious ecclesial problems that greatly destroys the image of the RCC and diminishes the moral credibility of the Catholic hierarchy.

The Structural Limitations of the Seminary Against Pedophilia

Inadequate Seminary Screening Methods

Seminarians with pedophilic disorder can oftentimes pass the seminary screening tests. And once admitted to the seminary, they cannot just be expelled without apparent cases of child sexual abuse. Currently, Catholic seminaries generally lack professional people or experts such as psychologists, psychiatrist, and other type of social scientists who specialized in pedophilia and ephebophilia to detect people who have these tendencies while undergoing the celibate seminary training.

Pedophilia is a condition acquired by people before they enter the seminary (Greely 2004; Martin 2017; Plante 2020). Thus, stringent screening and detection methods for seminary applicants become necessary to prevent and weed out the undesirables. Pedophilia is difficult to treat once aspirants have already joined the seminary formation. Catholic seminaries lack experts to treat the complex disorder of pedophilia, which has been recognized by psychiatrists as difficult to treat. Thus, the seminary screening process is crucial to prevent the entry of clerical candidates with pedophilic tendencies.

Preventing the entry of pedophiles to the seminary and their ordination requires that seminary formators should possess some expertise on pedophila and get some assistance from experts to strictly block pedophile seminarians' entry to the priesthood.

> The ongoing clergy sexual abuse crisis in the Catholic Church has led to calls for major changes in the psychological evaluation of seminary applicants. Unfortunately, there is increasing agreement among scholars that the current, standard psychological testing is not effective in ferreting out sexual difficulties in the general population, much less in seminary candidates.
>
> *(McGlone and Sperry 2020, 262)*

Among the major shortcomings is the lack of communication between the major stakeholders: vocation, formational personnel, and psychologists and a uniformly applied, standardized battery that emphasizes "suitability" with little or no focus on the "fit" of candidates for a particular diocese or religious order . . . [It needs] realistic approaches to increase the effectiveness and predictability of such evaluations and offer an innovative plan for large-scale postdoctoral training and certification of psychologists to provide evidence-based psychological evaluations of seminary candidates.

Currently, seminaries have various psychological tests and interviews but inadequate to eliminate undesirable candidates, including pedophiles. They have their own limitations such as lack in long-term research and longitudinal studies to follow-up initial findings. Lassi et al. (2022), for instance, had made a study to provide an analytic review of psychological tests used in the admission process of candidates to the Catholic priesthood or religious life. Of all empirical studies, articles, and diagnostic tools evaluated in the study, only 0.7% of all production is represented by observational and longitudinal and correlational studies. They argued that "cross-sectional studies, meta-analyses and systematic reviews are needed to detect validated screening

Child Clerical Sexual Abuse, Pedophilia, & Seminary Formation **167**

tools and longitudinal and correlational studies to evaluate the results of educational processes over a period to correct them" (Lassi et al. 2022).

In seminary screening, interviews to identify pedophile tendencies is also difficult to achieve as all applicants declare that they are heterosexuals. Like gay and heterosexual applicants who may not have been called to celibate priesthood but married priesthood, especially if same-sex marriage is allowed in the RCC, pedophile individuals can blend well in their social environment (Freiburger 2010). The psychological examinations and interviews are ineffective to detect their attraction to children. Since pedophilia can be regressive, that is, a sexual attraction to both women and children and fixated, that is, a sexual attraction exclusively for children, screening process can even be more complicated. The regressive type can indeed appear as heterosexuals as many of them are attracted to women. In fact, some of them are married. Thus, they can appear as healthy heterosexual people when applying in the seminary.

Further, pedophile individuals are not directly affected by celibacy in seminary training, especially for fixated ones whose sexual attraction is solely for children. Celibate seminary formation can serve as a cover for their pedophilic orientation, which does pose a problem for their treatment. Given the absence of the necessary and effective interventions in seminary formation to detect and treat pedophilic seminarians, the seminary can then serve as a breeding ground or incubation that can heighten their pedophilic desires for children that can translate into cCSA when deviant opportunities occur after ordination.

The seminary formation could be a struggle for pedophile individuals as there are no apparent potential victims inside the seminary environment during the long years of training. With the stringent supervision of seminary formators that opposes any open violations to chastity and celibacy, pedophile seminarians would therefore repress their pedophilic tendencies during the seminary formation that can further deteriorate their sexual and mental health. This repression, however, will eventually "explode" into real cases of cCSA as a compensatory behavior once these seminarians are ordained and become near to children in their clerical ministries.

Given the lack of adequate behavioral surveillance in the parish against sexual abuse comparable to the strict supervision of seminarians' life inside the seminary, pedophile priests can then become dangerous predators who prey on children under their care. As Böhm et al. (2014) argue, once seminary graduates with pedophile tendencies become priests and live independent lives in the parish or ministry, their repressed sexual needs will find a way to victimize children for satisfaction. Clerical celibacy can give them awesome spiritual powers to get the confidence of parents and become near to their vulnerable children.

168 Major Forms of Clerical Sexual Abuse and Seminary Formation

Lastly, cCSA, which constitutes the smallest fraction of the total CSA cases in the RCC, could not be resolved by married priesthood but by strict screening of candidates to the priesthood in the seminary and immediate dismissal of pedophiles from seminary formation once identified and outright dismissal from clerical state once abusive priests are proven guilty.

Lack of Experts and Program for Pedophilia

In addition to inadequate seminary screening tests and interviews, as well as the lack of professionals and experts inside Catholic seminaries who can competently handle pedophilia, seminary programs to process and treat pedophilia during seminary formation are also apparently absent. Seminary formators are usually clerics who are trained in the disciplines of philosophy and theology. Only few priests are trained as professional psychologists and psychiatrists who can handle pedophilia, and they are commonly assigned in psychological clinics and treatment centers but not in seminaries.

The principles of the new Program for Priestly Formation, Sixth Edition by the United States Conference of Catholic Bishops (USCCB) recommend that:

> [t]he rector should also make provision for the availability of psychological and counseling services during the stages of formation. He ensures that those employed as counselors for seminarians are professionally licensed or certified; are well versed in and supportive of the Church's expectations of seminarians, especially concerning celibacy; and will not encourage behaviors contrary to Church teachings.
>
> *(USCCB 2022, para. 5)*

Despite this recommendation, which can probably be addressed in developed countries such as the United States, there are other hundreds of seminaries around the world that cannot afford the services of expert and licensed counselors and psychologists who can effectively deal with the sexuality problems of seminarians. Psychologists and psychiatrists may be tapped during screening process but not usually during seminary formation in a long-term basis to detect and treat seminarians with sexual issues such as pedophilic tendencies. Thus, the lack of concrete and effective interventions for pedophilic disorder inside seminary formation is a consequence of the lack of in-house experts who can effectively deal with this type of problem.

Moreover, "pedophilia is a serious chronic and lifelong psychiatric disorder, with significant comorbidity with other paraphilic disorders" (Cohen and Galynker 2002, 1). It is extremely difficult to treat, requiring intensive, long-term, and comprehensive, and possibly lifetime treatment (Cohen and Galynker 2002). Therefore, it is also doubtful if seminaries can effectively treat pedophilia during seminary formation even if they hire in-house experts to intervene given the complexity of this disorder.

The World Health Organization (WHO) classifies pedophilia as a mental or psychiatric disorder. Sex offenders have entrenched cognitive and affective deficits related to their sexual disorders (Renaud et al. 2011). With the scarcity of professional psychologists, psychiatrists, and other relevant experts who can assist seminary fathers, screening and treating seminarians with pedophilia become more complicated to deal with before they become priests.

> There is no evidence to suggest that pedophilia can be changed. Instead, interventions are designed to increase voluntary control over sexual arousal, reduce sex drive, or teach self-management skills to individuals who are motivated to avoid acting upon their sexual interests.
>
> *(Seto 2009, 391)*

Treatment for pedophilia is not currently available in Catholic seminaries. Pedophile CSA remains the most complex and difficult type of CSA in the RCC, resulting in the misconception that homosexuality has something to do with it, thus blaming homosexual priests as the primary cause of CSAs in the Church.

Pedophilia is also "a disorder of public concern because of its association with child sexual offense and recidivism" (Scarpazza 2023, 1). "In order to treat individuals with pedophilia who are at risk of committing offenses, disclosure of the attraction must first take place" (Jimenez-Arista and Reid 2023, 214). But this seems impossible for seminary applicants and seminarians to reveal their pedophilia without being rejected or expelled from the seminary. Furthermore, some seminarians who may not be aware that they have this pedophilic orientation will probably deny having pedophilia to formators, specifically regressive ones who are also attracted to women.

Regressed and Fixated Pedophiles

What further complicates the process of identifying individuals with pedophilic tendencies in seminary screening process due to a lack of competent experts is that pedophilia is generally classified into two types: the regressed and fixated. Freiburger (2010) contends that pedophiles can be either regressed or fixated. The regressed pedophiles are often described as individuals who usually have sex with adults of the opposite sex but may engage in sexual relations with children if they feel emotionally rejected or extremely stressed by their age-appropriate partners. That is why some regressive pedophiles are married. In this case, regressed seminarians with this tendency can assert as heterosexuals with normal attraction to women when applying in the seminary.

Fixated pedophiles, on the other hand, are pedophiles whose sexual drives are directed solely towards children. "They are usually seen as much more dangerous because they are more likely to become chronic sexual predators, aggressively manipulating children into their sexual lives" (Freiburger 2010, 15). But this is not apparent during seminary screening and training without experts who can identify this problem. Thus, the celibate seminary training can only repress this dangerous drive instead of arresting it, which can be translated into actual cCSA cases once ordained and exposed to deviant opportunity structures that allow them to be with children in their ministry without effective guardians.

In a published book entitled *Pedophilia, Hebephilia and Sexual Offending against Children: The Berlin Dissexuality Therapy (BEDIT)*, Klaus Beier (2021) also claims that pedophilia can be latent and repressed. Those with sexual interest with prepubescent minors or children do not inevitably lead to offenses against children. Some can keep their desires in their fantasies and do not act them out on the behavioral level until the right opportunity comes. Thus, it is highly probable that fixated pedophile seminarians only repressed their sexual desires for children inside the highly regulated seminary formation but can become highly dangerous predator priests when ordained who can molest innocent children under their pastoral care in the parish or ministry.

Blending Abilities of Pedophiles

The blending abilities of pedophiles who enter the seminary also pose a serious problem to seminary formators, who are not usually trained in dealing with pedophilia. Pedophiles are individuals who can usually blend well with their social environment. They can appear as educated and respectable people (Freiburger 2010). In a celibate priesthood, they can blend well in a community of celibate heterosexual and homosexual priests. The ability to appear normal in personality, attitude, and appearance as heterosexuals is what makes pedophiles difficult to identify during seminary screening process and formation. In seminary entrance tests and interviews, for instance, pedophile applicants can claim as healthy heterosexuals unless proven otherwise by experts.

The current exclusive seminary training that suspends the adult socialization of seminarians can greatly deprive aspirants with latent pedophile tendencies to develop their personality and overcome these tendencies in normal social settings. John Jay College (2004) investigation revealed that the 474 priest offenders who were classified as pedophiles and ephebophiles do not constitute the majority for all the sexual offenders against adolescent boys in the RCC. "Many gay men who have sex with other adult men are also attracted to adolescent boys, just as there are many adult men who have sexual relations with adult women and are also attracted to post-pubescent girls" (Fitzgibbons and O'Leary 2011, 256). However, gay and pedophile priests only constitute a small percentage of the total CSA cases in the RCC. But pedophile priests are highly dangerous pastors, especially the fixated ones, when assigned with children in the parish and ministry without effective guardians.

In sum, the exclusive and all-male seminary formation with no special programs and interventions as well as experts on pedophilia can then serve as an "incubator" that represses and intensifies pedophilic drives, which can be ready "to erupt" into covert child sexual abuse after ordination. Since seminarians are generally cloistered in semi-monastic environment with strong behavioral surveillance by seminary formators, pedophilic tendencies can intensify without the normal socialization in society and effective treatment.

Pedophilia in Catholic seminaries whether regressed or fixated can remain unaddressed in the current clerical formation system with the lack of effective screening protocols, in-house experts, and programs before and during seminary formation. To take a proactive stance to detect and eliminate pedophile individuals before they are ordained is a better move for the Catholic hierarchy and seminary formators than allowing pedophiles to be ordained and to commit child sexual abuse scandals that can greatly tarnish the moral credibility of the RCC and destroy the lives of innocent children. cCSA in the RCC necessitates investing in improving screening protocols and hiring the best experts in pedophilia to detect and eliminate pedophile individuals during clerical training, disallowing them to join the ranks of good and spiritual priests in the RCC.

Implication of Seminary Flaws to Clerical Ministry Against cCSA

Occurrence of cCSA Before Discovery and Diocesan Response

The transition from celibate seminary structure to clerical ministry is always problematic for Catholic priests, especially for those without the rare gift of clerical celibacy and with repressed sexuality during clerical training. The structural flaws in seminary formation are further magnified in clerical ministry once the newly ordained priests are assigned in the parish without effective guardians against CSA. In a study published in a book entitled *The First Five Years of the Priesthood: A Study of Newly Ordained Catholic Priests* by Dean Hoge (2002), the first five years in the priesthood was portrayed as a difficult transition period for new celibate priests who needed to adjust to the lonely life of the parish, specifically to difficulties in adjusting to fellow older priests in the parish. They were also disposed to live parallel lives with their bishops, who appear as distant figures.

If the seminary with its strict surveillance by formators can allow pedophile seminarians to escape the drag net and get ordained, how much more if they become priests and assigned to the semi-autonomous social structure of the parish with the lack of powerful supervisors against pedophilia. They can covertly commit cCSA with the weak social bonding with fellow priests and their bishops in dioceses. A strong social bond with fellow priests can actually deter sexual deviance. If pedophiles with their blending abilities can escape the detection system of the seminary, they can easily do so in the semi-autonomous parish structure with no strict behavioral surveillance, lay empowerment to regulate clerical behavior, and absence of experts and programs for pedophilia.

Detecting and defrocking pedophile priests are complex and difficult processes to achieve before actual cases of cCSA are committed, given the weak monitoring system that is actively participated by the laity in parishes and dioceses. Thus, sexually abusive pedophile priests can continue their molestation without early detection and effective ecclesial intervention and sanction. As Karen Terry (2008, 567) claims:

> [T]he average priest with an allegation of abuse waits 11 years before the first known abuse occurs. Analysis of the duration of abusive behavior showed great variation in combinations of length in years and number of victims; some abused many victims for a short period of time, whereas others abused few victims for a long period of time. That said, generally, the more victims abused by a priest, then the longer his abusive career.

The parish is generally designed to provide spiritual services and sacraments to the faithful. It has no program and professional personnel who can deal with pedophile priests in the ministry before they commit child abuse. In the absence of effective lay empowerment in the RCC, lay people in the parish are generally helpless to formally investigate and sanction pedophile priests to avoid cover-ups by bishops who are normally sympathetic to their clergy. With the present ecclesial set-up, it is usually the bishop who has the plenary ecclesial power in the diocese who can directly investigate and sanction his pedophile priests, although victims and their relatives can go to civil courts to seek justice.

Without formal governance powers, the laity is passive in proactively preventing cCSA to occur in the RCC. Only the local bishop, who possesses monarchial powers in his diocese (Doyle 2006), has the discretion whether to elevate the cCSA case to Rome for further investigation or just send his pedophile priests to treatment centers and/or assign them to other parishes or temporarily transfer or incardinate them to distant dioceses abroad. Thus, bishops with this discretionary power are usually blamed by the media and the public for covering up cCSA cases and sending sexually abusive priests, such as pedophiles to treatment centers as a response to CSA. As Terry (2008, 567) contends:

> Treatment for abusive priests was a more common response. Nearly 40% of the priests with allegations of abuse received treatment, and some

Child Clerical Sexual Abuse, Pedophilia, & Seminary Formation **173**

received multiple types of treatment. Records show that 1,627 priests received some type of treatment and that there were 3,041 instances of treatment. Priests with more than one allegation of abuse were more likely to participate in treatment, despite the severity of the offense(s) committed. Types of treatment varied, and the most common forms were psychotherapy, specialized treatment for clergy sex offenders, general treatment, specialized program for sex offenders, evaluation without treatment, relapse prevention, and spiritual counseling.

(Terry 2008, 563–564)

Weak Detection System for cCSA in the Parish and Cover-Ups

Since Catholic pedophile priests commonly commit child abuse before they are discovered and dealt with by their Catholic bishops, it implies that the parish and diocese, just like seminaries, have no specialized system for the early detection and prevention of pedophilia before innocent children are abused: "Church response to the abuse varied, and one major difficulty in evaluating the response was the length of time from abusive incident to the time of reporting" (Terry 2008, 563). Victims usually are afraid to report cCSA to their parents and authorities because of the grooming and pressure by their abusers.

The common social pattern for pedophile CSA in the RCC is that cCSA would first be committed before it is discovered by the public and the media. This implies that the RCC in the diocesan level has no effective system to identify pedophile priests and immediately defrock them and allow criminal prosecution in civil courts to prosper to seek justice for innocent victims. Seeing CSA as an internal church matter, bishops usually hide cCSA to avoid scandals in the Church. Because of priest shortage, sympathy to their fellow priests, and other informal normative standards (Ballano 2016), they also tend to just send their abusive priests to treatment facility and/or transfer them to other assignments in the diocese or locations abroad beyond the jurisdiction of secular courts.

Kevin Lewis O' Neil (2020, 745), for instance, claims that

throughout the second half of the twentieth century, Latin America became something of a dumping ground for U.S. priests suspected of sexual abuse, with north-to-south clerical transfers sending predatory priests to countries where pedophilia did not exist in any kind of ontological sense.

Thus, the receiving dioceses that normally have no prior information of the background of the arriving pedophile priests would later encounter similar problems of cCSA in their jurisdictions, thus continuing the institutional culture of child sexual abuse and cover-up in the RCC: "Catholic priests who sexually abused minors were transferred to other parishes without disclosing the actual reason for their transfer" (Armbruster 2022, 61). Thus, Jodi Death (2015, 96)

174 Major Forms of Clerical Sexual Abuse and Seminary Formation

aptly describes the RCC's response to CSA and recommends exploring the RCC's institutional culture to understand and prevent cover-up of CSA in the RCC:

> One area explored in international inquiries is the role of institutional culture and the occurrence of cover-up of CSA by clergy by Catholic officials. This has resulted in criticism of Catholic institutions for covering up CSA by clergy through extreme levels of secrecy; the movement of perpetrators from parish to parish, or school to school; silencing victims through legal clauses in settlements; poor record keeping practices; failing to cooperate with Police investigations; dissuading victims from going to Police with complaints; ignoring and disbelieving victims and privileging the word of Clergy denying the abuse; and the vehement and costly defense of clergy accused of abuse through both civil and criminal cases.

Truly, cover-up of CSA cases, especially pedophile priests abusing children, could have been prevented to avoid public scandals and public shaming of Church officials for their cover-ups and silencing of victims if the seminary formation is effective in weeding out early individuals with pedophilia. If there is also a proactive action by Church authorities to immediately dismiss seminarians and priests with this serious malady and mental disorder. Thus, the RCC needs to invest more in providing the seminary the necessary resources and funds for effective screening protocols against applicants with pedophilic tendencies, specialized training on pedophilia for seminary fathers, as well as hiring experts and professionals to craft interventions to detect early cases of pedophilia inside the seminary, and empowering qualified laity to participate in monitoring clerical behavior in the parish to detect and initiate formal investigation in the RCC against cCSA.

The proactive move of early detection and expulsion of seminary candidates with this mental disorder is necessary to prevent the ordination of pedophiles and cCSA in the RCC; thus, sparing the RCC from public condemnation and accusation of cover-up of CSA cases. Discovering of pedophile tendencies early can have more chances to eliminate pedophilia before and during seminary formation with its TI structure and panoptic behavioral monitoring compared to the autonomous and functional parish, which has no organized authority and direct social control to supervise clerical behavior to prevent pedophile CSA.

Conclusion and Recommendation

This chapter has shown that the celibate seminary formation has structural flaws in terms of adequate testing and detection system as well as expertise and personnel to deal with candidates with pedophilic tendencies before and during seminary training to prevent pedophile seminarians to become priests.

Applicants and seminarians with pedophilia can blend well with their environment, repress their attraction to children, as well as hide under the cloak of clerical celibacy to avoid public suspicion and detection of their mental disorder that is highly dangerous for innocent children in the parish.

What makes pedophilia further difficult to detect is that all seminary applicants usually declare themselves as heterosexual. Those with regressive pedophilia, who are also attracted to women and who may not be personally aware that they have this condition during seminary formation, can appear as sexually normal and healthy individuals. Pedophilia also has no immediate cure for pedophilia. Psychologists and psychiatrists generally view pedophilia as a serious mental condition that requires a lifetime treatment. With the lack of experts and active and effective professional intervention during clerical formation, the exclusive seminary training will only become an incubation for Catholic pedophile priests who are sexually repressed and thus more likely to commit cCSA as compensatory behavior when the right opportunity comes during clerical ministry.

To strengthen the ecclesial drive against pedophile CSA, the RCC needs to invest more in terms of resources, specialized training on pedophilia for seminary fathers, and hiring of in-house experts for seminary screening and formation to detect and weed out pedophiles. Moreover, the RCC should consider an alternative seminary training by reinstating the apprenticeship type of clerical training that allows married priesthood and immersion in the social world for seminary formators to realistically detect pedophilia. Candidates with pedophile tendencies will have more chances to be discovered and dismissed from priestly formation early if tempted to commit child abuse rather than being exclusively housed in seminary formation.

A proactive move by Catholic bishops that can prevent more child abuses, sexual scandals, and accusations of cover-up CSA if pedophiles are expelled during seminary formation. It is also more costly and damaging to the RCC if pedophiles are ordained rather than being discovered and dismissed early before ordination. Lastly, lay leaders with expertise on child sexual abuse and pedophilia should also be included in a committee in the parish or diocese that monitors and investigates cCSA with real ecclesial powers to vote and to represent the hierarchy in civil cases and ecclesial cases that should reach up to Rome.

References

Adubale, Andrew A., and Oyaziwo Aluede. 2017. "A Survey of Counselling Needs of Seminarians in Catholic Major Seminaries in Nigeria." *Asia Pacific Journal of Counselling and Psychotherapy* 8 (1): 29–40. https://doi.org/10.1080/21507686. 2016.1260610.

Anderson, Colt. 2004. "When Magisterium Becomes Imperium." *The Journal of Theological Studies* 65 (4): 741–766. https://doi.org/10.1177/004056390406500403.

Armbruster, Andre. 2022. "On the Undisclosed Transfer of Abusive Catholic Priests: A Field Theoretical Analysis of the Sexual Repression Within the Catholic Church and the Use of Legitimate Language." *Critical Research on Religion* 10 (1): 61–77. https://doi.org/10.1177/20503032211015282.

Ballano, Vivencio O. 2016. "Enforcing the Canon Law: Normative Pluralism and Clerical Abuse in the Catholic Church." *Mabini Review* 5: 28–43.

Ballano, Vivencio O. 2019. *Clerical Sexual Abuse in Catholic Hierarchy: A Sociological Exploratory Study on Social Disorganization*. Singapore: Springer Nature.

Ballano, Vivencio O. 2023. *In Defense of Married Priesthood: A Sociotheological Investigation of Catholic Clerical Celibacy*. London: Routledge.

Beier, Klaus M. 2021. *Pedophilia, Hebephilia and Sexual Offending against Children: The Berlin Dissexuality Therapy (BEDIT)*. Cham: Springer.

Benkert, Marianne, and Thomas P. Doyle. 2009. "Clericalism, Religious Duress, and Its Psychological Impact on Victims of Clergy Sexual Abuse." *Pastoral Psychology* 58: 223–238. https://doi.org/10.1007/s11089-008-0188-0.

Berry, Jason. 1992. *Lead Us Not Into Temptation: Catholic Priests and Sexual Abuse of Children*. New York: Image Books.

Böhm, Bettina, Hans Zollner, Jörg M. Fegert, and Hubert Liebhardt. 2014. "Child Sexual Abuse in the Context of the Roman Catholic Church: A Review of Literature from 1981–2013." *Journal of Child Sexual Abuse* 23 (6): 635–656. https://doi.org/10.1080/10538712.2014.929607.

Camargo, Robert J., and John Allan Loftus. 1992. "Child Sexual Abuse Among Troubled Clergy: A Descriptive Summary." *Paper Presented at 100th Annual Convention of the American Psychological Association*, Washington, DC., August 1992, Toronto, Canada.

Cohen, Lisa J., and Igor I. Galynker. 2002. "Clinical Features of Pedophilia and Implications for Treatment." *Journal of Psychiatric Practice* 8 (5): 1–14.

Cozzens, Donald. 2002. *Sacred Silence: Denial and the Crisis in the Church*. Collegeville, MN: Liturgical Press.

Cozzens, Donald. 2006. *Freeing Celibacy*. Collegeville, MN: Liturgical Press.

Cravatts, Richard. 2007. "L.A. Sex Abuse Settlement Leaves Troubling Questions Unanswered." *The State Journal-Register*, July 25, 2007. www.sj-r.com/story/news/2007/07/25/l-sex-abuse-settlement-leaves/47782055007/.

Dale, Kathryn A., and Judith L. Alpert. 2007. "Hiding Behind the Cloth: Child Sexual Abuse and the Catholic Church." *Journal of Child Sexual Abuse* 16 (3): 59–74. https://doi.org/10.1300/J070v16n03_04.

Death, Jodi. 2015. "Bad Apples, Bad Barrel: Exploring Institutional Responses to Child Sexual Abuse by Catholic Clergy in Australia." *International Journal for Crime, Justice and Social Democracy* 4 (2): 94–110.

de Weger, Stephen Edward. 2022. "Unchaste Celibates: Clergy Sexual Misconduct Against Adults – Expressions, Definitions, and Harms" *Religions* 13 (5): 1–27. https://doi.org/10.3390/rel13050393.

Doyle, Thomas P. 2006. "Clericalism: Enabler of Clergy Sexual Abuse." *Pastoral Psychology* 54 (3): 189–213. https://doi.org/10.1007/s11089-006-6323-x.

Doyle, Thomas P., and Stephen C. Rubino. 2004. "Catholic Clergy Sexual Abuse Meets the Civil Law." *Fordham Urban Law Journal* 31: 549–615. https://ir.lawnet.fordham.edu/ulj/vol31/iss2/6.

Fitzgibbons, Richard M. D., and Dale O'Leary. 2011. "Sexual Abuse of Minors by Catholic Clergy." *The Linacre Quarterly* 78 (3): 252–273.

Frawley O'Dea, Mary Gail. 2004. "Psychosocial Anatomy of the Catholic Sexual Abuse Scandal." *Studies in Gender and Sexuality* 5 (2): 121–137. https://doi.org/10.1080/15240650509349244.

Frawley O'Dea, Mary Gail. 2008. "Perversion of Power: Sexual Abuse in the Catholic Church." *Journal of Psychological Trauma* 7 (3): 206–211. https://doi.org/10.1080/19322880802266854.

Freiburger, Dr. James. 2010. *Clergy Pedophiles: A Study of Sexually Abusive Clergy and their Victims*. Bloomington, ID: Author House.

Garland, Diana R. and Christen Argueta. 2010. "How Clergy Sexual Misconduct Happens: A Qualitative Study of First-Hand Accounts." *Social Work & Christianity* 37 (1): 1–27.

Giami, Alain. 2020. "Institutions' Approach to Sexuality, A Necessity Between Care and Sexual Rights." *Soins. Psychiatrie* 41 (330): 12–16. https://doi.org/10.1016/s0241-6972(20)30100-6. PMID: 33353601.

Goffman, Erving. 1968. *Asylums: Essays on the Social Situation of Mental Patients and Other Inmates*. 1st ed. New York, NY: Anchor Books.

Gorrell, Paul. 2006. "The Roman Catholic Pedophilia Crisis and the Call to Erotic Conversion." *Theology & Sexuality* 12 (3): 251–262. https://doi.org/10.1177/1355835806065380.

Greely, Andrew. 2004. *Priests: A Calling in Crisis*. Chicago: University of Chicago Press.

Guhin, Jeffrey, Jessica McCrory Calarco, and Cynthia Miller-Idriss. 2021. "Whatever Happened to Socialization?" *Annual Review of Sociology* 47 (1): 109–129. https://doi.org/10.1146/annurev-soc-090320103012.

Henslin, James. 2013. "Chapter 3: Socialization." In *Instructor's Manual, Essentials of Sociology*. London: Pearson.

Hoge, Dean R. 2002. *The First Five Years of the Priesthood: A Study of Newly Ordained Catholic Priests*. Collegeville, MN: Liturgical Press.

Hoy, Wayne K., and Anita E. Woolfolk. 1990. "Socialization of Student Teachers." *American Educational Research Journal* 27 (2): 279–300. https://doi.org/10.3102/00028312027002279.

Jenkins, Philip. 1996. *Pedophiles and Priests: Anatomy of a Contemporary Crisis*. Bridgewater, NJ: Replica Books.

Jenness, Valerie, and Julie Gerlinger. 2020. "The Feminization of Transgender Women in Prisons for Men: How Prison as a Total Institution Shapes Gender." *Journal of Contemporary Criminal Justice* 36 (2): 182–205. https://doi.org/10.1177/1043986219894422.

Jimenez-Arista, Laura E., and Duncan B. Reid. 2023. "Realization, Self-View, and Disclosure of Pedophilia: A Content Analysis of Online Posts." *Sexual Abuse* 35 (2): 214–240. https://doi.org/10.1177/10790632221099256.

John Jay College Report. 2004. "The Nature and Scope of Sexual Abuse of Minors by Catholic Priests and Deacons in the United States 1950–2002." *USCCB*. www.bishop-accountability.org/reports/2004_02_27_JohnJay/

Keenan, Marie. 2011. *Child Sexual Abuse and the Catholic Church: Gender, Power, and Organizational Culture*. 1st ed. London and New York: Oxford University Press.

Kennedy, Eugene. 2001. *The Unhealed Wound*. New York: St. Martin's Griffin.

Lassi, Steffano, Lisa Asta, Amedeo Cencini, Ernesto Caffo, and Hans Zollner. 2022. "Reviewing the Use of Psychological Assessment Tools in the Screening and Admission Process of Candidates to the Catholic Priesthood or Religious Life." *Spirituality in Clinical Practice* (Advance online publication). https://doi.org/10.1037/scp0000305.

Lothstein, L. M. 1995. *Treating Clergy Who Sexually Abuse Minors: A 16-Year Experience in the Professionals and Clergy Program at the IOL*. https://static1.squarespace.com/static/57c231996b8f5bf91e0c091e/t/58542f72e6f2e1c538f276b8/1481912178735/treating+clergy+who+sexually+abuse+minors.pdf.

Martin, James, S. J. 2017. "It's Not About Celibacy: Blaming the Wrong Thing for Sexual Abuse in the Church." *America: The Jesuit Review*, December 15, 2017. https://www.americamagazine.org/politics-society/2017/12/15/its-not-about-celibacy-blaming-wrong-thing-sexual-abuse-church.

McGlone, Gerard, and Len Sperry. 2020. "Psychological Evaluation of Catholic Seminary Candidates: Strengths, Shortcomings, and an Innovative plan." *Spirituality in Clinical Practice* 7 (4): 262–277. https://doi.org/10.1037/scp0000240.

O' Neill, Kevin Lewis. 2020. "The Unmasking of a Pedophilic Priest: Transnational Clerical Sexual Abuse in Guatemala." *Comparative Studies in Society and History* 62 (4): 745–769. https://doi.org/10.1017/S0010417520000274.

Plante, Thomas G. 2020. "Clergy Sexual Abuse in the Roman Catholic Church: Dispelling Eleven Myths and Separating Facts from Fiction." *Spirituality in Clinical Practice* 7 (4): 220–229. https://doi.org/10.1037/scp0000209.

Rashid, Faisal, and Ian Ian Barron. 2018. "The Roman Catholic Church: A Centuries Old History of Awareness of Clerical Child Sexual Abuse (from the First to the 19th Century)." *Journal of Child Sexual Abuse* 27 (7): 778–792. https://doi.org/10.1080/10538712.2018.1491916.

Renaud, Patrice, Christian Joyal, Serge Stoleru, Mathieu Goyette, Nikolaus Weiskopf, and Niels Birbaumer. 2011. "Real-Time Functional Magnetic Imaging – Brain-computer Interface and Virtual Reality: Promising Tools for the Treatment of Pedophilia." *Progress in Brain Research* 192: 263–272. https://doi.org/10.1016/B978-0-444-53355-5.00014-2.

Robinson, T. 1994. "Shadows of the Lantern Bearers: A Study of Sexually Troubled Clergy". *Paper presented at the 23rd International Congress of Applied Psychology*, July 1994, Madrid.

Rosetti, Stephen. 2002. "Five Misconceptions on Abuse Child Sexual Abuse and the Catholic Church." *America: The Jesuit Review*, April 22, 2002. www.americamagazine.org/politics-society/2002/04/22/fivemisconceptions-about-child-sexual-abuse-and-catholic-church.

Royal Commission into Institutional Responses to Child Clerical Sexual Abuse. 2017. "Final Report." https://www.childabuseroyalcommission.gov.au/final-report.

Scarpazza, C., C. Costa, U. Battaglia, C. Berryessa, M. L. Bianchetti, I. Caggiu, O. Devinsky, S. Ferracuti, F. Focquaert, A. Forgione, F. Gilbert, A. Pennati, P. Pietrini, I. Rainero, G. Sartori, R. Swerdlow, and A. S. Camperio Ciani. 2023. "Acquired Pedophilia: International Delphi-Method-Based Consensus Guidelines." *Translational Psychiatry* 13: 11. https://doi.org/10.1038/s41398-023-02314-8.

Scheper-Hughes, Nancy, and John Devine. 2003. "Priestly Celibacy and Child Sexual Abuse." *Sexualities* 6 (1): 15–40. https://doi.org/10.1177/1363460703006001003.

Scott, Susie. 2010. "Revisiting the Total Institution: Performative Regulation in the Reinventive Institution." *Sociology* 44 (2): 213–231. https://doi.org/10.1177/0038038509357198.

Scott, Susie. 2011. *Total Institutions and Reinvented Identities*. London: Palgrave McMillian.

Seto, Michael. 2009. "Pedophilia." *Annual Review of Clinical Psychology* 5 (1): 391–407.

Sipe, A. W. Richard. 1990. *A Secret World: Sexuality and the Search for Celibacy*. 1st ed. East Sussex: Brunner-Routledge.

Sipe, A. W. Richard. 1994. "The Problem of Sexual Trauma and Addiction in the Catholic Church." *Sexual Addiction and Compulsivity* 1: 130–137.

Sipe, A. W. Richard. 2010. "Beneath the Child Abuse Scandal." *National Catholic Reporter*, July 22, 2010. https://www.ncronline.org/news/accountability/beneath-child-abuse-scandal.

Swaminath, Surabhi, Raluca M. Simons, and Mason L. Hatwan. 2023. "Understanding Pedophilia: A Theoretical Framework on the Development of Sexual Penchants." *Journal of Child Sexual Abuse*: 1–17. https://doi.org/10.1080/1053871 2.2023.2236602.

Terry, Karen J. 2008. "Stained Glass: The Nature and Scope of Child Sexual Abuse in the Catholic Church." *Criminal Justice and Behavior* 35: 549–569.

USCCB (United States Conference of Catholic Bishops). 2022. "Principles of the New PPF Bulletin: Psychology in Admission & Formation, Volume 17." In *Program for Priestly Formation*, edited by USCCB. Washinton, DC: USCCB.

Wills, Gary. 2000. *Papal Sin: Structures of Deceit*. New York: Doubleday.

Wills, Gary. 2001. *Papal Sin: Structures of Deceit*. New York: Image.

Yip, Andrew K. T. 2003. "Sexuality and the Church." *Sexualities* 6 (1): 60–64. https://doi.org/10.1177/1363460703006001007.

PART IV

Alternative Clerical Training and Apprenticeship

9

EXPLORING ALTERNATIVE CLERICAL TRAINING AND MARRIED PRIESTHOOD IN CURRENT AGE

Introduction

The Roman Catholic Church (RCC) documents on clerical formation often stress the importance of authentic human formation vis-à-vis spiritual, academic, and pastoral training for new priests: Pope Paul VI (1965) contends, "Therefore, by a wisely planned training there is also to be developed in the students a due human maturity" (para. 11). Despite this papal goal of developing the human maturity of new priests, the current exclusive seminary formation inadvertently produces immature priests who would become vulnerable to clerical sexual abuse (CSA) once ordained and exposed to deviant opportunities in the parish.

The current clerical training that still retains that the exclusive, all-male, and semi-monastic seminary institution that is generally separated from the real world seems problematic to the psychosexual maturity of seminarians. However, Vatican II's document *Optatam Totius* [Decree on Priestly Training] still reaffirmed the importance of the exclusive seminary institution established by the Council of Trent in the 16th century as a community of young men. It states that, "Under the rector's leadership they are to form a very closely knit community both in spirit and in activity and they are to constitute among themselves and with the students that kind of family that will answer to the Lord's prayer" (Pope Paul VI 1965, para. 5).

Originally, clerical training in the RCC since the time of Christ is generally by apprenticeship wherein candidates lived their normal social life while undergoing spiritual and academic formation under a veteran priest or bishop in their diocese. But this structure was changed when the Council of Trent established the seminary as an exclusive institution for priestly training to

DOI: 10.4324/9781032722474-13

protect "endangered youth" or young seminarians from the temptations of the city, removing them from the world in order to fortify and strengthen their priestly vocation (Schuth 2016). Although experiments on seminary formation are currently explored in some dioceses after Vatican II to make clerical formation more attuned to the current age, the basic social structure of an all-male and communal social organization under the strict supervision of seminary fathers is still generally visible in these innovations.

In the light of the growing clerical sexual abuse (CSA) in the RCC and scientific studies that showed that most sexual offenders in the Church are immature heterosexual priests who abuse children, adolescents, and adults, regardless of age and gender, some scholars began to investigate the structural contribution of the present celibate seminary formation, which is organized in what Erving Goffman (1968) calls "total institution" (TI), to the persistence of CSA in the RCC (e.g., Sipe 1990, 2003; Frawley O'Dea 2004; Keenan 2015; Ballano 2023). Catholic seminaries that developed through the years kept their basic TI structure that suspends the normal adult socialization of priestly candidates in the real world and emphasizes the spiritual formation of seminarians: "Even when more attention was gradually paid to instruction, the spiritual aspect was still stressed, and the professors were all spiritual directors" (Fagan 1965, 269).

Structurally, the present "seminary was meant to train people to the life of prayer and to help them acquire virtues like regularity, dignity, and a sense of obedience" (Fagan 1965, 270). However, this seminary focus on spirituality often results in the neglect of human and sexuality development by basically housing seminarians in an exclusive institution that disallows open discussion on sexuality issues and social interaction with women. Thus, the current celibate seminary system as a TI (Goffman 1968) that isolates heterosexual seminarians from their normal adult socialization with women in society can largely contribute to their psychosexual immaturity, making them weak in behavioral control on sexual matters.

The Catholic celibate seminary training aims to inculcate into the minds of seminarians the social construct of the perfect male clerical masculinity that is overly idealistic that can also contribute to psychosexual immaturity. As criminologist and expert on CSA Marie Keenan (2015, 67) aptly observes:

> Within such a construct, the individual sees himself as a priest first and only secondly as a man. According to this perfect clerical template, clerical masculinity is based on purity and chastity. Celibacy is seen as a gift from God, available to all if one prays sufficiently. Sex and sexual expression are seen as a set of "acts," and sexual sins are based on lists of rules and regulations regarding these sex "acts." Sexual desire and emotional intimacy are seen as less relevant for priests, . . . Women and girls are seen as a threat to the celibate commitment.

Male heterosexual seminarians maybe well prepared academically, spiritually, and pastorally, but emotionally and sexually underdeveloped and unprepared to deal with their own emotional distress and sexual problems during formation and after ordination when assigned in the parish. Furthermore, this psychosexual immaturity of Catholic priests is also facilitated by the RCC's clerical culture of nondisclosure of emotion or emotional distress and prohibition of casual and overt talks on emotional problems and sexuality (Cozzens et al. 2004) that is being pursued in seminary training. Consequently, as seminary graduates, "priests do not and cannot talk about sex, sexual fantasies, or desires. Sexuality is censored and tabooed" (Armbruster 2021, 67).

Keeping seminarians in an abnormal social environment of the seminary with a prohibition on women and open talks regarding sexuality can indeed result in psychosexual immaturity (Frawley O'Dea 2004). CSA studies point to immature male heterosexual priests, especially diocesan clerics, who are trained by the current exclusive and celibate seminary training as the primary cohort of sexual abusers in the RCC, regardless of gender and age. The present celibate seminary social structure thus trains seminarians to be humanly immature and weak to deal with sexuality and emotional distress before they are ordained and assigned as diocesan priests, which is an enabler of CSA in the RCC.

Specifically, the perfect model of male celibate masculinity pursued by the RCC in seminary training does suit well with human experience when seminarians become priests. Keenan (2015, 68) notes the negative unintended consequences of the problematic celibate clerical masculinity the RCC wants to realize among its priests:

> In terms of lifestyle and environment, the men who embodied a model of Perfect Celibate Clerical Masculinity avoided and effectively denied their sexuality and sexual desire. They tried to become "holy and detached" and "sexless." They avoided relationships with women and friendships with men. They had few close friendships within the clergy and no close adult friendships outside of clerical life. They felt lonely and unfulfilled.
>
> *(Keenan 2015, 68)*

Keenan's research with priests in Ireland affirmed this when she discovered that clerics who became abuse perpetrators were formed by their seminary training and experiences that aimed "to embody a Perfect Clerical Celibate Masculine identity, losing their personal selves and integrity in the process" (Keenan 2015, 69). RCC's insistence of the current celibate and exclusive seminary training, thus, structurally contributes to the formation of immature priests who are prone to commit CSA. To address the psychosexual immaturity of diocesan clerics who are found to be the number one type of sexual offenders in the RCC (John Jay College Report 2004), the Catholic hierarchy and seminary formators should explore alternative clerical training that does not suspend the normal adult socialization of priestly candidates to minimize clerical immaturity and prevent CSA.

The Catholic seminary as the breeding ground for priests, which is the first line of defense of the RCC against CSA before real cases of sexual abuse can occur in the parish or clerical ministry. Creating an alternative clerical formation that allows married priesthood and encourages the psychosexual maturity of heterosexual priestly candidates can spare the RCC from sexual scandals that threaten the moral credibility of the Catholic hierarchy and destroy the spiritual image of the Church. The present semi-monastic seminary is structurally appropriate for religious and monastic priests but not for diocesan priests who normally live alone without a religious community in the parish (Ballano 2023).

In fact, the social structure of the current seminary system is largely copied from the communal and spiritual life of monasteries and religious organizations. It is structurally designed for religious and monastic priests who normally live and work with their religious communities that predominantly provide human and spiritual support to inhibit CSA. But this communal structure of the seminary is, however, unsuitable for diocesan clerics who would live and work alone most of the time in the parish without any intimate primary group or religious community to assist them in their personal and pastoral needs.

With the mandatory clerical celibacy, diocesan priests do not have an intimate group to lean on to support their psychosexual needs as well as regulate their behavior against the temptations of CSA in the parish. Thus, the reestablishment of married priesthood, which is recognized by the RCC as a valid social calling, is a doable alternative for diocesan priests who usually live a lonely life with higher risks of committing CSA in the parish. Research shows that sexual abuses are often committed by priests privately in their residences. In married priesthood, spouses and children of married clerics can provide direct social control and regulation to clerical behavior, thus removing the absolute privacy created by clerical celibacy that facilitates CSA.

This chapter will propose a major structural change and an alternative clerical training for Catholic diocesan priests based on apprenticeship system that allows married priesthood and normal socialization of priestly candidates in society. This alternative system of clerical training can enhance human and sexual maturity during clerical formation, which can proactively minimize the chances of CSA in the parish after ordination. Specifically, it suggests an inculturated and reestablished apprenticeship clerical training in dioceses that is adapted to contemporary society and culture. This inculturated training includes a strong academic training in sociology and the social sciences, adequate utilization of telepresence and information communication technologies (ICTs), updated canonical norms on clerical marriage and confluent relationships, and participation of lay leaders in a pool of credible experts and social scientists who are part of the formation team.

To achieve this goal, this chapter is structured into three major parts. The first part proposes a major structural change of the current celibate seminary training, introducing a modified, inculturated, and reestablished apprenticeship clerical training that is open to married diocesan priesthood and adjusted to the human formation of the current age. The second part suggests enhanced academic training in sociology and the social sciences under this modified apprenticeship clerical training. The third part explores the significance of adopting digital technology, promoting social networks, and utilization of telepresence in the reestablished apprenticeship system, given the limited resources and experts for clerical training in the RCC. The fourth part recommends new canonical provisions on clerical marriage and confluent relationship to stress that open and married priesthood implies serious clerical commitment and that promiscuous relationships of the current age are not allowed under the modified apprenticeship system. The last part emphasizes the importance of lay participation and empowerment in the alternative clerical training as well as in the continuing regulation of clerical behavior to prevent CSA in the RCC.

Reestablishing Apprenticeship in Contemporary Times

The suspension of the normal adolescent and adult socialization of seminarians has greatly contributed to the immaturity of diocesan priests who will be assigned to the autonomous secular world of the parish after ordination. Indeed, young seminarians who entered the seminary at a young age and were trained not to have sex of any kind, talk about sex of any kind, or think about sex of any kind with no sufficient guidance on how to appreciate celibacy as a freely given choice could make them immature and become part of the main cohort of sexual abusers in the RCC (Frawley O'Dea 2004).

When the Council of Trent suspended the long tradition of apprenticeship training for ministers in the RCC, it was not guided by an appropriate preexisting social structure or "template" on how to adapt the clerical training of diocesan priests to the current circumstances of the time. With the strong influence of monasticism and religious life and the adoption of mandatory clerical celibacy in the 11th and 12th centuries, the Catholic hierarchy adopted instead the celibate, communal, and semi-monastic religious life as the overall structure for Catholic seminaries. It also adopted the TI structure that isolates clerical formation from the real social world, bracketing the human and sexual socialization of seminarians in society.

The adoption of celibate seminary training further closed the possibility of clerical formation for married priesthood. The main structural flaw of this

188 Alternative Clerical Training and Apprenticeship

celibate seminary system is the "abnormal" psychosexual socialization of heterosexual priests who are often cited in most CSA research as the main cohort of sexual abusers in the RCC (John Jay College 2004; Terry 2008; Frawley O'Dea and Goldner 2016; De Weger 2022). Thus, this implies that the TI structure of the current seminary system that requires diocesan seminarians to reside in the seminary is inadequate, requiring an alternative clerical training to reduce the risks of producing immature seminarians who would later commit CSA once ordained and assigned in the RCC.

Reestablishing the apprenticeship clerical training in contemporary times as an alternative method for diocesan priestly formation is appropriate but it should include (1) inculturation, (2) married and open priesthood, (3) normal socialization, (4) enhanced academic formation in sociology and the social sciences, (5) utilization of telepresence and digital networks, (6) new provisions on clerical marriage and confluent relationships, and (7) lay empowerment in clerical formation and supervision of clerical behavior in the ministry to prevent more sexual scandals in the RCC.

Inculturation and Clerical Training in Contemporary Age

"Inculturation has been a buzzword throughout the Catholic world . . . for decades" (Weigel 2019, para. 1). It is one of the most significant theological concepts of the Roman Catholic Church (RCC) after the Second Vatican Council (Vatican II), a universal council convened by Pope John XXIII in Rome from 1962 to 1965 to adapt the Church's life and teaching to modern times. It simply implies "inserting" or adapting the Christian message – and in this case, the RCC's teaching on priestly formation – to the prevailing culture of the current times. To implement Christ's original teaching on optional celibacy today that recognizes the two social callings of Catholic priesthood, that is, the married and celibate priesthood, inculturation and adaptation of clerical training in a particular culture of society are necessary.

In African culture that emphasizes patriarchal structure, for instance, married priesthood seems suitable than celibate presbyterate. Several ordained African priests and even bishops resisted clerical celibacy and left the RCC to get married and even set up their own churches. There seems to be a strong social resistance to celibacy within the African church. One African bishop, for example, left the RCC to marry and later provided leadership for many other priests who also left the celibate priesthood for married priesthood outside the Western Church. The Zambian Archbishop Emmanuel Milingo is an example of an African bishop who left the celibate priesthood and became married several years ago in a Unification Church ceremony. He left the RCC and became the leader of his married schismatic priests. Consequently, as many as 300,000 African Catholics followed him in his new church (Perriello 2013).

Adopting the old tradition of apprenticeship of priestly formation that started with Christ but suspended in the 16th century by the Council of Trent with the institution of the celibate seminary training requires inculturation of clerical training to the prevailing culture of society. Indeed, the old apprenticeship clerical formation since time of Christ implied adopting an "inculturated" and evolving clerical formation. As Shazad (2015, 16) argues,

> The style, structure, and method of forming future priests in the early period and throughout the Church history was established under the understanding, need, and circumstance of that time. But as it was passing, it became more formal and official in its approach and criteria.
>
> *(Shazad 2015, 16)*

In the New Testament, priestly formation pursued the apprenticeship model. Jesus Christ, the eternal High Priest (Heb 5:5–6), had a great multitude as followers or disciples (Mark 3:7–8) (Shazad 2015). The first clerical training was initiated by Jesus, acting as the first formator and the Twelve Apostles who became the first clerical candidates (Luke 6:12–16). As narrated by the four Gospels, Christ called his apostles, both married and celibate, to learn his life and ministry.

"In the first four centuries, there were no formal record and clear-cut program for the training of priests. Historians, researchers, and archaeologists cannot outrightly hint on any special institution that was set aside for the training of seminarians" (Daboh 2020, 138). Then "from the fourth to fifth centuries, most of the priestly formation was in the form of apprenticeships with local bishops or parish priests, while students stayed in their family homes" (Schuth 2016, 11).

The effort to set up a formal school for clerical training, though not an exclusive organization like a total institution, started to emerge in 12th and 13th centuries, the period when Lateral Councils also imposed the mandatory clerical celibacy for all Catholic priests. During the third Lateran Council in 1179, a priest was appointed to the cathedral to be responsible for the formation of local clerics. Then in the Fourth Lateran Council of 1215, the RCC required that this priest must be a theologian who would teach Scriptures and Pastoral theology (Papesh 2004). Later, the RCC created a separate benefice, which was attached to every cathedral Church, and a headmaster was hired to teach candidates to the priesthood (Orme 2006).

Although clerical formation before the advent of the seminary was largely informal with no fixed organization, one can notice that priestly training was not isolated from the world. Candidates were not housed in one exclusive institution. They were free to socialize with people from all walks of life outside their scheduled spiritual and academic training. They could also attend secular schools and freely interact with women. Under the apprenticeship style of clerical training, the normal adolescent and adult socialization of candidates, which is crucial for authentic human and sexual maturity, is not suspended or bracketed by an institution that can lead to psychosexual immaturity.

There are experiments and attempts to mimic the apprenticeship style in contemporary period. Some seminaries allow their seminarians to study in colleges as normal students and live in a common residence. They are allowed to mingle with women and ordinary people. This is indeed an improvement of the original TI structure that can enhance the human and sexual formation of seminarians. But this innovation still has an inherent limitation. Under this set-up, which is still basically following the RCC teachings on seminary formation, seminarians are still supervised by a set of formators who can sanction any breach of celibacy and open discussion on sexuality inside the formation house.

Inculturation implies an accurate and scientific understanding of society and culture before the Christian message can be adapted adequately. Thus, to achieve an incultured reestablishment of the apprenticeship of clerical training in the current age needs a sociological understanding of the general social patterns of global society and culture. One important distinction between Christ's time and the postapostolic and Medieval period is the quality and speed of social change happening in society. The olden times when apprenticeship was practiced is characterized what George Ritzer's (2010) calls "solidity." Things, information, beliefs, and values of people are "solid," "heavy," and largely "fixed." Thus, personal and societal changes were slow, and people's values, beliefs, and commitments were generally stable and fixed.

This societal pattern is in contrast with the current globalizing society, which is characterized by "liquidity" or constant change, that is, things, information, and people are always in a constant state of flux. What used to be "solid" and "stable" in social reality during the earlier historical periods became "light," "mobile," and "negotiable" in contemporary globalizing world (Ritzer 2010; Ritzer and Dean 2021). Thus, people's minds undergo cultural recycling, radically altering their personal and religious life – something that Vatican II has not foreseen when it affirmed the seminary clerical formation and mandatory clerical celibacy in the 1960s. Thus, inculturating clerical training and reestablishing the apprenticeship model require that the RCC dialogues and coordinates with sociologists and social scientists who are experts on contemporary society and culture.

Married Priesthood

One of the serious structural defects of the present celibate seminary training is the rejection of married priesthood for diocesan seminarians who might not have been called to celibate presbyterate. The imposition of mandatory clerical celibacy in the 12th century has effectively suspended the universal practice of married priesthood in the RCC, which has long been existing as a valid social calling of Catholic priesthood and a persistent custom in the universal church up to the present times (Ballano 2023).

But **Vogels** (1993, 110) argues that

> the calling to the priesthood as a vocation on the one hand can be combined with the social callings of either celibacy or marriage on the other. It should be also possible for these two social callings to co-exist side by side, as is indeed the practice of the Eastern Church.

Reestablishing the universal married priesthood in the RCC requires political will, support of the laity, and scientific thinking among the members of the Catholic hierarchy led by the Pope on the behavioral aspects of celibacy.

The current clerical training, denies the option for married priesthood in case candidates discover during seminary training that they do not have the gift of celibacy. The RCC inappropriately assumes that the gift of celibacy can be received by diocesan seminarians if they are open and obedient to seminary rules and get ordained after seminary training. Thus, in most cases, heterosexual seminarians who felt called to married priesthood are forced to adapt to the celibate seminary formation, which is inappropriate to their social calling.

Those who do not yet experience dating and romantic relationships before seminary training, for instance, which could probably be addressed in apprenticeship system that allows normal socialization, may comply with all the academic and spiritual requirements, and get ordained, and yet still sexually and emotionally immature and unprepared to deal the real challenges of diocesan priesthood such as temptations to commit CSA as compensatory behavior for repressed sexuality.

Clerical celibacy emerged as a significant enabler of CSA in an investigation sponsored by German Bishops' Conference that aims to identify the major structures that facilitate CSA in the RCC. It also revealed several structures and dynamics within the RCC that supported CSA, including the obligatory clerical celibacy, which facilitated clergy sexual abuse (Wamsley 2018). Since clerical celibacy is like a key and lock, those with unresolved personal issues before they enter the seminary cannot resolve them after ordination without violating the vow of celibacy (Adams 2011). Thus, the current celibate training becomes a structural obstacle for authentic human and sexual maturity of heterosexual diocesan candidates who have unresolved personal issues and who may be called to married priesthood.

Without an alternative clerical training that allows married priesthood and realistic immersion in social life, immature diocesan priests will continue to constitute the main cohort of clerical sexual abusers in the RCC (Frawley O'Dea 2004; John Jay College Report 2004). Allowing a universal married priesthood for diocesan priests requires creating a different clerical training

192 Alternative Clerical Training and Apprenticeship

that is not structured in a TI organization. This implies a clerical formation that allows the continuation of the normal adolescent and adult socialization of candidates while undergoing their priestly training to maximize human growth and sexual maturity, as well as adequate preparation for marriage after priestly training for those who decide to become married priests. Thus, the reestablishment of the apprenticeship style of clerical training that permits married priesthood and normal socialization becomes a necessary option for diocesan clergy today to resist CSA.

Open Priesthood

Knowing whether one has the gift of clerical celibacy or married priesthood requires discernment and personal decision. Thus, the new clerical training should be flexible enough to allow discernment and change of social calling in time. The candidates should be given the choice to remain celibate as diocesan priests, transfer to religious life, choose married priesthood after apprenticeship, or leave the apprenticeship training to get married. Those who left the apprenticeship training and became married men should be allowed to resume their apprenticeship training and become married priests after a good evaluation of the formators as *viri probati* or men of edifying Christian virtues.

In sociology and the social sciences, it is generally believed that people are historical and "open systems." They cannot foresee future events nor control them. Christ also taught the celibacy is a personal choice and God's gift, which can only be discovered by the person himself through discernment. To discover whether candidates have the charism of celibacy or married priesthood would entirely depend on the person's prayer and decision. God reveals himself through historical events and human experience to call people to the priesthood. And people respond to God's call through faith, prayer, and discernment and actualize it by entering clerical training and choosing whether they are called to celibate or married priesthood.

Allowing married priesthood in a new apprenticeship clerical training should take two forms for candidates to choose from. It can be a married priesthood that can be pursued by unmarried candidates or by married men or the so-called *viri probati* or married men with proven exemplary faith (O' Connell and Hansen 2019). In the case of unmarried candidates, it is desirable that they should finish their formation before marriage and ordination. Since this is an open clerical training and priesthood where diocesan candidates are allowed to have healthy relationships with women during formation, it is inevitable that marriage can take place before ordination. But they should be allowed to return to their training as married men and become married priests if they are proven by the formation team to be qualified. However, candidates who opt to remain celibate during and after the apprenticeship training may do so and should be encouraged by the formation team to join religious or monastic orders, which should take care of their celibate priesthood.

This inculturated and reestablished apprenticeship clerical training should recognize the significant difference between the vocation to marriage and married priesthood. Married priests with their families should be under an ecclesial social structure while married lay people are on their own in secular society. To prevent making married priesthood as a mere job or opportunity for social mobility, Canon law should be amended to allow married priests to live decent but frugal lives with the needs of their families taken care of by a special ecclesiastical committee or dicastery with diocesan subcommittees in the RCC, whose main ecclesial function is to administer to the material and financial needs of married priests.

Married priesthood, in addition to lay empowerment and lay regulation of clerical behavior, is an important key to address the persistence of CSA in the RCC, which is committed mostly by male heterosexual diocesan priests (John Jay College Report 2004). Married priesthood addresses the psychosexual needs of the parish clergy to resist loneliness and address the lack of intimate social bonding in diocesan priesthood. More importantly, it removes absolute personal freedom created by celibacy and provides direct social control to clerical behavior that can greatly inhibit sexual deviance such as CSA. Spouses and children of married priests can directly monitor clerical behavior to prevent or minimize CSA (Ballano 2023).

Research showed that CSA cases normally occurred privately in the priest's residence with no effective guardians. About 41% of all CSA cases privately occurred in the priest's residence (John Jay College Report 2004). The diocesan bishop who is supposed to be the guardian of his priests is often a distant figure. The presbyterate is also not a cohesive clerical community that can monitor CSA in the diocese. Some research showed that due to the lack of lay and family guardians who can monitor clerical activities, priest offenders usually find deviant opportunities to be alone with their victims (Sipe 1990; John Jay College 2004; Donze 2018). Therefore, if married priesthood is permitted in the RCC under this new apprenticeship clerical training, the absolute privacy enjoyed by celibate priests and opportunities for CSA would be reduced.

The power of clerical celibacy that enables abusive priests to be near to their potential victims can be tempered by the inquisitive eyes of their spouses, children, and relatives of married priests as well as by whatever monitoring system created by organizations of married priests in dioceses. If same-sex marriage is also allowed in the RCC, gay priests can be monitored also by their spouses and relatives to provide direct social control of their behavior to prevent CSA. Married priesthood can, therefore, produce the essential social controls, that is, the system of measures, suggestion, persuasion, restraint, and coercion, which pressures people to conform to conventional behavior (Sharma 2007) to counteract CSA in the RCC.

Allowing Normal Socialization

One of the main contributory factors of the persistence of CSA in the RCC is the immaturity of heterosexual diocesan priests who are trained in the exclusive, secluded, and semi-monastic seminary, which is detached from the real world. Since seminarians enter the seminary at a younger age, their normal adolescent and adult socialization is disrupted, which contributes to their abnormal psychosexual development. To prevent this, the normal socialization process of candidates joining the alternative and reestablished apprenticeship clerical should be unhampered. Aside from academic studies in secular or Catholic colleges or universities and spiritual and pastoral training with flexible or fixed schedules with their spiritual directors and formation team, candidates should be allowed to stay in their homes or student dormitories and interact with anyone, especially women. A healthy friendship, dating, and romantic relationship should be allowed by the formation team during the apprenticeship period if they do not hinder the clerical formation process.

A normal socialization process implies interaction with sociocultural agents such as parents, family members, schoolmates, relatives, friends, women, and the media (Henslin 2013; Terziev and Vaseliva 2022). In this new apprenticeship model, candidates' behavior should not be tightly monitored and controlled by the formation team. Candidates are responsible for their own actions and can freely confide to the formation team or their human and spiritual directors if problems arise. Under this new clerical formation set-up, it lay leaders in the parishes and dioceses are encouraged to help monitor the candidates' behavior with the authority to report to the rector or whoever is in-charge of clerical formation for any abusive behavior. Each candidate will be assigned to a particular spiritual director and expert counselor who will be responsible for processing their human and spiritual experiences.

Allowing candidates to live a normal social life in this new set-up can be a discovery phase or period for the formators, experts, and counselors to judge whether or not they are fit to the priesthood. For instance, formators or lay leaders can discover actual cases of child abuse by candidates before ordination. This can be addressed early by dismissing the candidate from the apprenticeship training and allowing the prosecution of the case, without waiting for them to become priests and commit child sexual abuse. With this system, cover-up of CSA cases by bishops and scandals that demoralize the RCC can be greatly minimized or prevented. Under the current seminary system with panoptic surveillance and lack of experts, the sexual tendencies and unresolved personal issues of candidates can just be repressed and suspended during the formation period but could "erupt" any time after ordination when the right deviant opportunities arise in the parish or ministry, giving serious pastoral problems to bishops on how to deal with CSA cases and avoid cover-ups and scandals in the RCC.

Academic Training in Sociology and the Social Sciences

One important area that is neglected in the current seminary curriculum to improve the empirical understanding of of priests on CSA is the sociological and social science educational training during clerical formation. Despite the major societal changes after Vatican II and the advent of the present technology-driven globalization that have transformed all aspects of social life, the RCC still retains the highly philosophical and theological academic training of future priests that lacks inculturation and incorporation of the growing influence of modern sociology and the social sciences in contemporary world. This is understandable since Catholic theology was well developed in a historical era of the Medieval period dominated by Western philosophy. The philosophical and theological synthesis of St. Thomas Aquinas that also led to the birth of philosophical theology (Elders 1990) continues to influence the normative theological training of Catholic seminaries (Bain 2023).

But the Medieval period that produced scholasticism, making theology as "the queen of all sciences" and philosophy as its handmaid, was vastly different from the growing complexity of today's globalizing society, characterized metaphorically by George Ritzer (2010) as an increasing "liquidity" of the world where goods, services, things, information, and even people are like "liquid" or water that can easily travel or move beyond national borders and flow around the globe. The invention of the Internet, the world wide web, and information communication technologies (ICTs) has further complicated the contemporary world: social world is now "split" into the old temporal space of face-to-face interaction and transaction and the new cyberspace where human communications become digital and characterized by telepresence (Steuer 1992; Strengers 2015).

Philosophy is still very relevant to the theological formation of priestly candidates. Since the Christian faith also deals with mysteries and dogmatic realities that are beyond the empirical research of science, philosophy is needed to provide a rational justification of the faith. However, it is incapable of guiding cannot guide priests and seminarians to scientifically understand the world and its challenges to celibate priesthood (Ballano 2023). The current clerical curriculum is still dominated by scholastic and Western philosophy.

Following the program of priestly formation of the United States Conference of Catholic Bishops in 2005, one Catholic college seminary in the United States such as, for instance, the Boromeo Seminary Cleveland, has a college academic program that is dominated by Greek and Western philosophy, without being sufficiently supplemented by sociology and social science courses in the curriculum. The usual seminary philosophy program

196 Alternative Clerical Training and Apprenticeship

encourages rational thinking according to Western and Catholic philosophical traditions but not empirical thinking that can only be taught by sociology and the social sciences:

> The philosophy curriculum consists of ten integrated courses or thirty hours of study, and they are ideally taken in sequence. Four are historical courses, covering ancient and medieval, modern, and contemporary philosophy. Six are systematic courses dedicated to important areas of philosophical inquiry: philosophy of nature, philosophy of the human person, philosophy of knowledge, ethics, logic, metaphysics, and philosophy of God.
>
> *(Borromeo Seminary Cleveland Website n.d., para. 2)*

The first year would orient college seminarians to the study of philosophy by providing an overview of its Western history. The second year begins with systematic courses devoted to different areas of philosophy. Themes investigated under these courses include the origins of the universe, cognitive psychology of religious belief, human uniqueness and immortality, artificial intelligence, moral responsibility and neuroscience, and the historical Adam. The third year continues these systematic courses by investigating the relation of the human person to the true and the good, studying theories of knowledge and ethical theory. The fourth year completes the student's systematic study of philosophy by studying metaphysics and philosophy of God (Borromeo Seminary Cleveland Website n.d., paras. 3–6).

Courses such as sociology, anthropology, and other social sciences, which are necessary to develop the empirical and scientific thinking and research skills of future priests, are apparently missing. Some theological claims and ethical principles of the RCC such as those of Catholic social teaching require empirical grounding to inculturate the Christian message to people's cultural orientation in society. The seminary's academic training needs to include more social science courses to develop the empirical mind of seminarians in order that they can understand the complexity of contemporary world and its challenges to Catholic priesthood.

In this new apprenticeship clerical training, candidates should therefore be allowed to take up sociology courses in colleges and universities to supplement their philosophical and theological training. It is also desirable that they take advanced degrees in sociology after ordination, instead of the usual licentiate or doctorate in sacred theology or canon law. Sociology can also greatly aid their pastoral work of priests on inculturation in the Church and probably can help develop the emerging sociological theology in Catholic scholarship. Basically, philosophy asks ultimate questions about life, but not empirical questions pursued by sociology and the social sciences to understand the behavioral aspects of the Christian faith and Catholic priesthood.

Lastly, sociology and the social sciences are the right tools to use rather than philosophy to fully understand the urgent and current moral issues that besieged the RCC such as CSA. Sociological research can sharpen the priestly candidates' empirical mind on clergy sexual misconduct. A special course on current scientific research and literature should also be included in the curriculum of the new apprenticeship priestly training. Currently, with the RCC's culture of nondisclosure of emotional distress and sexuality, seminary formators do not encourage seminarians to read scientific literature on human sexuality and CSA. But with the availability of digital networks today, candidates in apprenticeship training can be educated about CSA through a constantly updated literature posted in apprenticeship websites. The research materials can be published online through these websites and supervised by the formation team and lay experts. These sites should have interactive features to increase the sociological awareness of the candidates on the moral and criminal aspects of CSA in the RCC.

Utilization of Telepresence and Digital Networks

The invention of the Internet in the late 1980s and growing sophistication of Information Communication Technologies (ICTs) have led to a new form culture and social presence for Christians in the contemporary world – telepresence and its virtual reality (VR). The "existence of virtual space enhances connections among people through electronic linkages and allows people to exchange information even while they occupy different physical locations" (Yu and Shaw 2008, 410). ICTs can enable individuals to participate in distant activities through telepresence (Janelle and Hodge 2000).

Telepresence, a term invented by Marvin Minsky, is a technology-mediated presence. Jonathan Steuer (1992, 76) defines it as "the experience of presence in an environment by means of a communication medium." Telepresence implies "a feeling of presence in mediated environment rather than in the immediate physical environment" (Draper, Kaber, and Usher 1998, 356). To Meadows (2012, 165), "The current convergence of technologies, presence and telepresence are maximized by people through mobile technology, from smart phones to GPS-enabled devices has seamlessly connected people through cellular networks and wireless hotspots."

Unlike the previous eras such as the Medieval and Modern times, which totally relied on face-to-face interaction and personal presence, the current contemporary world is largely driven by technology and telepresence. Thus, it provides digital and social networks that allow people from distant places to participate and interact in an online group or community activity without physically leaving their temporal space. Most people today have smartphones with the Internet, which can easily be used to communicate through telepresence. Since apprenticeship training implies that the candidates are physically

198 Alternative Clerical Training and Apprenticeship

dispersed and are not housed in a seminary, telepresence and ICTs can then play a crucial role in communication and clerical formation.

The apprenticeship clerical training should incorporate digital technology and the telepresence of the ICTs and the use the cyberspace to prepare candidates to the current global culture of the secular world during clerical training and ministry in the parish. The use of digital technology in apprenticeship training saves a lot of financial resources for the RCC. For instance, the seminary can tap online networks to allow experts and professional psychologists abroad to participate in counseling and assisting candidates on their psychosexual issues. It is expensive for the formation team to hire and bring in experts from distant places to participate physically for the human formation of future priests. The current seminary clerical training despite attempts to introduce digital technology in academic training still lags in the use of the latest technological advances of the current age. This problem can probably be addressed in apprenticeship training where candidates will be more exposed to telepresence and ICTs in secular colleges and universities, which usually provide updated digital educational technologies and facilities that enhance their students' digital competence.

The RCC can also tap the ICTs to network, assist, as well as train candidates who reside in various parts of the diocese during the apprentice period. They can also be utilized for both lay and priest formators to monitor possible sexual abuse of candidates during and after clerical formation. Digital technologies are also useful surveillance tools for the laity to monitor clerical behavior to inhibit CSA in the parish. Since lay experts and social scientists who can truly assist the candidates' human and sexual development are usually expensive and rare to hire physically, especially by formation teams in developing countries, the utilization of telepresence and digital networks through online chat or video conferencing in apprenticeship training can greatly save financial resources for cash-strapped dioceses in poor countries.

Provisions for Clerical Marriage and Confluent Relationship

The greatest threat to both celibate and marriage priesthood is confluent relationships that can result in violations of priestly vows and CSAs. The current globalizing world encourages promiscuity and confluent love that challenges clerical celibacy and married priesthood. In a series of books published since 1990, the British sociologist Anthony Giddens (2002) explored the impact of globalization on the personal relationships and inner lives of those in the advanced capitalist societies in the West. To him, the constant flux and change in contemporary society have resulted in a type of love and relationship that is radically different from the concept of romantic love that predominates in the 1960s.

In contemporary society, Giddens noticed a shift from traditional relationships to the concept of "pure relationships," which are founded on a model of "confluent love." To him, confluent love is "pure relationship," a contingent and active type of love that is open, conditional, and free from constraints (Giddens 1992). Because of its contingency and impermanence, Bauman (2003) calls this kind of love "liquid love." Unlike romantic love, which is geared toward marriage and lifelong commitment, confluent love is contingent with no marital commitments.

Giddens (2002) characterized confluent love as pure and temporary relationship by two or more people whether heterosexual, homosexual, or any sexual orientation, if all the partners are sexually happy in the relationship until further notice. It is contingent as since the relationship is always subject to termination upon notice of any of the partners. Thus, confluent love encourages promiscuity and short-term sexual relationship and satisfaction with no commitment to marriage or celibate life.

All forms of contingent intimate relationships, regardless of gender and age, whether dyadic or group love, are forms of confluent love. This love relationship can also occur in physical and/or cyberspace. Confluent love challenges both celibate and married priesthood. Those who aim to inculturate apprenticeship and married priesthood in contemporary times need to consider this contemporary trend.

Thus, the reestablishment of apprenticeship clerical training, which exposes candidates to the real-world of confluent love in both temporal and cyberspace, needs the expertise of psychologists, sociologists, anthropologists, and other social scientists to assist spiritual directors in processing human problems and psychosexual difficulties faced by candidates during clerical formation. In the current semi-monastic and exclusive celibate training, problems related to sexuality and emotional distress are usually addressed within the context of spiritual direction with seminary spiritual directors who are non-experts in human psychology and social science.

Thus, a revived apprenticeship clerical training should intensify the participation of social scientists in the formation of clerical candidates. The contemporary world is vastly more complex than the Medieval world when the celibate seminary clerical formation was institutionalized or from the modern world when Vatican II retained it up to the present. The late Pope Benedict XVI has already forewarned priests of this type of love and sexual freedom that started in the all out freedom of 1960s which collapsed the previously normative standards regarding sexuality (Beswick 2019).

To stress that married priesthood is a serious religious commitment regardless of the social circumstances, the RCC should suspend or dismiss from the clerical state married clerics and products of this reestablished apprenticeship clerical training who are found unfaithful to their marriage vows by committing serious sins of adultery and liquid love. Canon law should also be updated to list as grave sins form of confluent love which should be given serious ecclesiastical sanctions. The current Code of Canon Law did not consider contemporary serious sins against marriage and celibacy in temporal space and cyberspace when it was codified in 1983.

Lay Empowerment in Clerical Formation and Behavior

The structural defect of the current seminary clerical training includes the lack of lay participation in priestly formation. Although there might be a few lay teachers in the seminary, they nevertheless do not participate in the evaluation and decision-making on the overall fitness of seminarians to the priesthood. To shift the formation of men away from clericalism to make servant priests, two American lay theologians who teach in seminaries, Colt Anderson and Christopher M. Bellitto (2019), have proposed a helpful list of reforms that included lay participation in seminary formation:

1 Until diaconal ordination, seminarians should dress as and be treated as they are, lay men.
2 Seminarians' classes of theology should be held with other lay and religious men and women.
3 The professional opinions of religious sisters and lay professors, professionals, and supervisors must be taken into real account when deliberating on whether a seminarian will proceed in formation and to ordination. These deliberative processes cannot be singularly in the hands of the clergy.
4 A seminary's board of trustees must have lay members who, again, have deliberative and not simply consultative votes.

(Keenan 2018, 133)

The lay empowerment introduced by Vatican II is not enough to enable the laity to participate in the governance and formal administration in the RCC, which is still monopolized by ordained and celibate clerics. The laity remains the docile flock of the hierarchy and cannot vote or participate in ecclesial decision-making (Ballano 2020). In seminary formation, lay people can only teach but could not participate in deciding whether seminarians are fit for the priesthood.

Pope Francis's latest move in allowing lay people and women to vote in church matters in the current synod on synodality is perhaps a tacit acknowledgment that Vatican II's lay empowerment needs real lay participation in ecclesial affairs, especially in power-sharing (Gomes 2023). Real lay empowerment in the sociological sense requires distribution of authority and not just an enlargement of the laity's apostolate in the RCC. The laity's passive participation in ecclesial governance is thus reflected in the absence of lay involvement in the seminary clerical formation. Most cases of CSA in the RCC after seminary formation occur because of the laity's lack of direct formal authority to monitor clerical behavior, initiate formal ecclesial investigation, and participate in deciding these cases from the diocese up to Rome.

Without the proactive and formal participation of the laity in ecclesial governance to regulate clerical behavior, cover-ups of CSA cases by bishops would be inevitable with the lack of a strong system of checks and balances in the RCC. Currently,

> lay people do not have much real power in church governance, as parish council and financial committees are 'consultative,' with the pastor presiding over them; their votes are not binding. Clericalism, hierarchicalism, and hegemonic masculinity will continue to shape church culture unless and until canon law is changed to reflect genuine equality and co-responsibility between the ordained and laity.
>
> *(Mescher 2023, 138)*

The formal lay participation in regulating priestly formation and ministry is necessary in this new apprenticeship clerical training. The proactive and real ecclesial powers for the laity can increase the RCC's checks and balances system against CSA, reducing the burden of the Catholic hierarchy to justify cover-ups of clergy sexual abuses. Vatican II has recognized that the realm of expertise of the laity is their being immersed in the world of "secular affairs" (Pope Paul VI 1964, #31). Lay people are, therefore, in the best position to objectively monitor and understand sexual abuses of the clergy in secular society without the "clerical camaraderie" that often results in cover-ups of CSA cases by bishops and fellow priests.

Under this new apprenticeship system, lay leaders who are randomly selected by the diocesan consultors and local bishop based on competence and personal integrity with fixed terms should be included in the clerical formation team. If the RCC would formally allow lay participation in ecclesial governance, these lay leaders should have the authority to vote and decide cases pertaining to clerical formation and clerical behavior even beyond the apprenticeship period. They should also be allowed to act as the rector or head of the apprenticeship formation team and decide in the selection of experts who will act as counselors for the human and sexual needs of the candidates. The bishop and the clergy of the diocese are, however, more competent to choose the spiritual directors of priestly candidates who will join the formation team.

Lastly, the power and duties of the apprenticeship formation team, which is participated by competent and expert lay leaders, can be expanded to monitor the behavior of apprenticeship graduates who became priests and worked in parishes. Since this team has the records and personal knowledge of the human and spiritual needs of these new diocesan priests, the members should also be tasked to monitor or regulate clerical behavior. To minimize overwork, a separate team in coordination with the formation team can also be constituted to exclusively follow up the psychosexual development of new priests as well as supervise clerical behavior and coordinate with church and civil authorities on CSA cases.

The creation of a special team, which is largely composed of lay people with expertise on sexuality and CSA, should not only be active at the parish and diocesan levels but must also in various ecclesiastical networks. This team should also in close coordination with other higher level special teams special teams that coordinate with episcopal conferences and with the Vatican bureaucracy to further investigate and decide CSA cases with finality. Normally, it is the Dicastery of the Doctrine and Faith (DDF), which is composed only of top clerics, that investigates and decides CSA cases with finality without lay participation. Thus, lay experts and leaders with competence on CSA and judicial proceedings should be appointed by the Pope in this dicastery with voting powers to avoid cover-up or mishandling of CSA cases. Indeed, effective lay empowerment and participation in formal ecclesial governance, clerical formation, and monitoring of clerical behavior against CSA can be a key to halt the enduring sexual abuses in the RCC.

Conclusion

This chapter has illustrated the structural flaws of the current celibate seminary formation that is structured in a TI set-up that can primarily lead to psychosexual immaturity of heterosexual diocesan priests, who are the main cohort of sexually abusive priests in the RCC as manifested in most CSA studies and investigations. With the institution of the seminary by the Council of Trent in the 16th century that suspended apprenticeship clerical training and the imposition of mandatory clerical celibacy, which became the foundation of the current celibate seminary formation, male heterosexual seminarians who may be called to married priesthood are forced to undergo the rigid exclusive all-male formation that suspends their normal adolescent and adult socialization and interaction with women. This abnormal environment and sexual repression can result in psychosexual immaturity and vulnerability to CSA once ordained and appointed in the parish without effective guardians.

To prevent more sexual scandals and CSA in the RCC, this chapter recommended the reestablishment of the apprenticeship clerical training for diocesan priests that is inculturated and adapted to contemporary times as an alternative method to the current celibate seminary formation. Celibate seminary training is only ideal for religious and monastic priests but not for diocesan priests. It thus suggested that the new apprenticeship clerical training should include (1) inculturation, (2) married and open priesthood for diocesan priests, (3) normal socialization, (4) enhanced academic formation in sociology and the social sciences, (5) utilization of telepresence and digital networks, (6) new provisions on clerical marriage and confluent relationships, and (7) lay empowerment in clerical formation and monitoring of priestly behavior to halt the persistent clergy sexual scandal in the RCC, mostly committed by psychosexual immature secular priests who are graduates of the exclusive, all-male, and celibate seminary formation.

References

Adams, Kenneth. 2011. "Clergy Sexual Abuse: A Commentary on Celibacy." *Sexual Addiction & Compulsivity: The Journal of Treatment & Prevention* 10 (2–3): 91–92. https://doi.org/10.1080/10720160390230583.

Anderson, Colt C., and Christopher M. Bellitto. 2019. "Two Former Seminary Professors Say the Current System Breeds an Ambition for Higher Office Known as 'Scarlet Fever.'" *La Croix International Website*, August 29, 2019. https://international.la-croix.com/news/religion/the-reform-seminaries-need/9812.

Armbruster, Andre. 2021. "On the Undisclosed Transfer of Abusive Catholic Priests: A Field Theoretical Analysis of the Sexual Repression Within the Catholic Church and the Use of Legitimate Language." *Critical Research on Religion* 10 (1): 61–77.

Bain, Eric. 2023. *The Lame Wing: Enlightenment Philosophy and Theology*, 30485234. Ave Maria: Ave Maria University ProQuest Dissertations Publishing.

Ballano, Vivencio O. 2020. "The Catholic Laity, Clerical Sexual Abuse, and Married Priesthood: A Sociological Analysis of Vatican II's Lay Empowerment." *Cogent Social Sciences* 6 (1): 1–17. https://doi.org/10.1080/23311886.2020.1813438.

Ballano, Vivencio O. 2023. *In Defense of Married Priesthood: A Sociotheological Investigation of Catholic Clerical Celibacy*. London and New York: Routledge.

Bauman, Zygmunt. 2003. *Liquid Love*. Cambridge: Polity Press.

Beswick, Emma. 2019. "Ex-Pope Benedict XVI Says, 'All-Out Sexual Freedom' of 60s to Blame for Clerical Sex Abuse." *Euronews*, December 4, 2019. www.euronews.com/2019/04/11/ex-pope-benedict-xvi-says-all-out-sexual-freedom-of-60s-to-blame-for-clerical-sex-abuse.

Borromeo Seminary Cleveland Website. n.d. "Curriculum." www.borromeoseminary.org/academics/philosophy/curriculum/

Cozzens, Donald, William Schipper, Merle Longwood, Marie M. Fortune, and Elaine Graham. 2004. "Clergy Sexual Abuse: Theological and Gender Perspectives." *Journal of Religion & Abuse* 6 (2): 3–29. https://doi.org/10.1300/j154v06n02_02.

Daboh, Habila. 2020. "The Evolution of Seminary Formation from the Apostolic Era to the Council of Trent: A Critical Appraisal." *JORAS* 10: 137–156.

de Weger, Stephen Edward. 2022. "Unchaste Celibates: Clergy Sexual Misconduct against Adults – Expressions, Definitions, and Harms." *Religions* 13 (5): 1–27. https://doi.org/10.3390/rel13050393.

Donze, Caroline. 2018. "Breaking the Seal of Confession: Examining the Constitutionality of the Clergy-Penitent Privilege in Mandatory Reporting Law." *Louisiana Law Review* 78 (1): 266–310. https://digitalcommons.law.lsu.edu/lalrev/vol78/iss1/12.

Draper, John V., David B. Kaber, and John M. Usher. 1998. "Telepresence." *Human Factors: The Journal of the Human Factors and Ergonomics Society* 40 (3): 354–375. https://doi.org/10.1518/001872098779591386.

Elders, Leo J. 1990. *The Philosophical Theology of St. Thomas Aquinas*. Leiden: Brill.

Fagan, Seán. 1965. "The New Approach to Seminary Training." *The Furrow* 16 (5): 267–276.

Frawley O'Dea, M. G. 2004. "Psychological Anatomy of the Catholic Sexual Abuse Scandal." *Studies in Gender and Sexuality* 5 (2): 121–137. https://doi.org/10.1080/15240650509349244.

Frawley O'Dea, Mary Gail, and Virginia Goldner. 2016. "Abusive Priests: Who They Were and Were Not." In *Predatory Priests, Silenced Victims: The Sexual Abuse Crisis and the Catholic Church*, edited by Mary Gail Frawley O'Dea, and Virginia Goldner. London and New York: Routledge.

Giddens, Anthony. 1992. *The Transformation of Intimacy*. Oxford: Blackwell.

Giddens, Anthony. 2002. *Runaway World: How Globalisation Is Reshaping Our Lives*. London: Profile Books.

Goffman, Erving. 1968. *Asylums: Essays on the Social Situation of Mental Patients and Other Inmates*. 1st ed. New York, NY: Anchor Books.

Gomes, Sebastian. 2023. "Synodality Is Working: Women Getting a Vote at the Vatican Is the Latest Proof." *America: The Jesuit Review*, May 3, 2013. www.americamagazine.org/faith/2023/05/03/pope-francis-synod-women-vote-245214

Henslin, James. 2013. "Chapter 3: Socialization." In *Instructor's Manual, Essentials of Sociology*. London: Pearson.

Janelle, D. G., and D. C. Hodge, eds. 2000. *Information, Place, and Cyberspace Issues in Accessibility*. Berlin: Springer.

John Jay College Report. 2004. "The Nature and Scope of Sexual Abuse of Minors by Catholic Priests and Deacons in the United States 1950–2002." *USCCB*. www.bishop-accountability.org/reports/2004_02_27_JohnJay/.

Keenan, Marie. 2015. "Masculinity, Relationships and Context: Child Sexual Abuse and the Catholic Church Catholic Church." *Irish Journal of Applied Social Studies* 15 (2): 64–77.

Meadows, Philip R. 2012. "Mission and Discipleship in a Digital Culture." *Mission Studies* 29 (2): 163–182. https://doi.org/10.1163/15733831-12341235.

Mescher, Marcus. 2023. "Chapter 8: Clergy Sexual Abuse as Moral Injury: Confronting a Wounded and Wounding Church." *Journal of Moral Theology* 3 (CTEWC Book Series 3): 122–139. https://doi.org/10.55476/001c.72061.

O' Connell, Gerard, and Luke Hansen. 2019. "Synod Votes to Ordain Married Men, and to Protect Amazon's Indigenous Peoples and Rainforests. America:" *The Jesuit Review*, October 26, 2019. www.americamagazine.org/faith/2019/10/26/synod-votes-ordain-married-men-and-protect-amazons-indigenous-peoples-and.

Orme, Nicholas. 2006. *Medieval Schools: From Roman Britain to Renaissance England*. New Haven and London: Yale University Press.

Papesh, Michael L. 2004. *Clerical Culture: Contradiction and Transformation*. Collegeville, MN: Liturgical Press.

Perriello, Pat. 2013. "Trouble with celibacy in the church in Africa." *National Catholic Reporter*, August 26, 2013. www.ncronline.org/blogs/ncr-today/trouble-celibacy-church-africa.

Pope Paul VI. 1964. *Lumen Gentium* [Dogmatic Constitution on the Church]. Vatican: Vatican Archives.www.vatican.va/archive/hist_councils/ii_vatican_council/documents/vat-ii_const_19641121_lumen-gentium_en.html.

Pope Paul VI. 1965. *Optatam Totius* [Decree on Priestly Formation]. Vatican: Vatican Archives. www.vatican.va/archive/hist_councils/ii_vatican_council/documents/vat-ii_decree_19651028_optatam-totius_en.html.

Ritzer, George. 2010. *Globalization: A Basic Text*. Malden, MA and Oxford: Wiley-Blackwell.

Ritzer, Geroge, and Paul Dean. 2021. *Globalization: A Basic Text*. 3rd ed. Hoboken, NJ and Sussex: Wiley-Blackwell.

Schuth, Katarina. 2016. *Seminary Formation: Recent History-Current Circumstances-New Directions*. Collegeville, MN: Liturgical Press.

Sharma, R. K. 2007. *Social Change and Social Control*. London: Atlantic.

Shazad, Waqas. 2015. "Formation for Priesthood and Challenges for the Church in Pakistan." *National Institute of Theology*. www.academia.edu/19331009/Formation_for_Priesthood_Challenges_for_the_Church_in_Pakistan.

Sipe, A. W. Richard. 1990. *A Secret World: Celibacy and the Search for Celibacy*. Collegeville, MN: Brunner/Mazel.

Sipe, A. W. Richard. 2003. *Celibacy in Crises*. New York and Hove: Brunner-Routledge.

Steuer, Jonathan. 1992. "Defining Virtual Reality: Dimensions Determining Telepresence." *Journal of Communication* 42 (4): 73–93. https://doi.org/10.1111/j.1460-2466.1992.tb00812.x.

Strengers, Yolande. 2015. "Meeting in the Global Workplace: Air Travel, Telepresence and the Body." *Mobilities* 10 (4): 592–608. https://doi.org/10.1080/17450101.2014.902655.

Terry, Karen J. 2008. "Stained Glass: The Nature and Scope of Child Sexual Abuse in the Catholic Church." *Criminal Justice and Behavior* 35: 549–569.

Terziev, Venelin, and Silva Vasileva. 2022. "The Role of Education in Socialization of an Individual." https://ssrn.com/abstract=4101387; http://dx.doi.org/10.2139/ssrn.4101387.

Vogels, Heinz-Jürgen. 1993. *Celibacy: Gift or Law?* Lanham, MD: Rowman & Littlefield.

Wamsley, Laurel. 2018. "German Bishops' Report: At Least 3,677 Minors Were Abused By Clerics." *NPR Website*, September 25, 2018. https://www.npr.org/2018/09/25/651528211/german-bishops-report-at-least-3-677-minors-were-abused-by-clerics.

Weigel, George. 2019. "Inculturation" and the Culture that is the Church." *First Things*. www.firstthings.com/web-exclusives/2019/10/letters-from-the-synod-2019-8.

Yu, Hongbo, and Shaw Shih-Lung. 2008. "Exploring Potential Human Activities in Physical and Virtual Spaces: A Spatio-Temporal GIS Approach." *International Journal of Geographical Information Science* 22 (4): 409–430. https://doi.org/10.1080/13658810701427569.

INDEX

Adubale, Andrew A. 76
Adubale, Oyaziwo 76
alternative clerical training 18–19,
52, 186–190; for diocesan married
priesthood 63–64; lay participation
in seminary formation 200–202; need
for 18–19; normal adolescent and
adult socialization 194–195; open
priesthood 192–193; provision of
confluent love 198–200; sociological
and social science educational
training 195–197; utilization of
telepresence and digital networks
197–198; *see also* apprenticeship
clerical training; married priesthood
Anderson, Colt 160
apprenticeship clerical training 11,
13, 31–32; abolishing 36–37, 162
(Council of Trent); benefits of 44–45;
digital technology, incorporating in
198; history of 32–35; and married
priesthood 105, 124, 126, 131,
192–193; opportunities for maturity
38–39, 69–70, 135; reestablishing
186–190, 199–203; and sociology
courses 196–197; *see also* seminary
clerical training
Armbruster, Andre 59

Beier, Klaus 170
Benedict XVI, Pope 12, 149, 199
Benkert, Marianne 159
Berry, Jason 161

Bevilacqua of Philadelphia, Cardinal
Anthony 141, 145
Bohm, Bettina 167
Boisvert, Donald 146
Bourdieu, Pierre 9
bracketing 18, 129, 187
Brandmuller, Cardinal 141

Camargo, Robert J. 158
Canon Law 199–200
Casibba, R. 49
celibate priesthood 11, 52–54, 99–100,
113, 128–129; in contemporary age
188–189; heterosexual and gay men
148–149, 152; saints and 109–110;
training 15, 163; and women seen as
obstacle/temptation 132–133
celibate seminary formation, foundation
of 52–54
celibate seminary training 7–10,
69–71, 95, 184; apprenticeship
model (*see* apprenticeship clerical
training); celibate male priesthood
model 10, 40–41; of heterosexual
seminarians 132–134; inculturation
and 188–190; internal and external
social control 9, 13; organizational
socialization of 16; primary negative
unintended effect of 63; psychological
process of screening seminary
applicants 70–71; psychosexual
formation 9; psychosexual
immaturity and 132–134, 184–185;

Index **207**

psychosexual underdevelopment and vulnerability 15; RCC's prescriptions 12; seminary structure 12–13; sociological approach 11–13; as a TI 71–75, 86, 163–164, 184; *see also* seminary clerical training

child clerical sexual abuse (cCSA) 157–158, 160, 163, 168; detection system 173–174; implication of seminary flaws in 171–174; *see also* pedophile clerical sexual abuse

Child Sexual Abuse of Australia 50

Chrysostom, St. John 34

clergy sexual misconduct against adults (CMMA) 122

clericalism 5, 29–30, 123

clerical marriage 95, 187, 188; provisions for and confluent relationship 198–200

clerical sexual abuse (CSA) 4–5, 21–22; celibate seminary training as enabler of 7–11; research and investigations 5–7; social resistance theory 19–21 sociological approach 11–13; socialization theory 16–17; total institution theory (TI) 16–19

compensatory behaviors 18, 50

compulsory masturbation 74–75, 109–110

confluent love 198–200

Council of Trent 6–7, 12, 31, 34–37, 39, 41, 43, 51, 94, 162

covert clerical resistance 40–42

Cozzens, Donald 78, 148; *The Changing Face of Catholic Priesthood* 140

Cravatts, Richard 133

Daniel, Kasomo 20

Devine, John 160

de Weger, Stephen Edward 122, 134

Dicastery of the Doctrine and Faith (DDF) 202

diocesan married priesthood, alternative clerical training for 63–64

Doyle, Fr. Thomas P. 44, 49, 54, 98, 159

Duffy, Fr. Eugene 12

emasculinity 52–53

ephebophilia 157

evangelization of humanity 3

Feierman, Jay 71, 146

fixated pedophiles 170; *see also* regressed pedophiles

Foucault, Michel 17

Francis, Pope 4, 200

Gartner, R. B. 121

gender socialization, seminary 68–69, 73; concept 126–127; of heterosexual seminarians 124–126; teaching males and females on expected mannerisms 127–129; as a total institution (TI) 130–131

gender training in seminary 76–78

Giddens, Anthony 10, 40, 198–199

Goffman, Erving 7, 17, 30, 40, 51–52, 72, 94, 96–97, 100, 162, 184; *Asylums* 17, 40; *The Presentation of Self in Everyday Life* 101; view of TI 17, 40

Goldner, Virginia 122

Grattagliano I. 49

Greeley, Father Andrew 140, 148

Greely, Andrew 133

hegemonic masculinity 53

heterosexual clerical sexual abuse and seminary formation: accused and found guilty 124; against adolescents and adults 121; causes 124–126; against children 121; against children and minors 121–122; gender socialization and 126–131; against girls and women 122–123; by immature priests 134–135; issue of psychosexual immaturity 132–134; multiple-cause explanation 123; single-cause explanation 123; sociological analysis 124; structural explanation of 123–124

heterosexual seminarians: compulsive masturbation 109–110; coping strategies 113; inappropriate gender socialization of 18, 31, 79–80, 83, 123–126; immaturity 123–126, 132–133, 135–136; of living double lives 105; engaging in hidden private life 96–97, 102, 108, 135; negative impact of clerical celibate seminary 99, 202–203; secret romance 112; repression of sexuality 133–134

hierarchicalism 5

Hoge, Dean 8; first five years in the priesthood 171

homophobia 78, 153

homosexual clerical sexual abuse and seminary formation 140–143;

208 Index

blaming homosexuals for CSA
145–146, 149–151; misconceptions
on 143–144; need for specialized
formation 151–153; RCC's stand on
147–149; same-sex marriage 143;
sociological connection between
homosexuality and CSA 141, 146
homosexuality 5, 61, 140–142,
145–146; RCC's stand on and
seminary formation 147–149
human maturity in priestly training
37–39; psychosexual maturity 61–62

Ignatius of Loyola, St. 35
Information Communications
Technologies (ICTs) 19
institutionalization of seminary, benefits
36–37, 70
Institutional Responses that Child
Sexual Abuse 49

Jenkins, Philip 158
John Jay College Report 50, 69, 122,
134, 158, 170

Keenan, James 5
Keenan, Marie 8, 69, 121, 125,
184–185
Khwepe, Nontsokile Maria
Emmanuela 77
Kohanski, Dan 41

Lassi, Steffano 166
Lateran Councils 34
lay participation in seminary formation
200–202
Li, Hankun 50
Liu, Lejing 50
Loftus, John Allan 158
Lothstein, Dr. Leslie 61, 146
Lothstein, L. M. 158

male celibate masculinity 185;
see also priesthood masculinity
mandatory clerical celibacy 5, 7, 21, 38,
50, 93, 96
manhood: clerical celibacy as sign of
true 78–80; inclusive masculinity
theory 77; traditional gender view
of 77
manicheanism 39
married priesthood 7–8, 11, 13–14,
21–22, 84, 93–94, 96–97, 190–192;

alternative clerical training for
63–65, 13, 135–136; as best mode of
social calling for RCC 43–45; change
from apprenticeship to clerical
41–42; clerical celibacy and social
resistance 99–100; disregarding
60–61; for diocesan homosexual
and heterosexual priests 149; living
double lives 105; in modern age
186–188; and open priesthood
192–193; same sex marriage 149,
152–153; third gender and 52–53;
training in the real world 135;
Vatican and 69–71; *see also* clerical
marriage; confluent relationship
Martel, Frederic 107
maturity *see* human maturity;
psychosexual maturity
McDevitt, Patrick 102
McGlone, G. 59
Melliot, David 72
Merton, Robert K. 39
Miller, Maureen C. 94
Mills, C. Wright 125
Mininni, G. 49
monasticism 39
Muller, Cardinal Gerhard 140

National Review for the Protection
of Children and Young People
(NRPCYP) 51
normal socialization in society: allowing
194–195; apprenticeship for healthy
124, 186–188, 191–192; inadequate
seminary courses as replacement
82–83; RCC insisting on separating
future priests from 123–124;
recognized before theologizing
129; and TI 16–18, 38–39, 58, 63,
85, 134;

O'Dea, Frawley 7, 71, 80, 87, 122, 134
open priesthood 192–193
Optatam Totius (Decree on Priestly
Training) 30, 35–36, 103, 183
optional celibacy 13

panopticism 17
panoptic surveillance 17, 59
Parsons, Talcott 37
passive social resistance of seminarians
and clerics 20, 93, 96–97, 100–103,
105–113; acts during formation

105–113; as everyday form of popular opposition 100; front stage or backstage 101–102; meanings and symbols 100; against obligatory clerical celibacy 101; seminary formation and 102–103

Pastores Dabo Vobis (I Shall Give You Shepherds) 13, 30, 151–152

Paul II, Pope John 3–4, 43

pedophile clerical sexual abuse 19–20, 31, 63, 121–122, 124, 133–134, 140, 143, 149–151, 157–159; celibate seminary formation and 164–165; common social pattern for 173; magnification of 158–159; method in screening 160, 165–168; methodology and theoretical foundation 161–165; socialization in priestly training and 161–163; structural causes of 159–161; structural limitations of seminary against pedophilia 165–171

pedophilia 143–145, 160–161, 168–169; behavioral monitoring and intervention against 165; blending abilities of 170–171; in Catholic seminaries 171; definition 157, 163, 166; fixated 170; regressed 169; regressive nature of 167; significance of age of child 158; treatment for 169; World Health Organization (WHO) classification 163, 169

perfect celibate clerical masculinity 95

Plante, Thomas G. 29, 122, 145

Presbyterorum Ordinis (Order of Priests) 7, 41, 70

Program for Priestly Formation, Sixth Edition 168

psychosexual immaturity of seminary graduates 42–44, 132–134, 184–185

regressed pedophiles 169

Reisinger, Doris 122

resocialization 38, 162

Robert, Goss 146

Robinson, T. 158

Roman Catholic Church (RCC) and clerical sexual abuse (CSA) introduction to topic 3–5, 21–22; celibate seminary training and CSA 7–10; main objectives an arguments 10–11; need for alternative clerical training 18–19; research 5–7;

seminary as a TI social structure 17–18; socialization theory 16; sociological approach 11–13; theoretical orientation 15; *see also* alternative clerical training

Rosetti, Stephen 19

Rovers, Martin 69

Royal Commission into Institutional Responses 50

Royal Commission into Institutional Responses to Child Clerical Sexual Abuse 158

Rubino, Stephen C. 98

Sacred Congregation for the Religious 148

Sands, Kathleen M. 123

Sarah, Cardinal Robert 12

Scardigno, R. 49

Scheper-Hughes, Nancy 160

Schuth, Sr. Katarina 30, 36

Scott, James 15, 19–20, 41, 97; *Weapons of the Weak* 93, 100

screening of seminary applicants 70–71; psychological process of 70–71; of seminarians with pedophilic disorder 160, 165–168

secondary data analysis (SDA) 15

Second Vatican Council (Vatican II) 6–7, 13, 19, 30, 35–36, 41, 43, 56–57, 69–71, 87, 94, 112, 183, 188, 199–201

semi-monastic seminary formation 43

seminary clerical training 35–37; Catholic institution as training ground 35; compulsive masturbation 109–110; consequences of shifting methods in 39–44; institutionalization of seminary, benefits 36–37, 70; living double lives 105–107; monastic method 36; negative unintended consequences of 59–63; psychological process of screening seminary applicants 70–71; psychosexual immaturity of seminary graduates 42–44; retention of 57–59; romantic relationships with women 110–113; seminarians' nightlife during 110–113, 135; sexuality development 70; socialization and human maturity in 37–39; watching online pornography 108–109, 113; *see also* celibate seminary training

210 Index

sexuality formation in seminary training
68–70, 72–73, 95; curriculum
80–86; dealing with parishioners'
sexuality problems 84–86; issue of
poor socialization 81–82; openness
concerning celibacy 87; priesthood
as sign of true manhood 78–80;
scarcity of professional counselors,
issue of 76; sexual intimacy 75–80;
sexual orientation 72, 86–88;
sexual problem of masturbation 76;
unrealistic training 82–84
sexually repressed immature priests 7
sexual repression 133
sexual scandals 4
sexual socialization 8
Sipe, A. W. Richard 4, 20–21, 30, 51,
94, 96–98, 101, 121, 158; *The Secret
World* 73
social bonding 19, 31
social control 51, 87; against clerical
sexual abuse (CSA) 18, 51–52,
62–63, 72; direct 44; impact of lack
of 43–44; internal and external 9, 13;
theories on crime and deviance 9, 32
social isolation of seminarians 40
socialization of seminarians 37–39,
72, 81–82, 124, 126–129, 187;
disruption of 59–60; exclusive,
abnormal, and all-male socialization
process 162; informal 103–104
socialization theory 161–163;
organizational 16; primary 16;
secondary 16
social learning 16–18, 126, 132
social resistance by seminarians 15,
19–21; active or manifest 93; among

Catholic clergy against celibacy law
94; clerical celibacy and 99–100;
forms of sexual misconduct as form
of 96–97, 105–113; passive 20, 93,
96–97, 100–103, 105–113
sociological imagination 6
Sperry, L. 59
Stanosz, Paul 71
Swanson, R. N. 52
Synod on Synodality 101

Terry, Karen J. 159
third gender construction 52–54, 78,
129–130
total institutions (TI) 16–17, 30, 34,
51–52, 94, 160, 162; as an exclusive
resocialization organization 40;
behavior in face-to-face private
interactions 17; characteristics of
54–56; compliance in 17; gender
socialization as 130–131; seminary
as TI social structure 12–14, 17–18,
56–57, 71–75, 86, 163–164, 184

United States Conference of Catholic
Bishops (USCCB) 168

Vogels, Heinz-Jurgen 41

Wan, Wei Wan 50
Wills, Gary 160
Witte Jr., John 53, 94

Yip, Andrew K. T. 124
Yocum, Sandra 51

Zollner, Jesuit Fr. Hans 5

Printed in the United States
by Baker & Taylor Publisher Services